W9-BSD-305

AFFLUENZA

AFFLUENZA

The All-Consuming Epidemic

John de Graaf
David Wann
Thomas H. Naylor
In association with Redefining Progress

Illustrations by David Horsey
Foreword by Scott Simon

BK BERRETT-KOEHLER PUBLISHERS, INC.
San Francisco

Copyright © 2001 by John de Graaf, David Wann, Thomas Naylor
All rights reserved. No part of this publication may be reproduced, distributed, or transmitted in
any form or by any means, including photocopying, recording, or other electronic or mechanical
methods, without the prior written permission of the publisher, except in the case of brief quota-
tions embodied in critical reviews and certain other noncommercial uses permitted by copyright
law. For permission requests, write to the publisher, addressed "Attention: Permissions Coordinator," at the address below.

Berrett-Koehler Publishers, Inc.
450 Sansome Street, Suite 1200
San Francisco, CA 94111-3320
Tel: (415) 288-0260 Fax: (415) 362-2512 www.bkconnection.com

Ordering Information
Quantity sales. Special discounts are available on quantity purchases by corporations,
associations, and others. For details, contact the "Special Sales Department" at the
Berrett-Koehler address above.
Individual sales. Berrett-Koehler publications are available through most bookstores.
They can also be ordered direct from Berrett-Koehler: Tel: (800) 929-2929; Fax: (802) 864-7626;
www.bkconnection.com
Orders for college textbook/course adoption use. Please contact Berrett-Koehler:
Tel: (800) 929-2929; Fax: (802) 864-7626.
Orders by U.S. trade bookstores and wholesalers. Please contact Publishers Group West,
1700 Fourth Street, Berkeley, CA 94710. Tel: (510) 528-1444; Fax (510) 528-3444.

Printed in the United States of America
Printed on acid-free and recycled paper that is composed
of 80% recovered fiber, including 30% post consumer waste).

Library of Congress Cataloging-in-Publication Data
De Graaf, John.
    Affluenza: the all consuming epidemic / by John De Graaf, David Wann, and Thomas H. Naylor;
in association with Redefining Progress; illustrations by David Horsey; foreword by Scott Simon.
        p. cm.
    "Based in part on the PBS television programs "Affluenza" and "Escape from affluenza."
    Includes bibliographical references and index.
    ISBN 1-57675-151-1
        1. Quality of life—United States. 2. Wealth—United States. 3. Consumption (Economics)—
United States. 4. United States—Social conditions—1980- 5. United States—Economic conditions—1981- 6. United States—Civilization—1970- I. Wann, David. II. Naylor, Thomas H.,
1936-. III. Affluenza (Television program: 1997). IV. Escape from affluenza (Television program:
1998). V. Title.

HN60 .D396 2001
306'.0973–dc21
                                                                                2001035016

First Edition
        06   05   04   03   02   01   10   9   8   7   6   5   4   3   2   1

Interior design and composition: Seventeenth Street Studios
Copyeditor: Judith Bess
Indexer: Rachel Rice

Photo credits:
The Surrender of the Joneses, Francine Strickwerda;
Skeen Family, Pearland Texas ©1994D Peter Ginter, Peter Menzel/Material World;
Yadev Family, Ahraura, India © 1994D Peter Ginter/Material World.

In memory of
DAVID ROSS BROWER
(1912-2000)

a giant of 20th Century thought and action on behalf
of the earth. He hoped that one day

We may see that progress is not the
Accelerating speed with which we multiply
And subdue the Earth, nor the growing number
Of things we possess and cling to.
It is a way along which to search for truth,
To find serenity and love and reverence for life,
To be part of an enduring harmony…

And in memory of
DONELLA MEADOWS
(1941-2001)
Scientist and sheep farmer, she pointed us all
in the direction of a more sustainable society.

CONTENTS

FOREWORD

When I was first approached to host the television program *Affluenza*, the idea sounded just about as appealing as a lukewarm cup of boiled root tea. I imagined a stern sort of brew that would make me cringe with every breath and sip, while earnestly pious activists in earth sandals and dun-colored parkas spun from discarded soda pop bottles hectored innocent bystanders strolling into coffee bars and shopping malls: "Materialist stooge! Self-gratifying spendthrift! Polluting pirate!" I opened their proposal determined to quickly fill my schedule with conflicting activities.

But I had worked with this production group before, liked and respected them. More: I enjoyed spending time with them. And then, I read. And I was impressed. The program they proposed had wit, feeling, and style. It was pointed without being overbearing. It had character. And it held my interest.

I enlisted. I didn't imagine that *Affluenza* would become wildly popular. At most, I thought it might present a few significant scenes and ideas to an interested audience. It would impart a warm feeling and then, like most broadcasting, evaporate, leaving only a small, wet spot in its place.

What I hadn't figured on was timing, timing. *Affluenza* aired in the late 1990s, a time when more Americans were feeling fatter bank accounts—and more hollowness inside. Shopping and stock market speculation were becoming the genuine national pastimes. But at the same time, greater numbers of Americans were seeking to cash themselves out of what was becoming to them a daily rough-and-tumble struggle for mere things. So, against all expectation (or at least mine), *Affluenza* generated a kind of small but fierce enthusiasm. Discussion groups were convened. Tapes and transcripts were passed around, read, and replayed. Viewers who were drawn in by unexpected flashes of wit in the program stayed around to find that their consciences could be tickled, too.

This book is the cheerful result of accumulated curiosities from people who would like to run some of *Affluenza*'s thinking through their mind and hearts. It is not a how-to book, so much as a what-if book. While it contains some staggeringly practical suggestions for small and large proposals that could reform our cities, reorder our tax code, and build new kinds of communities that emphasize sharing over competition, it is not a book that shakes a finger in our faces and reprimands hard-working Americans for wanting a little more comfort, elegance, and enjoyment in our lives. On the contrary. *Affluenza* respects those perfectly human desires, and seeks to create ways to make comfort, elegance, and enjoyment more genuine and durable than purchasable, perishable commodities. More than most start-ups or dot-coms, it creates something of real value—a new way of accounting for true happiness in our lives.

Scott Simon
Weekend Edition Saturday Host
National Public Radio

Washington, D.C.
February 2001

PREFACE

Most movies start with a book, but this book started with a movie. In 1996, together with Vivia Boe, a fellow public television producer, I set out to craft a documentary about the subject of overconsumption and its many not-so-benign consequences for American society. Our research told us the subject was a huge one, touching our lives as Americans in more ways than any other social or environmental issue. But how to make sense of it? How to present the issue in a manner so that viewers could see that multiple problems were caused by our consuming passion, and were all connected to each other?

After videotaping more than two-thirds of the program, we were still wondering how to weave together the wide range of material we had collected. Then, on a flight from Seattle to Washington, D.C. to do still more videotaping, I happened to see the word *affluenza* used in passing in an article I was reading. For me, it was like that moment in cartoons when the light bulb goes on over someone's head. This was it: affluenza. A single word that not only would make a catchy (pun intended) TV title, but suggested a disease resulting from overconsumption.

Vivia and I agreed that here was a way to make the impacts of overconsuming more clearly understandable—as symptoms of a virus that, in the United States at least, had reached epidemic proportions. We could then look at the history of this disease, try to understand how and why it spread, what its carriers and hot zones were, and finally, how it could be treated.

From that point on, we began to use the term, asking interviewees if the idea made sense to them. And indeed, real doctors told us they could see symptoms of affluenza in many of their patients, symptoms often manifesting themselves physically. A psychologist offered his observation that many of his clients "suffer from affluenza, but very few know that's what they're suffering from."

To be certain that *Affluenza* would be carried by as many PBS affiliate stations as possible, Vivia and I borrowed a page from the marketers and promoted it shamelessly. At a Chicago meeting of PBS programmers, we wore lab coats and stethoscopes, with name pins labeling us Dr. John, Affluenza Epidemiologist, and Dr. Vivia, Affluenza Epidemiologist. We passed out medicine vials labeled Affluenza Vaccine (containing candy). We wanted the programmers to know that our show would be entertaining as well as informative. With a teaspoon of sugar to make the medicine go down.

Our documentary, *Affluenza*, premiered on PBS on September 15, 1997, and was greeted with an outpouring of audience calls and letters from every part of the United States, making it clear to us that we had touched a deep nerve of concern. Viewers as old as ninety-three wrote to express their fears for their grandchildren, while twenty-year-olds recounted sad tales from the lower depths of credit-card debt. A cover story in the *Washington Post* Sunday magazine about people trying to simplify their lives introduced them as they were watching the program. A teacher in rural North Carolina showed it to her class of sixth graders and said they wanted to talk about it for the next two weeks. On average, the kids thought they had three times as much "stuff" as they needed. One girl said she could no longer close her closet door. "I've just got too many things, clothes I never wear," she explained. "I can't get rid of them."

CROSSING POLITICAL LINES

Though past criticisms of consumerism have come mostly from the liberal side of the American political spectrum, we were pleased to find that *Affluenza* spoke to the concerns of Americans of all political persuasions. The head of one statewide conservative family organization wrote to congratulate us, saying "this issue is so important for families." Ratings and audience response were as high in conservative cities like Salt Lake and Houston as they were in liberal San Francisco or Minneapolis. In colleges, where *Affluenza* is now widely used in many departments, the program is as popular at Brigham Young as at Berkeley. At Appalachian State University in Boone, North Carolina, students and faculty showed it to audiences in both poor mountain communities and upscale churches, recording audience comments and producing a video of their own called *Escaping Affluenza in the Mountains*.

THE WORLD IS WATCHING

In 1998, we followed *Affluenza* with a closer look at treating the disease called *Escape from Affluenza*. Since that time, both television programs have been widely shown throughout the United States and abroad. We've become convinced that this is an issue that troubles people *throughout the world*. We've heard from countries where we couldn't imagine anyone would be concerned about affluenza—Thailand, Estonia, Russia, Nigeria, for example—but where, indeed, citizens hoped to adopt what was good about the American lifestyle and avoid what was harmful.

An Islamic business magazine in Sri Lanka asked us for a short article about the disease. Activists in rural northern Burma wanted to translate the TV program into a local dialect called Kachin. A sixteen-year-old Israeli girl sought permission to

© 2001 by Joel Pett

project it onto the wall of a Tel Aviv shopping center. Seeing overconsumption as a disease, they said, helped them understand it better and explain it to others.

We had hoped affluenza would become a household word. That hasn't quite happened yet, but the term is certainly much more widely used. An Internet search before our PBS broadcast turned up about 200 cases of the word on the Web—all of them in Italian, where "affluenza" simply means affluence. Now one finds thousands of examples, referring, in the vast majority of cases, to overconsumption.

A SOCIAL DISEASE

But often with different emphases. Some writers have used the term primarily with reference to the spoiled children of the super-rich. Others to what they call "sudden wealth syndrome." Defined as such, it loses the social/political message we put forward and becomes a matter of purely personal behavior. In our view, however, the virus is not confined to the upper classes, but has found its way throughout our society. Its symptoms affect the poor as well as the rich, and our two-tiered system (with rich getting richer and poor poorer) punishes the poor twice. They are conditioned to want the goods life, but given very little possibility of attaining it. Affluenza infects all of us, though in different ways.

AFFLUENZA: THE BOOK

After the TV broadcasts, calls from three individuals convinced me of the need to write a book on the subject. Thomas Naylor, an economist, and David Wann, an environmental scientist, both suggested a collaboration, while Todd Keithley, a New York literary agent, added his opinion that such a book would find an eager readership. I was immensely gratified by the reaction to the *Affluenza* television specials. But television, even at its most informative, is still a superficial medium; you simply can't put that much material into an hour. And that's the reason for this book: to explain "affluenza" in more depth, with more examples, more symptoms, more evidence, more-thorough exposition. If you've seen the video, you'll recognize a few of the characters and stories. But this book represents three more years of research, updated data and additional stories.

In the jargon of consumer culture, it's "new and improved!"

A COUPLE OF QUICK CAVEATS

With apologies to other citizens of North and South America, we frequently use the terms "America" and "Americans" to refer to the United States and its citizens. We mean no disrespect to other Americans, but simply recognize the colloquial usage that the term has throughout the rest of the world. Further, we do not mean to imply in this book any generalized condemnation of wealthy Americans or of money itself. Used properly for the common good (as by members of the group, Responsible Wealth, for example—see Chapter 26), money can contribute to the health of our society instead of encouraging affluenza. Indeed, this book would not have been written without the financial support of generous individuals.

Happy reading!

John de Graaf
Seattle, Washington
December 10, 2000

ACKNOWLEDGMENTS

The authors wish to extend their heartfelt thanks to the following people:

To Vivia Boe, John's fellow producer on both the *Affluenza* and *Escape from Affluenza* television programs. Her insights and ideas strengthened those works immeasurably. To Scott Simon for his terrific work as host of *Affluenza*, and for the foreword to this book. To Chris De Boer, Francine Strickwerda, and Hope Marston, for their research and production interviews during the making of those programs. And to all the other people who worked on the programs, including all of John's longtime colleagues at KCTS Television..

To Susan Sechler, Vicki Robin, The Pew Charitable Trusts, The Merck Family Fund, The Summit Foundation, KCTS Television, Oregon Public Broadcasting, The New Road Map Foundation, and ITVS, whose support helped make those programs possible. To John Hoskyns-Abrahall and Winnie Scherrer at Bullfrog Films and Anne Robinson at PBS. To Peter Barnes, Leyna Bernstein, and Pam Carr, for their support at the Mesa Refuge writer's retreat, and to Mesa Refuge cowriters Jonathan Rowe, Terry Tempest Williams, and Carl Anthony, who helped think some of this through.

To all those people whose stories, words and ideas are included in this book. To Arnie Anfinson, Monique Miller, Wanda Urbanska (the host of *Escape from Affluenza*), Frank Levering, Cecile Andrews, and other friends in the voluntary simplicity movement. To those who read this manuscript and offered helpful input: Dawn Griffin, Trish Padian, Joseph Webb, Stuart Lanier, Scott Gassman, and Jennifer Liss. And to Robert Meier for research assistance.

To Paula Wissel, David de Graaf, and Oliver and Vivian de Graaf for their love, support and patience. To the memory of David Wann Sr., whose convictions drove his actions; to Marjorie Wann, a very wise and resourceful woman; and to Colin and Libby, who inspire Dave to keep working. To all of Dave's friends at Harmony Village, who supported this project in many ways, but especially to Macon and Ginny Cowles, Matt and Linda Worswick, Wendy Hanophy, Claire Lanier, Bob Paulson, and Edee Gail. To our agent Todd Keithley.

Special thanks to the Merck Family Fund, the True North Foundation, the Threshold Foundation, the Weeden Foundation, and the Fred Gellert Family Foundation, who supported the writing of this book.

To Joanne Kliejunas and everyone at Redefining Progress, who helped and trusted in us, and to Steven Piersanti and all of our friends at Berrett-Koehler Publishers, who believed in this book. For all those whose help we have failed to remember, we thank you and ask your forgiveness.

It took a village to write this book, but all the errors and omissions should be blamed only on the authors.

Introduction: what is affluenza?

Imagine, if you will, the following scene:

In his office, a doctor offers his diagnosis to an attractive, expensively dressed female patient. "There's nothing physically wrong with you," he says. His patient is incredulous. "Then why do I feel so awful?" she asks. "So bloated and sluggish. I've got a big new house, a brand new car, a new wardrobe, and I just got a big raise at work. Why am I so miserable, doctor? Isn't there some pill you can give me?" The doctor shakes his head. "I'm afraid not," he replies. "There's no pill for what's wrong with you." "What is it, doctor?" she asks, alarmed. "Affluenza," he answers gravely. "It's the new epidemic. It's extremely contagious. It can be cured, but not easily."

Of course, the scene is an imaginary one, but the epidemic is real. Amid the prosperity, the soaring economy and the superficial upbeat atmosphere marking the

dawn of a new millennium, a powerful virus has infected American society, threatening our wallets, our friendships, our families our communities, and our environment. We call the virus *affluenza*. And because the United States has become the
economic model for most of the world, the virus is now loose on every continent.

Affluenza's costs and consequences are immense, though often concealed.
Untreated, the disease can cause permanent discontent. Were you to find it in the
Oxford English Dictionary, the definition might be something like the following:

> **affluenza**, n. a painful, contagious, socially transmitted condition of overload,
> debt, anxiety, and waste resulting from the dogged pursuit of more.

We Americans have been pursuing more—more stuff, especially—for most of
our history. We've been doing it to the exclusion of most other values since the
"me" decade of the 80s, and like starving children at a smorgasbord during the last
several years of uninterrupted economic expansion.

EARTH IN THE BALANCE

Quietly, like some sort of unseen mind-snatcher, the virus has entirely consumed
American political dialogue. Consider Al Gore. In 1992, while still a Senator, he
wrote a popular book called *Earth in the Balance*. America, Gore noted then,

> is holding ever more tightly to its habit of consuming larger and larger quanti-
> ties every year of coal, oil, fresh air and water, trees, topsoil and the thousand
> other substances we rip from the crust of the earth, transforming them into
> not just the sustenance and shelter we need but much more that we don't
> need. . . . The accumulation of material goods is at an all time high, but so is
> the number of people who feel an emptiness in their lives.[1]

Americans, Gore suggested, had become addicted to stuff. Our civilization, he
wrote, promises happiness through "the consumption of an endless stream of shiny
new products. . . . . But the promise is always false." A year later, Al Gore was inau-
gurated as Vice President of the United States. During the ceremony, a soprano sang
the beautiful old Shaker hymn, *Simple Gifts*—("'Tis the gift to be simple, 'tis the gift
to be free . . ."). During the song, Gore nodded in agreement. Then, in the next couple of years, something happened. The mind-snatcher came and took Al Gore.

In the 1996 vice-presidential debate, Gore's opponent, Jack Kemp, vowed to
"double the size of the U.S. economy in the next fifteen years." Yet Gore never
questioned whether it would be a good thing for Americans to consume twice as
much. By the 2000 election, the transformation of Al Gore into an agent of affluenza was complete. In a presidential debate, he vowed to increase the size of the U.S.

economy by thirty percent in ten years. And what happened to Al Gore seems to be happening to all of us.

"Who wants to be a millionaire?" asks the hit ABC TV show. Apparently, nearly everyone. Our newspaper editors believe we can't get enough stories of twenty-something men and women who are already tycoons, having watched their shares of software stock soar in value, or having started some dot-com that, while never turning a profit, has attracted millions in investor capital.

Of course, there's a downside to this obsession, and in our hearts, most of us know it. Pollster Richard Harwood found that out in 1995, when he conducted a survey about American attitudes concerning consumption for the Merck Family Fund. "People are saying that we spend and buy far more than we need. That our children are becoming very materialistic, and that we're spending for what we want today at the expense of future generations and our own future," Harwood explains. "It crosses religious lines, age lines, race, income, and education. There is a universal feeling in this nation that we've become too materialistic, too greedy, too self-absorbed, too selfish, and that we need to bring back into balance the enduring values that have guided this country over generations. Values of faith, family, responsibility, generosity, friendship."[2]

NEEDING MORE PLANETS

In our view, the affluenza epidemic is rooted in the obsessive, almost religious quest for economic expansion that has become the core principle of what is called "the American dream." It's rooted in the fact that our supreme measure of national progress is that quarterly ring of the cash register we call the Gross Domestic Product. It's rooted in the idea that every generation will be materially wealthier than its predecessor, and that somehow, each of us can pursue that single-minded end without damaging the countless other things we hold dear.

It doesn't work that way. The contention of this book is that if we don't begin to reject our culture's incessant demands to "buy now," we will "pay later" in ways we can scarcely imagine. The bill is already coming due. At its most extreme, "affluenza" threatens to exhaust the earth itself. "We human beings, especially in this century, have been producing and consuming at a rate that far exceeds the ability of the planet to absorb our pollution or replenish the stock," says corporate critic Jeremy Rifkin.

Even one of Rifkin's favorite targets agrees. "The Earth can't withstand a systematic increase of material things," contends Robert Shapiro, CEO of the Monsanto Corporation. "If we grow by using more stuff, we'd better start looking for a new planet."

Make that several new planets. That's what scientists say would be needed if everyone on earth were to suddenly adopt the American standard of living.

CONNECTIONS

Consider the following scenario, as reported in a 1998 article in *Parade* magazine:

The US economy defied experts' predictions and stayed healthy despite a global financial crisis and the threat of presidential impeachment, thanks to the resilience and stamina of the American consumer. . . . There was plenty of bad news. . . . Much of the nation's weather was awful. Torrential rains in California, a devastating flood on the Ohio River, weeks of triple-digit heat in Texas, lethal ice storms in Virginia and the worst Atlantic hurricane season in 200 years. The 1997 poverty rate was still higher than in the early '70s. And although the federal deficit is gone, Americans are deeper in debt than ever...But nothing distracted us from the good news: high employment, low inflation, real wage increases and the best mortgage rates and gasoline prices in decades. . . . Consumer spending remained strong throughout the year, guaranteeing continued economic growth.

The best gasoline prices, awful weather; continued economic growth, persistent poverty; consumer confidence, spiraling debt. Are they all somehow connected? We think so.

In each of the past four years more Americans declared personal bankruptcy than graduated from college. Our annual production of solid waste would fill a convoy of garbage trucks stretching halfway to the moon. We have twice as many shopping centers as high schools. We now work more hours each year than do the citizens of any other industrial country, including Japan. Though we comprise only 4.7 percent of the earth's people, we account for twenty-five percent of its global-warming greenhouse gas emissions. Ninety-five percent of our workers say they wish they could spend more time with their families. Forty percent of our lakes and streams are too polluted for swimming or fishing. Our CEOs now earn 400 times as much as average workers, a tenfold increase since 1980. Since 1950, we Americans have used up more resources than everyone who ever lived on earth before then.

However unrelated they may seem, all of these facts are also connected, diverse symptoms of affluenza. Much of this book focuses on the United States because its citizens are the world's most profligate consumers. Yet what is happening in the United States is clearly beginning to happen elsewhere as the American lifestyle becomes the model for nearly all of the rest of the world. But other countries may actually have more of a choice than the United States does. Where affluenza is not so full-blown an epidemic, they can keep themselves from greater infection and preserve more balanced lifestyles. We believe there are lessons for every country and every person, rich and poor, to be found in America's mistakes. The global economy means that all of us are in this together and need to understand and control this disease.

SYMPTOMS

We have divided the book into three sections. The first explores many of the symptoms of affluenza, each—only half-whimsically—compared to a real flu symptom. Think of how you feel when you've got the bug. You're likely to be running a temperature. You're congested. Your body is achy. You may have chills. Your stomach is upset. You're weak. You might have swollen glands, even a rash.

In the Age of Affluenza, America as a society shows all of these symptoms, metaphorically at least. We present each as a chapter. We start with individual symptoms, then move to the social conditions, and finally turn to the environmental impacts of affluenza.

Some chapters may greet you with the shock of self-recognition—"Honey, that's me!" You might have noticed the conditions discussed in others taking hold of your friends. You might find some more troubling than others, worrying more about your children than about your Mother Earth. You might be well off materially, but continually stressed out or feeling like your life lacks purpose or meaning. Or you might be poor, and angry at your inability to give your children what marketers say they "gotta have" to fit in. You might have just felt the sting of insults from another driver, red-faced with road rage. Or watched bulldozers destroy the only open space left around your community—to make room for row upon row of identical new tract homes with three-car garages. If you're elderly, you may have noticed your children's inability to balance their checkbooks, and you may worry for their children. If you're young, you may be anxious about your own future.

Wherever you're coming from, we believe you'll clearly recognize that at least some of the symptoms of affluenza affect you. Then, as you read on, you'll begin to see how they're connected to others less obvious from your vantage point.

GENESIS OF THE DISEASE

In Part Two of this book, we look beneath the symptoms to search for causes. Is affluenza simply human nature as some would suggest? What was the genesis of this powerful virus? How has it mutated throughout history and when did it begin to reach epidemic proportions? What choices did we make as a society (between free time and stuff, for example) that deepened our infection? We look carefully at warnings from across time and cultures, and at early efforts to eradicate the disease with controls and quarantines.

Then we discover how spread of the disease has become not only socially accept-able, but encouraged by all the powerful electronic carriers our technological civi-lization keeps perfecting. We suggest that affluenza promises to meet our needs in inefficient and destructive ways. And we contend that an entire industry of pseudo-physicians, handsomely rewarded by those with a huge stake in the perpetuation of affluenza, conspire to keep the diagnosis of the disease and the extent of its symp-toms from reaching the general public.

CURING AFFLUENZA

But far be it from our intent to leave you permanently depressed. Affluenza *can* be treated, and millions of ordinary Americans are already taking steps in that direction. When we produced the TV version of *Affluenza* in 1996, trend tracker Gerald Celente put "Voluntary Simplicity" near the top of his list of movements that were rapidly gaining supporters. Richard Harwood's 1995 poll found that twenty-eight percent of Americans had already chosen to "downshift" materially in some fashion, with eighty-six percent of them saying they were happier as a result.

Celente predicted that fifteen percent of Americans would be practicing a "strong" form of voluntary simplicity by the year 2000. He's had to backtrack some as late '90s prosperity brought a new wave of consumer frenzy, but he still expects interest in simple living to resurface in a big way when the latest economic bubble bursts.

Even now, despite the counter tendency of surging consumer passion, increas-ingly harried lifestyles continue to produce rat-race refugees. Enough to make cor-porate marketers salivate over millions of potential new customers. Hence, companies urge us to "simplify" our lives by buying their products, and new publi-cations like Time-Warner's *Real Simple* (it would be more aptly called *Real Cynical*, as most of it is devoted to ads for expensive products) build an audience of 400,000 subscribers before printing their first issues.

What that says to us is that there are a lot of people out there looking for answers to affluenza. Part Three of this book is devoted to offering you some answers we've found.

As with symptoms, we look at treatments starting with the personal and advanc-ing to the social and political. Our treatments, too, employ the medical metaphor. We start like you do when you've got the flu, with bed rest, aspirin, and chicken soup—individual prescriptions already being popularized by the "new frugality" and "voluntary simplicity" movements.

We encourage a restored interest in the natural world outdoors, with its remarkable healing powers. We agree with Gerald Celente. "There's this commercial out," he says, "and it shows this middle-aged man walking through the woods pumping his arms, and all of a sudden in the next cut, there he is on the back porch, woods in the background, walking on this treadmill that must have cost a fortune. It doesn't make sense. It was so much nicer walking through the woods and it cost nothing at all."[3]

We suggest strategies for rebuilding families and communities, and for respecting and restoring the earth and its biological rules. We offer "political prescriptions," with the belief that some well-considered legislation (to reward frugality and punish waste, for example) can help create a less affluenza-friendly social environment and make it easier for individuals to get well and stay that way.

We also present preventive approaches, including vaccines and vitamins, to strengthen our personal and social immune systems. And we suggest an annual check-up. Ours comes in three phases:

1. You can test how you're doing personally in staying well.

2. You can help your community assess its own true health, using indices of sustainability developed by several American cities.

3. And finally, as a people, we can find a truly useful substitute for our current, outmoded, measure of national health, the Gross Domestic Product (GDP).

We recommend an index called the Genuine Progress Indicator (GPI), currently being fine-tuned by Redefining Progress, an Oakland, California think-tank. Using multiple indices to discover how we're doing, the GPI paints a different picture of our real success as a society. While GDP has risen steadily throughout our history, the GPI has been falling since 1973.

LET'S BEGIN A DIALOGUE

There is little in this book that is truly new information, yet the issue in this "information age" isn't more information. It's how to make sense of what we already know. We offer a way of understanding seemingly disconnected personal, social, and environmental problems that makes sense to us—as symptoms of a perilous epidemic that threatens your future and that of generations to come. We don't expect you to agree with everything in these chapters, nor even to immediately convince you that affluenza is a real disease. Our intention is to encourage a national dialogue about the American consumer dream so that whatever choices you make about consumption are made with a clearer understanding of their possible consequences.

The message of this book isn't to stop buying; it's to buy carefully and consciously with full attention to the real benefits and costs of your purchases, remembering, always, that the best things in life aren't things.

PART ONE

Symptoms

CHAPTER 1

Shopping
fever

Gotta listen to me honey/gotta get all your
money/Gotta know just where I stand/
If you want to be my date/Well you better
get it straight/I'm a big time shopping man. . . .
Baby come on, there's a whole lotta
shoppin' going on. . . .
Get that money out of your savings account/
There's a whole lotta shoppin' going on. . . .

—FOLKSINGER ALAN ATKISSON

It's Thanksgiving Day and eight-year-old Jason Jones has just finished stuffing himself with turkey, cranberry sauce, and pumpkin pie a la mode. He sits at his PC, frantically typing a list of presents he hopes to receive from Santa Claus for Christmas. He plans to deliver the list to Santa the next day, opening day of the Christmas shopping season, and, incidentally, of affluenza season. Jason's list contains ten items, including a trip to Disney World, a mountain bike, a cell phone, a DVD player, and several compact disks.

Jason is no dummy; he doesn't really believe in Santa Claus, but he knows his parents give him what he asks Santa for, so he gets up bright and early on Friday to play the game. Jason and his mother, Janet, set out in their Lincoln Navigator and, half an hour later, arrive at the All-Star Bazaar, where thousands of people are already fighting for the remaining parking spots nearest the entrance.

The mall is jam-packed with frantic holiday shoppers, unwitting and at-risk in an affluenza hot zone, armed only with credit cards and checkbooks. In one store, a crowd gathers to watch two parents duke it out over the last remaining Dino-Man, the latest hot kids' toy, a doll with the body of a weightlifter and the head of a Tyrannosaurus (and selling faster than Beanie Babies). In a corner, a mother sobs, knowing she got there too late to get a Dino-Man for her son. "I knew I should have camped out here last night," she wails. Other customers, already exhausted, sit on benches by the bottom of an escalator, beside mountains of merchandise, looking both tense and bored.

It takes Jason nearly an hour to get through the line to Santa's lap and deliver his list. His mom leaves him in the video arcade with a roll of quarters while she makes the rounds of the dozens of shops in the mall. Hours later, on the way home, they stop at Blockbuster's to rent a couple of movies so Jason won't complain of boredom that night. Though the day is sunny and warm, unusually so for late fall, even the park in Jason's upper-middle class subdivision is devoid of kids. There are plenty of children in this neighborhood of young professionals. But if they're not shopping, they're indoors communing with Nintendo Play Stations or The Cartoon Network. It's a tough choice for Jason, but he's tired of the games he has so he turns on the TV.

Jason is, admittedly, an imaginary, composite kid. But his experience at the mall is far from atypical. In 1999, according to the National Retail Foundation, Americans spent nearly $200 billion on holiday gifts, more than $850 per consumer. Affluenza season, the month between Thanksgiving and Christmas, generated twenty-five percent of all retail profits

Most Americans tell pollsters they want less emphasis on holiday spending and gift-giving. A third cannot even remember what they gave their significant other the previous year, and many cannot pay off their Christmas debts until the following summer, if then. Yet the urge to splurge continues to surge. It's as if we Americans, despite our intentions, suffer from some kind of Willpower Deficiency Syndrome, a breakdown in affluenza immunity.

MALL MANIA

Since World War II, Americans have been engaged in a spending binge unprecedented in history and fueled to a frenzy by the booming economy of the past several years. We now spend nearly $6 trillion a year, more than $21,000 per person, most of it on consumer goods, which account for two-thirds of the recent growth in the U.S. economy. For example, we spend more on shoes, jewelry, and watches ($80 billion) than on higher education ($65 billion).[1] On a five-day shopping trip to Paris, the wife of Florida governor Jeb Bush spent $19,000, though she reported only $500 of it to U.S. Customs.[2] But she's not alone in her passion for shopping.

In 1986, America still had more high schools than shopping centers. Less than fifteen years later, we have more than twice as many shopping centers as high schools. In the Age of Affluenza (as we believe the decades surrounding the Second Millennium will eventually be called), shopping centers have supplanted churches as a symbol of cultural values. In fact, seventy percent of us visit malls each week, more than attend houses of worship.[3]

Our equivalent of Gothic cathedrals are the megamalls, which continually replace smaller shopping centers, drawing customers from ever-greater distances. Typically, they cover areas of fertile farmland that formerly produced bumper crops instead of traffic jams. Indeed, forty-six acres of prime American farmland are lost to "development" every hour. When a new megamall opens, the pomp and ceremony rival anything Notre Dame or Chartres might have witnessed in medieval times.

The Super Mall in Auburn, Washington, opened to a stampede of 100,000 shoppers in October 1995. The crowd gathered under an imitation of Washington's 14,410-foot Mt. Rainier. Rising above the Super Mall's front entrance, the imitation mountain provided one show which the real thing could not: a display of fireworks, set off as soon as the ribbon-cutting ceremony was over.

In a spirit of boosterism that would have impressed Sinclair Lewis' Babbitt, speaker after speaker extolled the wonders of the new shopping center, the biggest in the state. "The number of shoppers expected to visit here over the next year exceeds 1.2 million," bubbled Auburn's mayor, adding that "committed shoppers can shop till they drop in 1.2 million square feet of shopping space." Along with a new race track and casino in the area, the mall was expected to become a "destination attraction" for vacationers from the entire western United States and Canada. It would, they said, create 4,000 jobs and "improve the quality of life throughout the region." Thirty percent of the expected business would come from tourists who would each spend about five hours and more than $200 at the mall.[4]

FUN FOR THE WHOLE FAMILY

The thousands of eager shoppers on hand for the opening wore bored and impatient expressions during the speeches, but pushed eagerly through the open doors when the rhetoric stopped. One woman said she was "really excited about the mall because this is something we haven't had in this part of Washington. We were waiting for something like this."

"We said 'if we build it, they will come,' and they did," gushed a happy shopkeeper. Another explained that its hardwood floors "add a little sense of excitement to the mall. They're much easier than walking on tile or granite and make the Super Mall really special." She hoped children would enjoy it, "because shopping has become such a family experience that's really important."

Really. And it's a good thing, too, since we Americans now spend six hours a week shopping and only forty minutes playing with our kids.[5] "Shopping malls have really become the centers of many communities," says Michael Jacobson, founder of the Center for the Study of Commercialism in Washington, D.C. "Children as well as adults see a shopping center as just the natural destination to fill a bored life."[6]

WHAT ELSE MATTERS

"If you've seen the mall, you've seen them all," sneer critics like Jacobson, but "committed shoppers" (some psychologists say they *should* be committed) disagree. They're willing to jet across the country for new shopping experiences. So much so that some airlines now offer package flights to shopping Meccas like Potomac Mills, a giant "discount" mall divided into sections that are euphemistically labeled "neighborhoods." Potomac Mills bills itself as the "number one tourist attraction in Virginia," with more visitors each year than Shenandoah National Park, itself the most visited American National Park.

The host of *Affluenza,* Scott Simon, visited Potomac Mills while filming the television program. Shoppers were eager to answer his questions about where they came from and what they thought of the mall. None of the people Simon talked to were sweating profusely. But all seemed infected by shopping fever, often the first symptom of affluenza.

Two women from Dallas, Texas, said they'd been at the mall for three days straight, while their husbands golfed nearby. "We're always looking for a bargain. You've got to know the brands and we have experience, we're proud to say," they proclaimed. "I didn't need anything. I just went to shop," said a man with a cart full of merchandise. "Whatever I like I buy." "I bought a lot more than I planned to," another woman admitted. "You just see so much."

Yes, you do, and that's the idea. It's why big malls sell much more per square foot than do their smaller counterparts. Seeing so much leads to impulse buying, the key to mall profitability. Only a quarter of mall shoppers actually come with a specific product in mind. The rest come just to shop. "What else matters?" asked one of the ladies from Dallas, only half in jest.

"I came here with one overriding interest, to spend money," said a proud teenage girl, who was getting rid of the hundred dollars her mother had given her for this particular spree. "I like to shop," she explained. She's not alone. One poll found that ninety-three percent of teenage American girls rate shopping as their favorite activity.[7]

An older couple passed by with a shopping cart piled to the brim. "This is only half of what we've purchased," the man said cheerfully. "We brought a long list of things to buy," his wife added, "and then we bought a lot of stuff that wasn't on the list." Impulse. They were examining the fold-out map Potomac Mills provides to shoppers, saying, "we'd be lost without it."

But Potomac Mills is a mere mini-mall compared to the Mall of America in Bloomington, Minnesota. With 4.2 million square feet of shopping space, our biggest mall ("Where It's Always 72 Degrees!") spreads over an area the size of seventy-eight football fields. It employs 10,000 people and attracts forty million visits a year. The Mall of America is more than metaphorically a cathedral; some people even get married there. It is also a world-class affluenza hot zone.

In the Age of Affluenza, nothing succeeds like excess. "Good malls are usually the most profitable kind of real estate there is," says one Los Angeles real estate consultant. "Good malls are money machines."[8] "Good," he points out, means bigger. Because of that, the frenzy to attract megamalls pits city against city, each offering sweetheart deals in hopes of capturing tax revenues later on. To win such deals, mall developers compete for the most-profitable stores. According to *The Sacramento Bee,* the Seattle-based Nordstrom Company received $30 million in direct subsidies and incentives to put a store in Roseville, California's Galleria Mall. Why? "Nordstrom's does the highest sales per square foot in the industry," says mall developer Michael Levin. Most people, says Levin, will only drive about half an hour to a mall, "but with Nordstrom, they will drive much farther."[9]

HOME SHOPPING

Of course, these days you don't have to drive at all (or fly either) to shop, though most people still do. But while malls, and vast discount megastores like Wal-Mart and Costco, still boast growing sales (and still drive smaller, locally owned stores out of business), Americans are doing a whole lotta shopping right from their couches. Some forty *billion* mail-order catalogs flooded our homes last year, about 150 for every one of us, selling everything from soup to nuts (to refrigerators to underwear). "Buy Now, Pay Later," they shout. While some of us resent their arrival, most Americans eagerly await them and order from them with abandon. In some cases, we even pay for the catalogs (such as Sears') so that we can pay for what's in them.

Then there are the home shopping channels. Critics mock them as presenting a continual succession of baubles on bimbos, but for a sizeable percentage of Americans, they're the highlight of our cable TV systems, and highly profitable. And to think someone once called TV "a vast wasteland." That was before the shopping channels, of course.

Mail-order catalogs and shopping channels carry a lot more than products. They are highly effective carriers of affluenza. Next time a catalog comes, check it with a high-powered microscope.

CYBER SHOPPING

In the past several years, of course, a new affluenza carrier has come online. And it threatens to outdraw malls, catalogs, and shopping channels combined. The intense frenzy with which the ubiquitous Internet has been embraced as a shopping center can only be compared to that which followed the discovery of gold in California and Alaska, or the Texas oil boom. Twenty percent of Americans now spend at least five hours a week online and much of that time is spent shopping—a majority of Internet sites are now selling something.

During the 1999 affluenza season, consumers spent $10 billion online, three times what they spent only a year earlier. Now that's growth! For the year, e-sales topped $33 billion. That's still only a tiny fraction of total retail sales, but soon Internet shopping should eclipse catalog sales. Everything imaginable (and some things unimaginable) can now be bought online.

A REAL E-MAN

Proof of that is to be found in the adventures of DotComGuy (formerly Mitch Maddox—he had his name legally changed), a twenty-six-year-old Dallas man who has vowed not to leave his home for a year, while making all his purchases online. Maddox found regular shopping too slow for his tastes, and too much like work. He says he told his "low-tech parents" he could "live off the Internet for a year and never leave my apartment." Now, thousands of "DotComHeads" hang out at his Web site to watch this e-male shop. But he doesn't just buy online, he sells as well: DotComGuy merchandise including T-shirts, mouse pads (of course!), baseball hats, bumper stickers, and cake mix. "This is the Internet. This is a forum for e-commerce,"[10] he says, in answer to all those foolish people who thought it was an information highway.

SHOPPING AS THERAPY

When Scott Simon visited Potomac Mills, the mall was running one of the cleverest ad campaigns we've ever seen, featuring an alluring actress named Beckett Royce, whose persona combined bubble-headed ditziness with winking "joke's on you," sophistication. "Shopping is therapy," she intoned, lying on a couch. "Listen to that little voice in your head: SHOP, SHOP, SHOP."

Royce's monologues mocked the shopping channels and catalog shopping, but definitely not shopping at Potomac Mills. She pranced between its aisles, grabbing item after item, then adding up what she'd bought and chirruping, "I *spaved* a hundred dollars!" "Spaving" means spending and saving at the same time, she explained, suggesting that at Potomac Mills everyone could become a "spaver."

"The more you buy, the more you save," proclaims an ad for the Bon Marche, a Seattle department store. As our next chapter demonstrates, large numbers of Americans apparently believe this mathematical impossibility. Beckett Royce is no fool; she gets paid plenty to persuade the credulous that "spaving" works. Simple mathematics persuades otherwise. But then, math scores have been falling.

And, as we discover in our next chapter, the road to bankruptcy is *spaved* with good intentions.

CHAPTER 2

A rash of bankruptcies

Uh oh, we're in the red, dear
On our credit card it shows
Christmas is almost over
But the debit line still grows.

—"ALTERNATIVE" CAROL
from the Center for a New American Dream
(to the tune of "Rudolph,
the Red-nosed Reindeer")

On the Monday after Thanksgiving, Janet Jones, Jason's mom, drops him off at school, winds her way through heavy traffic back to the mall—a fairly new one, built in 10 B.P. (Before Pokemon)—and enters, eyes wide for the sales. She carries the wish list Jason wrote for Santa Claus. Making sure Mom knew what he wanted, Jason printed a copy of the list for her and left it, as if by accident, on his bed.

The first purchases go fine, and by her reckoning Janet has soon saved a hundred dollars, but when she tries to buy the mountain bike, there's a hitch. "I'm sorry," says the smiling clerk, "but you're over your limit on this card. Do you have another?" Momentarily embarrassed, Janet reaches in her purse. "No problem," she says. "I've got several." She remembers that slogan, "Some things are priceless, but for everything else there's Master-Card," and hands hers to the clerk, who runs it through a scanner. "Sorry," the young woman says with a sympathetic look. "Same results. Insufficient credit remaining."

Janet looks quickly around, hoping no one has seen her in this predicament, and, muttering "there must be some mistake," walks out of the bicycle shop.

On the way home from the mall, she passes the offices of Consumer Credit Counseling Service, and wonders if it might be time.

If she'd gone inside, she would have found things humming. These days, Consumer Credit Counseling Service (CCCS), a network with 1,100 offices in several countries, gets plenty of referrals—people who have gotten themselves deep in debt and haven't yet seen any light at the end of the tunnel.

PLASTIC NATION

According to Marielle Oetjen, a member of the CCCS staff in Colorado Springs, "One of the first things we do when people come here is cut up their credit cards. The whole availability and ease of credit makes it hard for people to remember that they're dealing with real money."[1]

Oetjen removes a large box from a shelf and pours the contents on the floor— hundreds, perhaps thousands, of cut-up credit cards. The average American now possesses five or more, for a nationwide total of well over a billion. The more you have, the more you're likely to be offered. Thomas' son was recently sent an offer for one, and he's only twelve! A steady stream of such offers fills American mailboxes, each offer with its own incentives: frequent flyer miles, introductory low interest rates, lower minimum payments. According to the *Guinness Book of World Records*, one American now has a whopping 1,262 credit cards, a dubious honor.[2]

"There's a lot of marketing ploys from the credit card companies to not only encourage customers but have those customers carry as much debt as possible," says Oetjen. That's how the companies (banks) make their money. Say you spend $2,000 on a typical credit card (eighteen percent interest), and make minimum payments to pay it off. It will take you eleven years, and you will end up paying double the original price. And that's if you never buy anything else with the card.

"The credit card companies push instant gratification," Oetjen points out. "Buy it now, don't worry about it. Pay it off in little monthly installments. You can take as long as you want. You can handle it. That's the ethic that's being pushed. That's what most of the folks that come in here get caught up in."

In fact, fewer than a third of Americans avoid interest by paying off their credit card balances each month. The average American household carried $7,564 in credit card debt during the year 2000. Even college students average $2,500. Total American credit card indebtedness tripled in the 1990s.[3]

The news was even worse for Cindy and Keaton Adams, an attractive young couple with two children who were in many ways typical Consumer Credit Counseling Service clients. They turned to CCCS when they found themselves $20,000 in debt and unable to make credit card payments. "We started out thinking we could finance the world," Keaton says. "And we tried, but it didn't work."[4]

It almost never does.

It all started when Keaton got a Mervyn's credit card at the age of eighteen. "With that," he says, "I managed to get a VISA card and Cindy managed to get a VISA card and we ended up with lots of VISA cards." They began buying plenty of things, all on credit. Besides credit card purchases, they found a way to get financing for new cars. "But it wasn't just 'let's get a nice $8,000 car,'" Cindy confesses. "It was 'let's try and finance an $18,000 car. The nicest car we can get.'"

But what they got was deeper and deeper into debt, until finally a debt collector just asked, "Why can't you pay your bills?" Keaton says it made him stop and think. When the debt collector suggested Consumer Credit Counseling, he took her advice. It was hard to watch their credit cards being cut up, Keaton and Cindy say now, but they're glad someone did it.

IS AMERICA BECOMING A DEBTOR'S PRISON?

The situation that faced the Adams family is not all that unusual these days. According to the *Los Angeles Times*, Americans are "straining under record debt loads amassed in a spending binge powered by the booming economy."[5] Current bankruptcy rates exceed those experienced during the Great Depression.

Rising debt, says one economist, is the "soft underbelly" of the U.S. economy. A soft underbelly covered with little red dots, as shopping fever leads to another affluenza symptom, a rash of bankruptcies. Six million Americans are as close to bankruptcy as the Adamses were. Each year, in fact, more than a million people— up from 313,000 in 1980, and including one in every seventy Americans—file for personal bankruptcy, more than graduate from college. That's been the case since 1996. On average, the debt load for such filers equals 22 months of income.[6] In response to the situation, lending institutions have successfully lobbied Congress to make it harder to declare bankruptcy, while at the same time they continue to push their customers toward financial ruin.

In 1980, U.S. household debt stood at sixty-five percent of disposable income. Today, the two figures are virtually equal. "Families are overextending themselves as never before as indicated recently when total household debts surpassed total after-tax incomes for the first time in history," writes *Los Angeles Times* reporter Leslie Earnest. "The biggest fear is what will happen to many families loaded with debt when the economy falters and jobs disappear—a scenario that would certainly drive up bankruptcies and foreclosures."[7]

A national *LA Times* poll (May 2000) found that eighty-four percent of Americans thought the economy was doing well, but four out of ten reported "some or much difficulty" paying their bills. And this is in *good* times. Elizabeth Warren, coauthor of *The Fragile Middle Class*, warns that "the next time the economy contracts . . . bankruptcies will explode."[8]

A PENNY SAVED—BARELY

There is a strange irony at work in contemporary America: The more incomes rise across the board, the less we save. It should be the other way around. Fatter paychecks ought to leave more dollars for savings accounts. Not so. When the film *Affluenza* was produced, Americans were saving just under four percent of their incomes, half the German rate and only a quarter that of Japan. That seemed, at the time, very bad news, since the savings rate had been about ten percent as recently as 1980. But today our national savings rate hovers near *zero,* and in some months falls below that line.[9] Meanwhile, impoverished Chinese, Indian, and Pakistani workers save a quarter of their incomes.

Advertisements often use exaggeration to touch popular social chords. Consider, for instance, the back cover of a recent *USA Weekend* magazine. An attractive woman, identified as "Veronica Lynn, Beverly Hills, FL, Doral Smoker," smiles from one half of the page while she is quoted on the other half as saying, "It lasts longer than my paycheck."[10] "It," in this case, is a Doral cigarette, the product the ad is selling. The underlying message is none too subtle: paychecks don't last long in contemporary America.

The United States of America. Land of history's biggest five-minute paychecks. But why worry? Light up. If you've already got affluenza, what's a little cancer?

WILL BOOMERS GO BUST?

Harvard University economist Juliet Schor points out that most Americans live without any adequate financial cushion. "Sixty percent of families," Schor writes, "have so little in the way of financial reserves that they can only sustain their lifestyles for about a month if they lose their jobs. The next richest can only hold out for about three and a half months."[11]

Some economists suggest there's no cause for alarm. Half of all Americans now own stocks (though in most cases, not many), they point out, and could sell them if need be. In a time of surging stock prices, many higher-income, stock-owning baby boomers see no need to be thrifty. They are relying on selling their stocks at a hefty profit to take care of their retirement needs a few years from now. It's a risky gamble, argues Tip Parker, an economic consultant and author of *What If Boomers Can't Retire?* Rising stock prices depend on the ability of boomers to sell their stocks to the next generation of workers, who, they expect, will pay top dollar.

But there are problems with that scenario, suggests Parker. In the future, there will be fewer workers to buy the stocks, and retirees will have to sell more cheaply to unload them. Moreover, as the Crash of '29 made only too clear, stock prices can plummet as well as climb, and many of them are already overvalued and not backed up by real corporate earnings.

Other analysts suggest that the current rash of bankruptcies has come primarily among lower-income Americans unable to keep pace with inflation in a period of increasing financial stratification. But recently, even Microsoft millionaires have joined their ranks. Some had used their stocks—whose value had continued to rise—as collateral for loans to finance expensive vacations or homes. "I could call up Solomon, Smith, Barney any time to ask for $10,000," said one. But when the value of her stock began to fall, Solomon, Smith, Barney called her up—to demand repayment. By then, her debts were greater than the amount she could cash her stock in for.

So why are we spending so much more now? Stay tuned. . . .

CHAPTER 3

Swollen expectations

*Greed has infected our society.
It is the worst infection.*

—DOCTOR PATCH ADAMS

*I was sad because I had no onboard fax until I
saw a man who had no mobile phone.*

—*New Yorker* cartoon
BY WARREN MILLER, 1993

ake a walk down memory lane. Way down. If you're as old as we are,
your memories carry you back to the 1950s, at least. The Second
World War and the Great Depression were over, and America was on
the move. Suburban houses going up everywhere. New cars rolling from the assembly lines and out onto new pavement. Ground breaking for the National Defense
Interstate Highway System, soon to stretch from sea to shining sea. A TV dinner
(introduced in 1953) in every oven.

"It's a great life, eh Bob?" a man in a '50s commercial intones as a young couple
and their tow-headed son sit on a couch watching the tube. "And tomorrow will be
even better, for you and for all the people." Of course, the great life wasn't great for
the millions who were poor or discriminated against. And even for middle-class
America, it wasn't worry-free. On the same day in 1957 (October 4th) that *Leave It
To Beaver* premiered on American television, those pesky Russians shot Sputnik into

space. Nikita Kruschev promised to bury us "in the peaceful field of economic competition." We know how that came out.

But 1957 was important for another less-heralded reason. It was the year the percentage of Americans describing themselves as "very happy" reached a peak never to be exceeded for the rest of the 20th Century.[1] The following year, a year when Americans bought 200 million "hula hoops," economist John Kenneth Galbraith published an influential book calling the United States "the affluent society."

We *felt* richer then than we do now. Most Americans today don't really think of themselves as affluent, says psychologist Paul Wachtel, "even though in terms of Gross National Product we have more than twice as much as we did then. Everybody's house has twice as much stuff in it. But the feeling of affluence, the experience of well-being, is no higher and perhaps even lower."[2]

Liberal economists argue that since about 1973 the real wages earned by middle-class Americans haven't really risen much and, for many workers, have actually declined. Young couples talk of not being able to afford what their parents had. By contrast, conservative economists contend that the rate of inflation as calculated by the federal government has been overstated and, therefore, that real wages have actually risen considerably. But one thing is incontestable: *We have a lot more stuff and much higher material expectations than previous generations did.*

STARTER CASTLES

Take housing, for example. The average size of new homes is now more than double what it was in the 1950s, while families are smaller. LaNita Wacker, who owns Dream House Realty in Seattle, has been selling homes for more than a quarter of a century. She takes us on a drive through the neighborhoods near her office to explain what's happened.

She shows us houses built during every decade since World War II and describes how they've gotten bigger and bigger. Right after World War II, Wacker points out, 750 square feet was the norm (in Levittown, for example). "Then in the '50s," she says, "they added 200 square feet, so 950 was the norm." By the '60s, 1,100 square feet was typical, and by the '70s, 1,350. Now it's 2,300.

LaNita Wacker started selling homes in 1972, "right about the time we moved from a single bath to the demand for a double bath."[3] Two-car garages came in then too, and by the late '80s many homes were being built with three-car garages. That's 600 to 900 square feet of garage space alone, "as much square footage as an entire family used in the early '50s," Wacker says. "It would house an entire family. But we have acquired a lot of stuff to store."

To drive the point home, Wacker takes us by a huge home with a four-car garage. Expensive cars and a boat are parked outside. The owner comes out wondering why LaNita is so interested in his place. "I own Dream House Realty," she says. "And yours is a dream house." "It was built to the specifications of my charming wife," the man replies with a laugh. "So why four garages?" asks LaNita. "It's probably because of storage," the man replies, explaining that the garages are filled with family possessions. "You never have enough storage so you can never have enough garages," he adds cheerfully. LaNita asks if he has children. "They're gone now," he replies. "It's just me and the wife."

The four-car garage is an exception, no doubt. But everyone expects larger homes now. "A master bedroom in the '50s would be about 130 square feet," explains Wacker. "Now, even in moderately priced homes, you're talking about maybe 300 square feet devoted to the master bedroom."

In recent years more than ever, homes have become a symbol of conspicuous consumption, as beneficiaries of the recent stock market boom and unparalleled economic expansion have begun, in many communities, to buy real estate, bulldoze existing (and perfectly functional) homes and replace them with megahouses of 10,000 square feet and more. "Starter castles," some have named them. Others call them "Monster Homes."

On America's Streets of Dreams, the competition is fierce. McMansions . . . Double McMansions . . . Deluxe McMansions . . . Deluxe McMansions with Cheese . . . Full Garage Deals . . . each one a little bigger and glitzier, popping up like mushrooms in a frenzy of home wars. In places like the spectacular mountain towns of the West, many such megahomes are actually *second homes,* mere vacation destinations for the newly rich.

BETTER THAN TAIL FINS

A similar story presents itself with automobiles. In 1957, when Ford had a better idea called the Edsel, cars were big and chromey, but they were far from the sophisticated machines we drive today. A 1960 Ford commercial shows crowds of people admiring new Fairlanes, Thunderbirds, and Falcons, surrounded by twinkling stars as if touched by Tinkerbell. It is, the ad proclaims, "the Wonderful New World of Ford." But in that wonderful new world, much of what we now take for granted as standard automobile features wasn't even available in luxury models.

In 1960, for example, fewer than five percent of new cars had air conditioning. Now ninety percent do. Mike Sillivan, a veteran Toyota salesman in Seattle, says that "today, people's expectations are much higher. They want amenities—power

...AND THEY JUST GET BIGGER AND BIGGER AND BIGGER AND...

steering, power brakes as standard, premium sound systems."[4] The car of today is a different animal from that of a generation ago. Filled with computer technology. And, after a decade's hiatus following the "energy crisis" of the mid '70s, big is back.

Until the recent price hike, gasoline costs for Americans were at an all-time low in real dollar terms. Worries about fuel efficiency were forgotten as we bought gas-guzzling four-wheel drive wagons called sport utility vehicles (some call them Suburban Assault Vehicles). In the late '90s half of all new cars sold were SUVs and light trucks, exempted from federal fuel efficiency standards. Roomy, comfy, and costly, SUVs just keep getting bigger.

CAR WARS

Until recently, the 18-foot-long Chevy Suburban set the standard for gigantism. Now, not to be outdone, Ford has introduced the Excursion, a 7,000-pound titan that is a foot longer than the Suburban. Ford Motors Chairman William Ford even apologized for making so many SUVs, calling his Excursion "the Ford Valdez" for its propensity to consume fuel. He condemned SUVs as wasteful and polluting, but said Ford would continue to manufacture them anyway because they are extremely profitable.

"For a lot of people an SUV is a status symbol," says car salesman Sillivan. "So they're willing to pay the thirty- to forty-odd thousand dollars to drive one of these vehicles."

Never one to give up without a fight, General Motors has come charging back at Ford, acquiring ownership of the Hummer, a more luxurious version of the military transport vehicle used during the Gulf War. GM is "placing a big bet that the decade-long trend toward ever larger and more aggressive-looking sport utility vehicles would continue," according to *The New York Times*.[5] "It's like a tank with fashion," says one teenager quoted by the *Times*. The kid says he loves the Hummer because "I like something where I can look down into another car and give that knowing smile that says 'I'm bigger than you.' It makes me feel powerful." More than a foot wider than the Excursion, the Hummer retails for $93,000. GM predicts these behemoths will be especially popular in (we are not making this up) Manhattan, which is probably a good thing because you need to be on the viewing platform of the Empire State Building to see over them. But now what will Ford counter with, an even bigger SUV called The Extinction?

WEIGHTLESS TOURISM

Hummers on the streets of Manhattan. You might call them Saddam's revenge. Or Ho-Hummers, if you compare them with yet another way to drop nearly a hundred grand. Check out spacevoyages.com to find out what may be the ultimate in swollen expectations. Just plop down $98 K, including a $6 K deposit, and you, dear reader, can be an astronaut. Sometime between 2003 and 2005, you'll be able to take a two-hour trip on a rocket ship and spend about five weightless minutes in actual outer space. Besides that, you'll get an "original and exclusive Space Adventures suborbital flight certificate," a flight training suit, astronaut wings, a medallion, a travel bag, photos, and a lifetime membership in the Space Adventurers Club—all for less than a hundred thousand dollars. If that sounds like a deal, you might want to stick a thermometer in your mouth right away. Ten . . . nine . . . eight . . .

LET'S DO LUNCH

Consider food. The '50s did give us TV dinners. Turkey, peas, and mashed potatoes in a throwaway tray for sixty-nine cents, thank you Swanson's. As kids, we considered them delectable. Our standard diets were pretty bland. Exotic meant soggy egg rolls, chow mein, and chop suey. Mexican was tacos and tamales (how did we cope without chimichangas and chalupas?). Thai wasn't even part of our vocabulary. Now, city streets and even suburban malls sport a United Nations of restaurants.

We remember waiting for certain fruits and vegetables to be in season. Now, there is no season; everything is always available. When it's winter here, it's summer in New Zealand, after all. Yet we often feel deprived. Strawberries lose their flavor when you can have them all the time. More choices and more diversity certainly aren't a bad thing, but they come at a cost. The exotic quickly becomes common-place and boring, requiring ever newer and more expensive menus.

Take coffee. Until recently, we took it as watery brown stuff made bearable by gobs of sugar. Now, specialty coffees are everywhere. NPR radio host Scott Simon was surprised a few years ago when he stopped at a service station in rural Wash-ington State. In the station's mini-mart was an espresso stand with so many types of coffee drinks to offer that Simon longed for an Italian dictionary to identify them. No need. The kid behind the counter with his baseball cap on backwards knew them all.

Eating out used to be a special occasion. Now we spend more money on restau-rant food than on the food we cook ourselves. Swelling expectations. Swelling stom-achs too, but that's another symptom.

INVENTION IS THE MOTHER OF NECESSITY

Consider, also, the kinds of goods that were deemed luxuries as recently as 1970, but are now found in well over half of U.S. homes, and thought of by a majority of Americans as necessities: dishwashers, clothes dryers, central heating and air condi-tioning, color and cable TV.[6] And back in 1970, there were no microwave ovens, VCRs, CD players, cell phones, fax machines, compact discs, leaf blowers, Poke-mon, or personal computers. Now, more than half of us take all of these goods for granted and would feel deprived without them. Well, OK, so you wouldn't feel deprived without Pokemon.

There always seems to be a "better" model that we've just gotta have. Writing about Compac's new iPaq 3600 Pocket PC, *Seattle Times* technology reporter Paul Andrews warns that the iPaq, with its "sleek Porsche-like case and striking color screen," costs $500 more than an ordinary Palm Pilot. "But without the color dis-play, music, and photos of the iPaq, life seems pretty dull," he laments.[7]

And take travel. We drive twice as much per capita as we did a half century ago, and fly an amazing twenty-five times as much.[8] Middle-income Americans seldom ventured more than a few hundred miles from home then, even during two-week summer vacations. Now, many of us (not just the rich) expect to spend occasional long weekends in Puerto Vallarta, or (in the case of New Yorkers) in Paris. Every-where, humble motels have been replaced by elegant "inns," humble resorts by Club Meds. Now, "I need a vacation" means I need to change continents for a few days.

THE CHANGING JONESES

"Greed has infected our society. It is the worst infection," says the real Patch Adams, the doctor who was portrayed by Robin Williams in a popular Hollywood film.[9] He's right only to a degree. It may be fear rather than greed that primarily drives our swelling expectations. Fear of not succeeding in the eyes of others. In one magazine ad from the '50s, readers are encouraged to "keep up with the Joneses" by driving what they're driving: a Chevy. A Chevy sedan at that, not even a Corvette. Just about the cheapest car around, even then.

But the mythical Joneses don't drive Chevrolets any more. And they're no longer your next door neighbors either, folks who make roughly what you do. Economist Juliet Schor studied people's attitudes about consumption in a large corporation and found that most Americans now compare themselves with coworkers or television characters when they think about what they "need."

But corporations have become increasingly stratified economically in recent years. One frequently comes into contact with much-better-paid colleagues than oneself. Their cars, clothes, and travel plans reflect their higher incomes, yet set the standards for everyone in the firm.

Likewise, says Schor, "TV shows a very inflated standard of living relative to what the true standard of living of the American public is. People on television tend to be upper middle class or even rich, and people who watch a lot of TV have highly inflated views of what the average American has. For example, people who are heavy TV watchers vastly exaggerate the number of Americans with swimming pools, tennis courts, maids, and planes, and their own expectations of what they should have also become inflated, so they tend to spend more and save less."[10]

Schor says that as the gap between rich and poor grew during the 1980s, people with relatively high incomes began to feel deprived in comparison to those who were suddenly making even more. "They started to feel 'poor on $100,00 a year' as the well-known phrase puts it, because they were comparing themselves to the Donald Trumps and the other newly wealthy." It happened all the way down the income line, Schor says. "Everybody felt worse compared to the role models, those at the top." Polls now show that Americans believe they need $75,000 (for a family of four) just to lead a "minimum" middle-class life.

I'VE GOT MINE, JACK

In the years just after World War II the super-rich sought to conceal their profligacy, but since Ronald Reagan's first inaugural ball many have begun to flaunt it again. As economist Robert Frank points out, there's been a rush on $15,000 purses,

$10,000 watches, even $65 million private jets. Twenty million Americans now own big-screen TVs costing at least $2,000 each. Some buy their children $5,000 life-size reproductions of Darth Vader and $18,000 replicas of Range Rovers, $25,000 birthday parties and million-dollar Bar Mitzvahs.[11]

Thus from the hot zones of popular culture and stratified workplaces, our new Joneses—consciously or otherwise—spread the affluenza virus, swelling our expectations as never before. And stuffing us up.

CHAPTER 4

Chronic

congestion

A house is just a pile of stuff
with a cover on it.

—GEORGE CARLIN

It's nine o'clock at night, and Karen and Ted Jones, a double income couple in their forties, are peering through a flickering flashlight beam at boxes of stuff, stored a few months earlier at U-Stuff-It, the self-storage facility near their house. He's rooting for a missing report his boss needs the next day, while she's foraging for a painting a friend gave her, because the friend is coming to visit.

"I feel kind of like a burglar," she comments in a low voice, rummaging through a box of Christmas decorations and vaguely familiar objects. "Why?" he asks. "This is our stuff. We're just lucky to be able to afford this space, aren't we?" She's not totally convinced. Lucky their stuff can overflow somewhere, with the garage and aluminum shed already popping their nails and rivets. But lucky to be paying $105 a month for 100 square feet of space? Lucky to have so much stuff? She's not sure.

ALL STUFFED UP

Karen and Ted are by no means alone. There are now more than 30,000 self-storage facilities in the country, offering over a billion square feet of relief for a legion of customers starting home businesses, combining households, getting organized after the move, or just unable to stop buying. The industry has expanded fortyfold since the 1960s, from virtually nothing then to $12 billion annually now, making it larger than the U.S. music industry.[1]

We're all stuffed up, literally! In our homes, workplaces, and streets, chronic congestion has settled into our daily lives—chaotic clutter that demands constant maintenance, sorting, displaying, and replacing.

So which box is that wretched report in?

WHEN HOUSES BECOME LANDFILLS

For Beth Johnson, the acquisition of stuff goes beyond mere frivolity. A recovered hoarder, she once had an addictive relationship with objects. Like up to two million Americans who compulsively save everything from bottlecaps to fast-food wrappers to utility bills, her house was a "landfill" with only a narrow path through all the stuff she couldn't part with. Now, after pulling her own life back together, she runs "Good Riddance Clutter Workshops" to help others recover from the disorder.

"Hoarders are often unable to hold jobs because they are so easily sidetracked," she says. "They see value in just about any object, and are afraid to throw something away because they fear they are throwing away a piece of themselves." To modify the behavior and reclaim the lives of hoarders, Beth often goes into victims' houses, helping them put all the magazines in one box, or all the junk packaging in one room. If twenty-year-old bills can be parted with, the next step is to bid good riddance to ten-year-old bills.[2]

In a world filled with clutter, we too easily become overwhelmed, lose our way, and get swept along in a current that carries us to the mall for more stuff, or to the car dealership for a new car—nothing down.

CAR CLUTTER

Denver resident Dan Berman, like many Americans, could take his two midsize SUVs to the jagged peak of the mountain, as in the TV ads, but not into his own garage. Neither vehicle would fit in the fifty-year-old brick garage, so he ripped it down and built one suitable for a new millennium. Some of his neighbors in Denver's solid Washington Park haven't gotten around to that yet. Driving past the old neighborhood's homes, you see $40,000 Excursions and Navigators grazing at curbside, desperate for exercise. But in a clogged-up metropolitan area like Denver, they aren't likely to get much.

Americans have reached a new milestone. We now live in a country that has more cars (203 million) than registered drivers. But with that dubious distinction come highway speeds of twenty miles an hour or less at rush hour—speeds that waste $60 billion a year in lost time and fuel. Stuck in traffic recently, Dave imagined all the cars on the highway suddenly disappearing, leaving just people standing there on the road. It wouldn't appear to be so jammed up, then—just a bunch of people walking to work, or taking part in . . . a parade!

What happened? America used to be the place where both the pizza delivery person and the ambulance driver could get there before it was too late. In our brave new world of clutter, both are trapped in traffic. (Rule of thumb, circa 2001: The shortest distance between two points is always under construction.) In a short story by a South American writer, traffic is so hopeless that drivers abandon their cars and start foraging for food in neighboring villages. Eventually they start growing crops by the roadside. A baby is conceived and born before traffic begins to move again. While congestion hasn't yet reached quite that level in the United States (or South America), it may not be a bad idea to put a few packages of seeds in the glove compartment, just in case.

METRO FOLLIES

The mother of all traffic jams is in Los Angeles, where Interstate 5 crosses I-10, 60, and 101. More than half a million vehicles log-jam through this stretch daily—not a pretty sight. Los Angeles residents spend eighty-two hours a year stuck in traffic, compared to a national average of thirty-four hours for urban drivers. L.A. drivers also waste 120 gallons of gas per capita annually owing to congestion,[3] and are also forced to breathe marginal air and listen to fast-talking traffic reports. Boston's "Big Dig," designed to bury Boston's central artery under the city like a subway of cars, will siphon taxpayer dollars for another fifty years. Its $14 billion—and counting—price tag is more than thirty times the 1975 estimate.

When it comes to traffic jams, we're all in it together, but some traffic engineers think only they hold the key to getting us back out. Rather than opting to reorganize our communities so less travel is necessary, the engineers are still road-crazy after all these years. Having already paved over two-thirds of Los Angeles, their sights are set on St. Louis, Tucson, and Colorado Springs. However, recent studies by the Texas Transportation Institute and others prove that the major cause of congestion is neither a lack of roads nor population growth but an increase of up to sixty-five percent in driving, largely caused by sprawl. Researchers concluded that *every ten-percent increase in the highway network results in a 5.3-percent increase in the amount of congestion.* Like a medication with serious side effects, building new roads may just make things worse.

With the highways all clogged up, drivers are increasingly "jumping ship" into our neighborhoods, cutting down alleyways and across vacant lots like Steve Martin's character in the movie *L.A. Story.* However, mechanical engineers think they have a more pragmatic, high-tech solution: "Smart cars" and "smart highways." One of them suggests automated highways on which vehicles equipped with specialized sensors and wireless communications systems could travel under computer control, at densely packed intervals. "Once traveling in automated mode, the driver could relax until the turnoff. At this point, the system would need to check whether the driver could retake control, and take appropriate action if the driver were asleep, sick, or even dead."[4] It's comforting to know that we may reach our destinations even if we're DOA. But doesn't it seem a little like a car cartoon? In a way, it's mass transit, except "smart highways" would be American style, *individualized* mass transit, resulting in high levels of individualized consumption as well as high levels of expensive road construction and maintenance.

STUFF WARS AT THE AIRPORT

If American homes crammed with stuff are the metaphorical equivalent of congestion in the lungs, and car traffic is the plugged arteries, planes must be the sneeze that propels affluenza carriers (that's us) through the air. Between 1988 and 1998, air travel increased by thirty-five percent and for the foreseeable future, the sky's the limit for air-travel profits.

At the airport—once our delayed flight is finally ready to go—we plead with the airline attendant to be able to carry on one more bag, but are reminded, sternly, of policies designed to protect the passenger. Stuff Wars is in full swing. The airlines have determined that we'll fly no matter how packed the flights, and how miniature the complimentary bags of peanuts. Their strategy is "More people, less stuff"— cram passengers in with as little carry-on luggage as possible. Meanwhile, passengers have another agenda—to keep their stuff with them so they don't have to wait for it at the baggage claim, and so they can access laptops, cosmetics, and emergency rations.

"Please do not leave your baggage unattended . . . " drones the voice on the PA as you wait in line to get through security. What's going on here? Everybody's obsessed with stuff! Your carry-on luggage is allowed to be only twenty by forty inches, and they need to x-ray it, label it, inspect it, and cross-examine you about it. Why can't they be more understanding? That's your *stuff*, symbolizing who you are. Don't they care who you are? Not really. Remember, you're a passenger, not a person.

The height of Stuff Wars madness can be experienced when the aircraft lands and the captain rings the bell signifying it's time to unfasten your seat belt, jump out of your seat, bump your head on the overhead compartment, and scramble for your stuff!

THE SKY *IS* FALLING

In the movie *The Gods Must Be Crazy,* a Coke bottle falls from the sky and disrupts the social structure of a peaceful tribe of Bushmen in Africa's Kalihari desert, unaccustomed to the artifacts of Western culture. In Southgate, California, the detached "nose wheel" of an airplane recently fell from the sky and impacted the ground in front of a market, barely missing a woman entering a church. Don't look up—the sky IS falling!

Even space is jam-packed with stuff. More than seven million pounds of spaceship pieces are hurtling around the planet at 22,000 miles an hour. At that speed, a piece of space debris the size of a small marble has the kinetic energy of a 400-

pound boulder dropped from 100 feet. To get out beyond the hazards of Earth's space clutter, future astronauts may spend much of their time dodging bullets of space junk.

Meanwhile, back on Earth, space junk collectors like Jim Bernath of British Columbia anxiously await the descent of more debris, to add to their collections. Bernath already owns chunks of comets and bits of the "Canada Arm," a device built to retrieve satellites. He's especially hopeful that a piece of the junked MIR space station may fall somewhere in Canada—possibly right into his own backyard.[5]

ANALYZING THE AMERICAN DREAM: WHERE CLUTTER COMES FROM

America's 102 million households—the authors' among them—currently contain and consume more stuff than all other households throughout history, put together. Behind closed doors, we churn through manufactured goods and piped-in entertainment as if life were a stuff-eating contest. Despite tangible indications of indigestion, we keep consuming, partly because we're convinced it's normal. Writes columnist Ellen Goodman, "Normal is getting dressed in clothes that you buy for work, driving through traffic in a car that you are still paying for, in order to get to the job that you need so you can pay for the clothes, car and the house that you leave empty all day in order to afford to live in it."[6]

Erich Fromm reminds us about the potential risk of settling for normal: "That millions share the same forms of mental pathology does not make those people sane."[7] And Jim Hightower defines "status quo" as "this mess we're in." As compared to what a sane society would be—grounded in natural rhythms, social cooperation and trust—the Dream we are dreaming is so abnormal that it keeps behavioral anthropologists working overtime, trying to figure out what we think we are doing. The Alfred P. Sloan Foundation recently set aside $20 million to examine the American lifestyle, primarily by carefully observing the daily behavior of Homo sapiens *americanus*.

For example, anthropologist Jan English-Lueck tries to make sense of child behavior as it relates to lifestyle. "When I shadow a three-year-old around, on the surface, that wouldn't seem to be an encapsulation of our culture," she said. "But when that three-year-old turns to his little sister and says, 'Don't bother me, I'm working,' that's worth overhearing."[8] Has the child already made the connection between hours spent working and all the stuff his parents accumulate in the house?

At the University of Arizona another crew of anthropologists has been studying America's garbage since 1973. Garbologists core-drill Tucson landfills and sort through obsolete naval aircraft carriers, trying to make sense of our everyday arti-facts. "We might think of the pattern of modern trash as a tangible record of human consumption," said William Rathje, the program's founder. "Future generations will marvel at the stuff that flows through our lives. The container of a frozen dinner that's cooked and eaten in minutes persists for hundreds of years."[9]

As in a monster movie, more stuff begins to take shape as we sit daydreaming about the perfect living room, the perfect body, or the neighborhood's sexiest lawn mower. Daydreams like these all require a steady stream of products that need to be hunted and gathered. On the vacation after next, maybe we'll hit the ski slopes in Colorado or hike in northern Italy, but before then we'll need to acquire a detailed checklist of expensive equipment. In the book *High Tech–High Touch*, author John Naisbitt and coauthors describe some of the items necessary for "adventure travel." "High-tech gear is available for every conceivable need, for every conceivable journey: digitally perfect-fit hiking boots, helmets with twenty-seven air vents, hydration packs, portable water purifiers, bike shorts with rubber-ized back-spray-repelling seats…"

SHAMEFUL STUFF

Most of us can relate to the dizzying array of technologically correct equipment and apparel. Do you have the right stuff? Does anyone? Some bicycling friends recently asked Dave to ride with them. His cut-off khaki shorts stuck out like a bor-der collie at a greyhound track beside their shiny spandex, but he just kept ped-dling. Even more "shameful" was the day his computer crashed and sank, taking years of data down with it. A vandal-generated message appeared suddenly on Dave's computer screen, insulting him by name, and within a few hours a repair-man pronounced the computer "toast." Even the emergency floppy disks he fed into the machine were spit out with a growl. The computer was only a few years old, but somehow Dave felt a sense of techno-shame that he wasn't properly equipped to fend off the virus. His penalty for not being state-of-the-art? $2,000 in cash to replace the deceased, useless computer.

Dave's neighbor, eighty-year-old political and social activist Ginny Cowles, appreciates the value of e-mail and the Internet, but she finds she can only read the screen well when she tilts her head up to bring the lower half of her bifocals to the task. "I think I may have to get a new pair of glasses to wear just when I'm on the computer," she said recently, with some frustration in her voice. "It's anoth-er example of how stuff always seems to require more stuff."

CHAPTER 5

The stress of excess

We hear the same refrain all the time from people: I have no life. I get up in the morning, daycare, eldercare, a 40 minute commute to work. I have to work late. I get home at night, there's laundry, bills to pay, jam something into the microwave oven. I'm exhausted, I go to sleep, I wake up and the routine begins all over again. This is what life has become in America.

—TREND-SPOTTER GERALD CELENTE

We are a nation that shouts at a microwave oven to hurry up.

—JOAN RYAN,
The San Francisco Chronicle

A ffluenza is a major disease, there's no question about it,"[1] says Dr. Richard Swenson of Menomonie, Wisconsin, who practiced medicine for many years before changing his focus to writing and lecturing. A tall, bearded, deeply religious man, Swenson began over a period of time to conclude that much of the pain in his patients' lives had psychological rather than physical roots. "And after about four or five years, the whole idea of *margin* came to the surface," he says. He found that too many of his patients were stretched to their limits and beyond with no margin, no room in their lives for rest, relaxation, and reflection. They showed symptoms of acute stress.

"It could be physical symptoms," Swenson recalls. "Headaches, low back pain, hyperacidity, palpitations in the heart, unexplained aches and pains. Or it could be emotional problems like depression, anxiety, sleeplessness, irritability, yelling at your boss or at your colleagues or your kids. There were all kinds of behavioral symptoms like driving too fast or drinking too much or screaming too much or being abusive. I recognized that they didn't have any space in their lives, they didn't have any reserves. The space between their load and their limits had just disappeared. I couldn't take an X-ray to find this thing, but nevertheless it was there. And it was a powerful source of pain and dysfunction in people's lives."

POSSESSION OVERLOAD

Swenson observed that many of his patients suffered from what he now calls "possession overload," the problem of dealing with too much stuff. "Possession overload is the kind of problem where you have so many things you find your life is being taken up by maintaining and caring for things instead of people," Swenson says. "Everything I own owns me. People feel sad and what do they do? They go to the mall and they shop and it makes them feel better, but only for a short time. There's an addictive quality in consumerism. But it simply doesn't work. They've gotten all these things and they still find this emptiness, this hollowness. All they have is stress and exhaustion and burnout, and their relationships are vaporizing. They're surrounded by all kinds of fun toys but the meaning is gone." "Tragedy," observes Swenson, "is wanting something badly, getting it, and finding it empty. And I think that's what's happened."

TIME FAMINE

There's been an almost imperceptible change in American greetings over the past two decades. Remember how when you used to say "how are you?" to the friends you ran into at work or on the street, they'd reply "fine, and you?" Now, when we ask that question, the answer is often "busy, and you?" (when they have time to say, "and you?") "Me too," we admit. We used to talk of having "time to smell the flowers." Now we barely find time to smell the coffee. "The pace of life has accelerated to the point where everyone is breathless," says Richard Swenson. "You look at all the countries that have the most prosperity and they're the same countries that have the most stress."

Tried to make a dinner date with a friend recently? Chances are you have to look a month ahead in your appointment calendars. Even children now carry them. Ask your coworkers what they'd like more of in their lives and odds are they'll say "time." "This is an issue that cuts across race lines, class lines, and gender lines," says African-American novelist Barbara Neely. "Nobody has any time out there."[2] We're all like the bespectacled bunny in Disney's *Alice in Wonderland*, who keeps looking at his watch and muttering, "No time to say hello, goodbye, I'm late! I'm late! I'm late!"

By the early 1990s, trend-spotters were warning that a specter was haunting America: time famine. Advertisers noted that "time will be the luxury of the 1990s." A series of clever TV spots for US West showed time-pressed citizens trying to "buy time" at a bank called 'Time R Us' or in bargain basements. One store offered customers "the greatest sale of all TIME." A weary woman asked where she could buy "quality time." "Now you CAN buy time," the ads promised. "Extra working time with mobile phone service from US West."[3]

More working time. Hmmm.

We thought the opposite was supposed to be true: that advances in technology, automation, cybernation, were supposed to give us more leisure time and *less* working time. Remember how all those futurists were predicting that by the end of the 20th Century we'd have more leisure time than we'd know what to do with? In

1965, a U.S. Senate subcommittee heard testimony that estimated a workweek of from fourteen to twenty-two hours by the year 2000.[4]

We got the technology, but we didn't get the time. We have computers, fax machines, cell phones, e-mail, robots, express mail, freeways, jetliners, microwaves, fast food, one-hour photos, digital cameras, pop tarts, frozen waffles, instant this and instant that. But we have *less* free time than we did thirty years ago. And about those mobile phones: They do give you "extra working time" while driving, but make you as likely to cause an accident as someone who's legally drunk. Progress? And then there are those leaf blowers . . .

THE HARRIED LEISURE CLASS

We should have paid attention to Staffan Linder. In 1970, the Swedish economist warned that all those predictions about more free time were a myth, that we'd soon be a "harried leisure class" starved for time. "Economic growth," wrote Linder, "entails a general increase in the scarcity of time."[5] He continued, "As the volume of consumption goods increases, requirements for the care and maintenance of these goods also tends to increase, we get bigger houses to clean, a car to wash, a boat to put up for the winter, a television set to repair, and have to make more decisions on spending."[6]

It's as simple as this: increased susceptibility to affluenza means increasing headaches from time pressure.

Shopping itself, Linder pointed out "is a very time-consuming activity." Indeed, on average, Americans now spend nearly seven times as much time shopping as they do playing with their kids. Even our celebrated freedom of choice only adds to the problem.

BRAND A OR BRAND B?

Consider the average supermarket. It now contains 30,000 items, two and half times as many as it did twenty years ago.[7] Picture yourself having to choose between a hundred types of cereal, for instance (or almost any other item). You can decide by price, grabbing what's on sale: by flavor—sweet sells—or by nutrition—but then, what counts most? Protein? Cholesterol? Calories? Added vitamins? Fat? Dietary fiber? Or you can give in to your child's nagging and buy the Cocoa Puffs. You can reach for tomato juice, confident that you're getting vitamins and antioxidants and only fifty calories per serving. But don't look at the "sodium" column— you won't be able to allow yourself any more salt for the rest of the day without feeling guilty.

So many choices. So little time. Linder said this would happen, and he warned that when choices become overwhelming, "the emphasis in advertising will be placed on ersatz information," because "brand loyalty must be built up among people who have no possibility of deciding how to act on objective grounds."[8] Ergo, if you're a marketer, hire a battery of psychologists to study which box colors are most associated by shoppers with pleasurable sex. Or something like that.

OVERWORKING AMERICANS

Linder argued that past a certain point, time pressure would increase with growing productivity. But he wasn't sure whether working hours would rise or fall. He certainly doubted they'd fall as much as the automation cheerleaders predicted. He was right. In fact, there seems to be some pretty strong evidence that Americans are actually working more now than they did a generation ago.

Using labor department statistics, Harvard economist Juliet Schor argues that full-time American workers are now toiling 160 hours—one full month—*more*, on average, than they did in 1969. "It's not only the people in the higher income groups—who, by the way, have been working much longer hours," says Schor. "It's also the middle classes, the lower classes, and the poor. Everybody is working longer hours."[9] Indeed, according to the International Labor Organization, in October of 1999 the United States passed Japan as the modern industrial country with the longest working hours. Forty-two percent of American workers say they feel "used up" by the end of the workday. Sixty-nine percent say they'd like to slow down and live a more relaxed life.

NO TIME TO CARE

Moreover, Schor says, "The pace of work has increased quite dramatically. We are working much faster today than we were in the past. And that contributes to our sense of being overworked and frenzied and harried and stressed out and burned out by our jobs." In the fax lane, everybody wants that report yesterday. Patience wears thin rapidly when we get used to a new generation of computers.

Several years ago, Karen Nussbaum, former president of 9 to 5, a clerical workers union, pointed out that "Twenty-six million Americans are monitored by the machines they work on, and that number is growing. I had one woman tell me her computer would flash off and on: YOU'RE NOT WORKING AS FAST AS THE PERSON NEXT TO YOU!"[10] Doesn't just thinking about that make your blood pressure rise?

Sometimes the speedup reaches utterly inhumane levels. Clandestine video footage recently shot inside a slaughterhouse shows fully conscious cows being skinned alive and having their legs cut off while struggling for freedom. In a signed affidavit, one employee said, "The chain goes too fast, more than 300 cows an hour. If I can't get the animal knocked out right, it keeps going. It never stops. The cows are getting hung alive or not alive. I can tell some cows are alive because they're holding their heads up. They just keep coming, coming, coming . . . " The video provides gruesome evidence that the speed of American production, driven by an insatiable desire for more, virtually guarantees us no time to care.

CHOOSING STUFF OVER TIME

Juliet Schor reminds us that the United States has seen more than a doubling of productivity since World War II. "So the issue is: what do we do with that progress? We could cut back on working hours. We could produce the old amount in half as much time and take half the time off. Or we could work just as much and produce twice as much." And, says Schor, "we've put all our economic progress into producing more things. Our consumption has doubled and working hours have not fallen at all. In fact, working hours have risen."[11]

Not everyone agrees with Schor about longer working hours. John Robinson, who runs the Americans' Use of Time Project at the University of Maryland, claims that "time diaries" kept by employees (they record how they spend each minute of every workday) actually show a decrease in working hours. But Robinson does agree that most working Americans "feel" more time-pressured than ever.[12] Much of their increased leisure, he says, has been consumed in watching television—and thus in absorbing even more exhortations to consume.

Either way, the experience of time famine intensifies, driven by longer, or at least, more demanding, working hours, and the competing time requirements associated with the care and feeding of stuff. Something has got to give. For many Americans, it's sleep. Doctors say more than half of all Americans get too little sleep—an average of an hour too little each night. We average twenty percent less sleep than we did in 1900. And that takes a toll on health.[13] So does our urgency about time.

HEART ATTACKS WAITING TO HAPPEN

The intake examination at the Meyer Friedman Institute in San Francisco is like none other in a doctor's office. A nurse runs prospective patients through a series of questions about their relationship to time. "Do you walk fast? Do you eat fast? Do you often do two or more things at the same time?" She also notes their physical responses to her questions. "Something you do a lot," she tells one interviewee, "is what we call expiratory sighing, as if you're emotionally exhausted or don't even want to think about the matter I'm asking you to talk about."[14]

The nurse tabulates the answers provided by patients and gives them a score, which, for most, puts them squarely in the category which, years ago, Meyer Friedman called the "Type A" personality. The more Type A someone is, the more likely that person is to suffer from what Friedman calls "time urgency." "We've also called it hurry sickness in the past," Bart Sparagon, the mellow, soft-spoken doctor who directs Friedman's clinic, says slowly. "It's as if people are struggling against time."[15]

"I have a vivid image of an advertisement for a famous journal about financial affairs," Sparagon adds, with a look of resignation. "It's a picture of men in suits carrying briefcases, leaping over hurdles, with this hostile, tense look on their faces, and it's an ad suggesting that if you buy this magazine, you can win this race. But when I see that picture, I know those men are racing toward a heart attack. I mean, do you *want* to win that race?"

Along with time urgency, the racers usually are afflicted with what Meyer Friedman terms "free-floating hostility." Everything that causes them to slow down—in their pursuit of money or other symbols of success—becomes an enemy, something in their way, an obstacle to overcome. "I think that time urgency is the major cause of premature heart disease in this country," Meyer Friedman once declared.[16] The more Type A a person is, he believes, the greater that person's risk of cardiac arrest.

Affluenza is certainly not the only cause of time urgency. But it is a major cause. Swelling expectations lead to a constant effort to keep up with the latest products, to compete in the consumption arena. That, in turn, forces us to work more, so we can afford the stuff. With so many things to use, and the need to work harder to obtain them, our lives grow more harried and pressured. As one pundit put it, "If you win the rat race, you're still a rat." And you may be a dead one.

In recent years, many scientists have come to believe that viruses and other infections make us more susceptible to heart attacks. Their conclusions have come from studying influenza viruses. But if Meyer Friedman and his theories about Type A personalities are right, they should look more closely at affluenza as well.

CHAPTER 6

Family convulsions

There is a tension between materialism and family values.

—TED HAGGARD,
Pastor, New Life Church, Colorado Springs

Affluenza is a family problem. In a variety of ways, the disease is like a termite, undermining American family life, sometimes to the breaking point. We have already mentioned time pressures. Some studies suggest that over the past generation, the time parents spend with their children has declined by as much as forty percent. One study found that American couples now find just twelve minutes a day to talk to each other![1] Then, too, the pressure to keep up with the Joneses leads many families into debt and simmering conflicts over money matters that frequently result in divorce. Indeed, the American divorce rate, despite reaching a plateau in the 1980s, is still double what it was in the '50s, and family counselors report that arguments about money are precipitating factors in ninety percent of divorce cases.[2]

FOR RICHER . . .

Take, for example, the case of Keaton and Cindy Adams, the couple we introduced you to in Chapter 2. They almost let affluenza tear their marriage apart. "Our wedding was so good we almost have it paid off," said Keaton, six years after they were married. "And that's where the whole ball started rolling."[3] And so it rolls for many young Americans—thousands shelled out for one big extravaganza, that public pledge of eternal fidelity, "for richer or for poorer."

First, of course, it's for richer. Presents from friends and family—microwaves, blenders, towels, toasters (never out of fashion), dinnerware, Tupperware, tea kettles, and a whole lot more (leaf blowers?). Plus a roomful of wrapping paper, used once and cast aside. Then the wedding bills come due.

After their wedding, Keaton and Cindy began buying lots of other things for their home, all on credit. They bought all kinds of expensive furniture and the obligatory "home entertainment center." "What's another $25 a month?" says Keaton, explaining their thought process at the time, one all too common in American families. "And then we found ourselves making minimum payments all over the place to the point where we couldn't. And we started to get two months behind, three months behind."

In a short time, they were $20,000 in debt, with no hope of paying it off. "The arguments ensued, we started fighting," Keaton recalls. "We were screaming divorce. Finally we ended up reaching a breaking point."

For millions of American families, their story would, no doubt, sound familiar. But it has (so far, at least) a happy ending. The Adamses sought help from Consumer Credit Counseling Service in Colorado Springs, where they lived at the time, and brought their spending and financial crisis under control. Cindy Adams says they've learned a hard lesson. "It's OK not to have the newest thing, the latest style," she now believes. "Our home doesn't have to be in tip-top condition. It lets us focus on things that are more important than stuff."

SOCIALLY SANCTIONED ADDICTION

Mike and Terri Pauly, family counselors in Colorado Springs, say they see many couples who get themselves into situations like that faced by Keaton and Cindy Adams. It starts, Mike says, "with trying to acquire as many things as possible. It's a major stressor right now in couples. There is a real addictive cycle that families get into where they go out and spend money in order to feel good about themselves. I have a number of couples I've worked with recently who are having lots of problems, but who come in on Monday and say 'We had a great weekend. And it's because we went out and spent a lot of money. We went to the mall and spent five hundred dollars on different things and we had a great time.'"[4] Shopping as therapy. But as a pyschotropic drug, it ultimately doesn't work.

The time comes, Mike Pauly points out, "when there's no more money left on the credit card and they get into that position of feeling backed against the wall. They start feeling stress and tension in their relationship." It's a problem, Mike says, "that's a lot like racism. It's all-pervasive, it's everywhere, and people don't realize it."

But unlike racism, the addiction to stuff isn't challenged in our society. In fact, says Terri Pauly, "It's a very socially acceptable way to be addictive, to get a temporary high, to feel good. I'm feeling depressed today, let's go shopping. As far as society goes it's sanctioned. They get a lot of social reinforcement for it."[5] "And yet," adds Mike, "just like with a drug or with alcohol, when it wears off it's still the same old world and people have to deal with that emptiness inside, which is really what causes people to go out and spend."

FINDING SOMEBODY BETTER

In addition to family conflicts brought on by overspending, Terri and Mike say they see another way by which rampant consumerism or affluenza weakens marriages. "The choices available to people in terms of products are so overwhelming," Terri contends. "Whether you're going to buy a car or a bagel, there's so many choices. There's a feeling when you've bought something that maybe you didn't make the right choice, maybe you missed something. And it can't help but carry over into relationships with people, that there's got to be somebody better out there."

"I see that a lot in my practice," adds Mike. "People come in and say they met someone at work or their relationship started at work and they divorced their spouses and got together. But once the wrapping was off it wasn't as new and different and wonderful as it was in the beginning when everyone was dressed up and powdered and looked perfect. So they go back to the company to find some other toy to play with, someone new, someone different."

Shopping for partners.

Ted Haggard, Pastor of the 5,000-member evangelical New Life Church in Colorado Springs, shares the Paulys' concerns. "Everything we watch," says Haggard, "is always promoting dissatisfaction. We need a new stereo, a new upgrade of our computer system, a better car, a bigger house. I think the societal discontent we're seeing is fed by the materialistic society we're living in."[6]

"The whole idea of using a thing and then throwing it away and getting another one, is affecting us all as people," Haggard believes. "We start looking at other people and saying that if they don't give us pleasure, they are disposable. I think the trend is dangerous and I think we need to have old values where we live in the same house as long as we can, where we keep material items as long as we can, and where we are faithful to each other."

In the use-it-once-and-throw-it-away, planned-obsolescence world of American consumer culture, it should not be surprising that attitudes formed in relation to products eventually get transferred to people as well.

Out of sight, out of mind. Moreover, family life strains under the stress of excess. As both parents work full-time and more to meet swelling expectations of the good life, then rush to maintain the frenetic lifestyles those expectations demand, nerves are frayed and tempers boil. In an ironic twist, the degeneration of family life leaves some partners spending *more* time at the office just to avoid the friction and turmoil back home, a phenomenon well-documented in *The Time Bind,* Arlie Russell Hochschild's study of workers' lives in a large corporation.

As Barbara Ehrenreich puts it in an endorsement of Hochschild's book, it's a "vicious cycle . . . the longer hours we work, the more stressful our home lives become; and the greater the tensions at home, the more we try to escape into work."[7] But the cycle frequently starts not with work, but with affluenza: often we work more because we want more. As a culture, at least, we have chosen money over time.

FAMILY VALUES OR MARKET VALUES?

There is yet another means by which affluenza pulls families apart. Glenn Stanton, the clean-cut, thirty-something director of a conservative family-support organization in South Carolina, calls it "the new homelessness." "We have people living in houses with one another but not connecting with one another," says Stanton.[8] They're not interacting because, quite simply, they all have their own toys to play with. "Dad is on the Internet," Stanton points out. "Mom's upstairs watching a movie on the VCR. The kids are downstairs playing video games. Everybody is connected to something outside the home even though they are physically within the home."

"The pressure that materialism is bringing to bear on the American family today is woefully underestimated but it is critically important," he argues. It wasn't something we expected to hear from Stanton, a former policy analyst for Focus on the Family, the largest Christian conservative organization in the United States.

Founded by Dr. James Dobson, a child psychologist whose radio program is heard by millions of people, Focus (FOF) is a mini-empire of conservative family advice based in Colorado Springs. Its operations are housed in a palacial hillside headquarters that might embarrass the Parthenon. Inside, the feel is expensive and dynamic. Tour groups learn about Dobson's vision for FOF, while the photographs lining the walls establish his connections to Republican stalwarts, including Ronald Reagan and Newt Gingrich.

Dozens of neatly dressed men and women respond to hundreds of phone callers every day, counseling them and sending out audiotapes, videotapes, and publications geared to teens, single parents, and other readers. "We get thousands of letters every week," said Stanton when we first met him at FOF. "People writing to us looking for help to hold their marriage together, their family together."

The ideology at Focus on the Family is decidedly free-market capitalist, but not without reservations, like those expressed by Stanton. "The market in a very real sense is hostile to the family," he contends. "It needs to expand itself. It needs to bring in new consumers. And quite tragically, it brings in new consumers at almost any price. Do we go after a sale even pitting child against parent? We would contend that that is too far."

THE CONSERVATIVE CONTRADICTION

Stanton and some other conservatives have begun to look carefully at what they see as an inherent tension between market values and family values. Edward Luttwak, a former Reagan administration official now with the Center for International and Strategic Studies, expresses his concerns about the issue rather bluntly. "The contradiction between wanting rapid economic growth and dynamic economic change and at the same time wanting family values, community values, and stability is a contradiction so huge that it can only last because of an aggressive refusal to think about it," says Luttwak,[9] author of the critically acclaimed book *Turbo-Capitalism.*

Luttwak calls himself "a real conservative, not a phony conservative." "I want to conserve family, community, nature. Conservatism should not be about the market, about money," he argues. "It should be about conserving things, not burning them up in the name of greed."

Too often, he says, so-called "conservatives" make speeches lauding the unrestricted market (as the best mechanism for rapidly increasing America's wealth), while at the same time saying "we have to go back to old family values, we have to maintain communities." "It's a complete non-sequiter, a complete contradiction, the two of course are completely in collision. It's the funniest after-dinner speech in America. And the fact that this is listened to without peals of laughter is a real problem."

"America," Luttwak contends, "is relatively rich, even Americans that are not doing that well are relatively rich, but America is very short of social tranquility, it's very short of stability. It's like somebody who has seventeen ties and no shoes buying himself another tie. The U.S. has no shoes as far as tranquility and the security of people's lives is concerned. But it has a lot of money. We have gone over to being a complete consumer society, a 100-percent consumer society. And the consequences are just as one would predict them. Mainly lots of consumption, lots of goodies and cheap things, cheap flights, and a lot of dissatisfaction."

Indeed, no system seems as effective as the unrestricted free market in delivering the most goods at the lowest prices to consumers. In the Age of Affluenza, such success has become the supreme measure of value. But human beings are more than consumers, more than stomachs craving to be filled. We are producers as well, looking to express ourselves through stable, meaningful work. We are members of families and communities, moral beings with interest in fairness and justice, living organisms dependent on a healthy and beautiful environment. We are parents and children.

Our affluenza-driven quest for maximum consumer access undermines these other values. To produce goods at the lowest prices, we lay off thousands of workers and transfer their workplaces from country to country in search of cheap labor. We shatter the dreams of those workers who are discarded, and often shatter their families as well. The security of whole communities is considered expendable. Lives are disrupted without a second thought. And as we shall see, children *are* pitted against parents, undermining family life even further.

CHAPTER 7

Dilated

pupils

We live in a material world,
and I'm a material girl.

—MADONNA

n 1969, when John was twenty-three, he taught briefly at a Navajo
Indian boarding school in Shiprock, New Mexico. His third-grade students were among the poorest children in America, possessing little
more than the clothes on their backs. The school had few toys or other sources of
entertainment. Yet John never heard the children say they were bored. They were
continually making up their own games. And though racism and alcoholism would
likely scar their lives a few years later, they were, at the age of ten, very happy and
well-adjusted children.

That Christmas, John went home to visit his family. He remembers the scene, a
floor full of packages under the tree. His own ten-year-old brother opened a dozen
or so of them, quickly moving from one to the next. A few days later, John found his
brother and a friend watching TV, the Christmas toys tossed aside in his brother's bedroom. Both boys complained to John that they had nothing to do. "We're bored," they

proclaimed. For John, it was a clear indication that children's happiness doesn't come from stuff. But powerful forces keep trying to persuade America's parents that it does.

THE CHILDREN'S MARKETING EXPLOSION

Susan, Jenny, and Emily, age ten, participate eagerly, punctuating the sound of rolling dice and moving plastic figures with shouts of "Yes!" and "My favorite store!" They're playing the game *Electronic Mall Madness*, from Milton Bradley. They jam their "credit cards" into the plastic ATM machine and withdraw play money to spend in the mall. The object of the game, which retails for $40, is to buy the most stuff and get back to the parking lot first. It's a good introduction to the happy-go-spending, affluenza-infected, life of today's children.

Spending by—and influenced by—American children twelve or younger recently began growing a torrid twenty percent a year, and is expected to reach $1 trillion annually within the next decade. Marketing to children has become the hottest trend in the advertising world. "Corporations are recognizing that the consumer lifestyle starts younger and younger," explains Joan Chiaramonte, who does market research for the Roper Starch polling firm. "If you wait to reach children with your product until they're eighteen years of age, you probably won't capture them."[1]

From 1980 to 1997 the amount spent on children's advertising in America rose from $100 million to $1.5 billion a year. Children are now also used effectively by marketers to influence their parents' purchases of big-ticket items, from luxury automobiles to resort vacations and even homes. One hotel chain sends promotional brochures to children who've stayed at its hotels, so the kids will pester their parents into returning.

For the first time in human history, children are getting most of their information from entities whose goal is to sell them something, rather than from family, school, or religion. The average twelve-year-old in the United States spends forty-eight hours a week exposed to commercial messages. The same child spends only about one and a half hours per week in significant conversation with his or her parents.[2]

Children under seven are especially vulnerable to marketing messages. Research shows that they are unable to distinguish commercial motives from benign or benevolent motives. One '70s study found that when asked who they would believe if their parents told them something was true and a TV character (even an animated one like Tony the Tiger) told them the opposite was true, most young children said they'd believe what the TV character told them.

What psychological, social, and cultural impacts are these trends having on children? Polls show that nearly ninety percent of American adults worry that our children are becoming "too focused on buying and consuming things."[3]

VALUES IN CONFLICT

In Minneapolis, psychologist David Walsh, author of *Selling Out America's Children,* teaches parents ways to protect their offspring from falling captive to commercialism. After years spent treating so-called "problem children," Walsh worries that childhood affluenza is reaching epidemic levels. He sees a fundamental collision of values between children's needs and advertising. "Market-created values of selfishness, instant gratification, perpetual discontentment, and constant consumption have become diametrically opposed to the values most Americans want to teach their children," says the grandfatherly Walsh, presenting his concerns with gentle passion.[4]

Advertising aimed at children is hardly a new phenomenon. By 1912, boxes of Cracker Jack already came with a toy inside to encourage children to ask for them. Long before television, children were saving cereal box tops to send in for prizes. Interestingly, the whole idea of children's TV programming came because advertisers were looking for ways to use the new electronic medium to sell their products. The first TV cartoon shows were created explicitly to sell sugared cereals.

Indeed, ninety percent of food ads on Saturday morning children's programs still hawk high-calorie, sugary, or salt-laden items. Combine that with the time children spend in front of the tube and it's not surprising that children today are far more likely to be obese (obesity rates among American children doubled in the 1980s alone) than they were in the early days of television.[5]

Today's children are exposed to far more TV advertising than their parents were—up to 200 commercials a day! But more importantly, perhaps, there's a big difference between today's ads and those of a generation ago. In the old ads, parents were portrayed as pillars of wisdom who both knew and wanted what was best for their children. Children, on the other hand, were full of wonder and innocence, and eager to please Mom and Dad. There was gender stereotyping—girls wanted dolls and boys wanted cowboys and Indians—but rebelling against one's parents wasn't part of the message.

KIDS AS CATTLE

Now the message has changed. Marketers openly refer to parents as "gatekeepers," whose efforts to protect their children from commercial pressures must be circumvented so that those children, in the rather chilling terms used by the marketers, can be "captured, owned, and branded." At a 1996 marketing conference called "Kid Power," held appropriately at Disney World, the keynote address, "Softening the Parental Veto," was presented by the marketing director of McDonald's.

Speaker after speaker revealed the strategy: Portray parents as fools and fuddy-duddies who aren't smart enough to realize their children's need for the products being sold. It's a proven technique for neutralizing parental influence in the marketer/child relationship.

Presenters at Kid Power '96 further revealed how marketers now use children to design effective advertising campaigns. Kids are given cameras to photograph themselves and their friends to see how they dress and spend their time. They are observed at home, at school, in stores and at public events. Their spending habits are carefully tracked. They are gathered into focus groups and asked to respond to commercials, separating the "cool" from the "uncool."

The "coolest" contemporary ads frequently carry the message delivered by Kid Power '96 speaker Paul Kurnit, a prominent marketing consultant. "Anti-social behavior in pursuit of a product is a good thing," Kurnit stated calmly, suggesting that advertisers could best reach children by encouraging rude, often aggressive behavior and faux rebellion against the strictures of family discipline.[6] There is, some critics say, a serious danger in this: If rude, aggressive behavior becomes the norm for children as they emulate advertising models, to what level will children have to escalate their aggressive activities to really feel they are rebelling?

SHOOTING THE NEIGHBOR'S CAT

None of that seems to matter to the marketers who advertise in *Electronic Gaming Monthly,* a magazine popular with kids who are avid video game players. When her eight-year-old son Arthur first showed her several of the ads, Caroline Sawe, a Seattle single mother, was shocked. Her son loves video games, but he was disturbed by an ad he saw in the May 1998 issue of *Electronic Gaming Monthly.* It was for a game called "Point Blank." Boldly splashed on the ad in giant print was the headline: MORE FUN THAN SHOOTING YOUR NEIGHBOR'S CAT. "I screamed when I saw it," Caroline Sawe recalls. "I think I scared Arthur, but I was so upset."[7]

The ad's copy was equally blunt: "Bang! Meow! Bang! Meow! Come on already. It's time you move up the food chain and take aim at something that sounds better when it explodes. . . . The directions are easy. If it's bigger than a pixel, shoot it." Caroline Sawe leafed through the magazine, growing even more horrified. Ad after ad glorified mindless violence. One, for a game called Vigilante 8, pictured a school bus armed with machine guns and missiles, commandeered by Molo, a "psycho" looking for revenge after being expelled from school. That one was especially disturbing because this was the same month that Kip Kinkel shot up his high school in Springfield, Oregon, killing two fellow students.

Caroline Sawe, a tall, passionate woman who immigrated to the United States from her native Tanzania, shakes her head sadly when she thinks about the ads and Arthur's exposure to them. Is this what she left her tribal homeland on the slopes of Mt. Kilimanjaro and came to America for? Are there no limits to what affluenza-afflicted marketers, looking to make quick profits by selling to children, will do?

GOTTA HAVE THE CLOTHES

The "anti-social" ads are targeted primarily at boys. For girls, the messages are more genteel, but still place products on a pedestal, above other values. A recent Sears ad is instructive: In it, actress and singer Maia Campbell tells girls, "You gotta believe in your dreams. You gotta stand up for yourself. You gotta be there for your friends. But, hey, *first* you gotta have something to wear. You *gotta* have the *clothes*." The ad shows Campbell modeling clothes collectively priced at $267.

Companies selling beauty products are targeting younger and younger girls. By the age of thirteen, twenty-six percent of American girls wear perfume every day. Christian Dior makes bras for preschoolers. Jeans ads feature preteen girls in sexual poses. Ad critic Laurie Mazur says such images "may have dangerous implications," pointing out that nearly half a million American children are victims of sexual abuse each year.[8]

TODAY'S LESSON IS BROUGHT TO YOU BY...

Not only are the messages different today, they aren't limited to print and television. As marketers attempt to get their message through the "clutter" of advertising aimed at children, they look to put ads in places where ads have never gone before.

In 1998, a student was suspended at Greenbrier High School in Georgia. His crime? Wearing a Pepsi T-shirt on "Coke Day in the Schools." It seems the 600 students at Greenbrier had been instructed to wear Coke T-shirts and spell out Coca-Cola on the school lawn to impress a visiting Coca-Cola executive and give the school a chance to win $500 from the soft drink company. If we had anything to say about it, it would have been the principal who was suspended, for allowing such a blatant commercial misuse of his school. But the incident at Greenbrier High is only the tip of an iceberg of commercialism that has penetrated deep into America's schools, allowing serious affluenza infections to follow close behind.

BETTER THAN STRAIGHT A'S

In the Age of Affluenza, voters demand tax cuts and reductions in public spending as their personal spending habits leave them with growing credit debt. Then too, many affluent families increasingly send their children to private schools, further reducing voter support for public school systems.

As funding for education tightens, school boards all across America have turned to corporations for financial help. In exchange for cash, companies are allowed to advertise their products on school rooftops, hallways, readerboards, book covers, uniforms, and buses.

A walk through the hallways of Colorado Springs high schools reveals a string of mini-billboards informing students that "M&Ms are better than straight A's" and encouraging them to "Satisfy your hunger for higher education with Snickers." The ads, critics say, constitute an endorsement by the schools of the very foods students are warned against in their health classes. School buses in Colorado Springs also carry ads, for 7-Up, Burger King, and the like, painted—by the students!—boldly on their sides. School superintendent Kenneth Burnley (who was chosen National School Superintendent of the Year for his policy allowing advertising in his schools) defends the ads, saying the money they provide is needed because voters in the prosperous, all-American city haven't passed a school bond since 1972. "People say I'd rather buy a boat than give money to the schools," explains Burnley.[9]

CASH CROPS?

"Children in our society are seen as cash crops to be harvested," explains Alex Molnar, a professor of education at the University of Wisconsin, Milwaukee, who has been investigating commercialism in the schools for many years.[10] Angry and articulate, Molnar readily displays his collection of "curriculum materials" created by corporations for use in the public schools.

Students find out about self-esteem by discussing "Good and Bad Hair Days" with materials provided by Revlon. They learn to "wipe out that germ" with Lysol, and study geothermal energy by eating Gusher's Fruit Snacks (the "teachers' guide" suggests that each student be given a Gusher, bite on it, and compare the sensation to a volcanic eruption!). They also learn the history of Tootsie Rolls, make shoes for Nike as an environmental lesson, count Lay's potato chips in math class and find out why the Exxon Valdez oil spill wasn't really harmful at all (materials courtesy of—you guessed it—Exxon) or why clear-cutting is beneficial—with a little help from Georgia-Pacific. Maybe we could turn around the steady decline of our children's SAT scores if we just asked them questions about good and bad hair days instead of about world geography.

In nearly half a million classrooms, 8.1 million children watch Channel One, a twelve-minute daily news program that includes two minutes of commercials. Viewing is mandatory for students because advertisers, who pay as much as $200,000 for a single thirty-second spot on Channel One, are told they can count on a "captive audience."[11]

CAPTIVE KIDS

As affluenza becomes an airwave-borne childhood epidemic, America's children pay a high price. Not only does the couch-potato-on-potato-chips lifestyle undermine our children's physical health, their mental health seems to suffer too. Psychologists report constantly rising rates of teenage depression and thoughts about suicide, and a tripling of actual child suicide rates since the 1960s.[12]

What kind of values do our children learn from their exposure to affluenza? In a recent poll, ninety-three percent of teenage girls cited shopping as their favorite activity. Fewer than five percent listed "helping others." In 1967, two-thirds of American college students said "developing a meaningful philosophy of life" was "very important" to them, while fewer than one-third said the same about "making a lot of money." By 1997, those figures were reversed.[13]

Asked about their "highest priority" in a recent poll taken at the University of Washington, forty-two percent of those polled cited "looking good/having good hair." Another eighteen percent listed "staying inebriated," while only six percent checked "learning about the world."

Jennifer Gailus and Olivia Martin would have been among the six percent. In 1996, Gailus, a vivacious former cheerleader, and her best friend Martin, who is quiet and serious, wrote a play called "Barbie Get Real," satirizing the hollow life of appearances and shopping they say had become rampant among their peers at Eastlake High School in affluent Redmond, Washington (the home of Microsoft).

Asked at the time why they wrote the play, Gailus summed up the pernicious effect affluenza has on children. "The kids in our high school," she said sadly, "take everything for granted. They think they've earned it and the world owes it to them. They'll just take, take, take, and they won't give anything back. And our society's going to crumble if we don't have people that give."[14]

CHAPTER 8

Community
chills

Everyplace looks like no place,
and no place looks like home.

—JAMES KUNTSLER, AUTHOR
The Geography of Nowhere

ou may have seen the ad. It's a fairly recent one for an SUV. It pictures a suburban street of identical, expensive ranch style houses with perfect lawns. The SUV being advertised is parked in the driveway of one of them. But in every other driveway is . . . a tank. A real tank. A big, deadly Army tank. It's a chilling ad, meant to remind us of how chilly our communities have become as our war of all-against-all consumer competition intensifies. Psychologically, it suggests that we need to drive something as strong as a tank to compete with all the other killer vehicles out there. But a classy, comfortable tank. Of course, the ad is an exaggeration. Our communities aren't this cold and hostile. Not yet. But there's a definite chill in the air . . . .

During the 1950s, Dave used to walk with his grandfather four or five blocks to the town square in Crown Point, Indiana, where the older man lived. Everyone knew his grandfather, even the guy carrying a sack of salvaged goods. Forty-five years later, Dave still remembers the names of his grandparents' neighbors, and the summer backyard parties they threw. But a sense of place and the trust that comes with it are disappearing from our towns and neighborhoods.

In 1951, we sat together with the neighbors, laughing at Red Skelton. In 1985, we still watched *Family Ties* as a family. But by 1995, each member of the family often watched his or her own TV as isolation and passivity became a way of life. What began as a quest for the good life in the suburbs degenerated into private consumption splurges that separated one neighbor from another, and one family member from another. We began to feel lost in our own neighborhoods. Huge retailers took advantage of the confusion, expanding to meet our demands for cheap underwear, hardware, and software.

The more we chased bargains and the paychecks that bought them, the more vitality slipped away from our towns. Now, if we want to experience Main Street—the way it was in the good old days—we travel to Disneyworld, to a faux community where smiling shopkeepers, the slow pace, and the quaintness remind us that our real communities were once close-knit and friendly.

How will Disney portray the good old days of the suburbs in future exhibits? Will they orchestrate background ambience—highway traffic, leaf blowers, and beeping garbage trucks—to make it more realistic? Will they recreate gridlock as "bumper-to-bumper cars," complete with cell phones to tell our families we'll be late for the next ride? Will our tour of the "gated community" require more tickets than rides through the "inner city" do? Will recreational and business opportunities that have sprung up in recent years be dramatized—businesses like Kid Shuttle, a taxi service for kids whose moms aren't home to take them to Tae Kwon Do? Will Disney hire extras to play the roles of other suburbanites who can't drive—elderly, disabled, and low-income residents, peeking out from behind living-room curtains?

BOWLING ALONE

Where can America's stranded nondrivers go in today's world? There's no colorful café down the block, or bowling alley or tavern, where neighbors can "be apart together, and mutually withdraw from the world," in the words of writer Ray Oldenburg.[1] Such "great good places" or "third places," that are apart from both home and work environments, are now often illegal—violations of zoning codes. The truth is, the term "community life" is perceived as archaic in a world so dominated by business and government.

"We've mutated from citizens to consumers in the last sixty years," says James Kuntsler, author of *The Geography of Nowhere*. "The trouble with being consumers is that consumers have no duties or responsibilities or obligations to their fellow consumers. Citizens do. They have the obligation to care about their fellow citizens, and about the integrity of the town's environment and history."[2]

Harvard political scientist Robert Putnam has devoted his career to the study of "social capital," the connections among people that bind a community together. He observed that the quality of governance varies with the level of involvement in such things as voter turnout, newspaper readership, and membership in choral societies. Recently, he captured the public's imagination by concluding that far too many Americans are "bowling alone" (compared to a generation ago, more people are bowling, but fewer of them bowl in leagues). Once a nation of joiners, we've now become a nation of loners. Only about half of the nation's voters typically vote in presidential elections. Only thirteen percent reported attending public meetings on town or school affairs, and PTA participation has fallen from more than twelve million in 1964 to seven million in 1995. The League of Women Voters' membership is down forty-two percent since 1969, and fraternal organizations like the Elks and Lions are endangered species.[3]

Volunteering for Boy Scouts is off twenty-six percent since 1970, and for the Red Cross, sixty-one percent. Overall, a record 109 million Americans are volunteering, but many of them do it "on the run," in shorter installments, so the total time volunteered has actually declined. The "fun factor" is a major stimulant in volunteering. If it's not fun, forget it. A 1998 study on volunteering revealed that thirty percent of young adults volunteered because it was fun, compared to eleven percent who said they were committed to the cause.[4]

Putnam concedes that membership has expanded in newer organizations such as the Sierra Club and the American Association of Retired Persons. But most members never even meet, he points out—they just pay their dues and maybe read the organization's newsletter. Internet chat groups, however convenient, are also faceless and fleshless. "Face-to-face connections are clearly more effective for building trust," he says. "Knowing the person you're talking to and taking personal responsibility for your view are crucial to having a conversation about public affairs."[5]

THE CHAINING OF AMERICA

Another symptom of civic degeneration is the disappearance of traditional civic leaders of community organizations. Bank presidents and business owners with longstanding ties to the community are bounced from positions of community leadership when the U.S. Banks, Wal-Marts, Office Maxes, and Home Depots come to town to put them out of business. And what do we get when the chains take over? Lower prices, cheaper stuff. But what we lose is the value of community

—a nonmaterial value, but more important for a high quality of life. We lose the personal touch.

For example, small businesses give a higher percentage of their revenues to charitable organizations than the big, absentee franchises do, and they offer a lot more in terms of local character and product diversity. At a locally owned coffee shop, you might see artwork from someone who lives down the street. The shop is *your* coffee shop. At your independent bookseller, you stand a much greater chance of finding books from small presses who publish a wider variety of books than mainstream publishers.

The "chaining of America" has happened so quickly that it's hard to believe the statistics. In 1972, independent booksellers claimed fifty-eight percent of all book sales, but by 1997, their share had fallen to just seventeen percent, and it continues to fall. Lowe's and Home Depot control more than a quarter of the hardware market, forcing many a neighborhood "Mr. Fixit" to wear corporate apron colors— if he's not "over-qualified." There are similar statistics for pharmacies, 11,000 of which have recently disappeared, as well as video stores, coffee shops, and office supply stores.

Overall, more than half a million franchise businesses in sixty different industries control thirty-five percent of the retail market.[6] By using economies of scale in purchasing and distribution, and being able to stay in the market even at a loss, the corporate retailers can drive out competition within a year, and in some cases less.[7]

In search of better buys and higher tax revenues, consumers and city council members typically sacrifice first Strip Avenue, then downtown to the franchise developers, forgetting that much of a franchise dollar is electronically transferred to corporate headquarters, while a dollar spent at the local hardware stays put in towns or neighborhoods. The value of the local dollar is multiplied many times as small businesses hire architects, designers, woodworkers, sign makers, local accountants, insurance brokers, computer consultants, attorneys, advertising agencies—all services that the big retailers contract out nationally. Local retailers and distributors also carry a higher percentage of locally made goods than the chains, creating more jobs for local producers.[8] When we buy from the chains, instead of a multiplier effect, we get a "divider effect."

In the year 2001 our social defenses are down. Distracted by material things and out of touch with social health, we watch community life from the sidelines. Hurrying to work, we see a fleet of bulldozers leveling a familiar open area next to the river, but we haven't heard yet what's going in there. Chances are good it's Wal-Mart, McDonald's, and Starbucks.

AL NORMAN, SPRAWL-BUSTER

"When I'm out of town," says Al Norman, "I come home to as many as a hundred e-mail messages from all over the world. Concerned citizens are asking me for information on how to stop the huge retailers from rolling over their towns like an asphalt roller." Norman spearheaded a Wal-Mart resistance campaign in his own hometown—Greenfield, Massachusetts—and won. After his story appeared in *Time, Newsweek,* the *New York Times,* and 60 Minutes, "My phone started ringing, and hasn't stopped. I've been to thirty-six states now, teaching home-town activists what tools are available."[9]

Norman's Web site lists about 100 successes, some of which he personally has coached to victory, but he's also very familiar with the defeats, and the socio-economic impacts that follow. "The *Adirondack Daily Enterprise* recently published an account of what has happened to retailers in Ticonderoga, New York, over the past eight months since Wal-Mart came to town," he said. "Business is down at least twenty percent at the drug store, jeweler, and auto parts stores, but the game's totally over at the Great American Market, the town's only downtown grocery store. First they cut their operating hours, then dropped the payroll from twenty-seven people to seventeen. This January, the grocery closed completely. Many of the people who shopped at the GAM were the elderly, low-income people without access to a car."

"I've been here 25 years," a downtown Sunoco station owner told Norman. "On the week before Christmas in prior years, you couldn't find a parking space on this street. This year, you could have landed a plane on it." Everyone's car was parked at the Mega-Mall. Norman recalls going into Henniker, New Hampshire, a town actively opposing an 11,000-square-foot Rite-Aid store. "It did my heart good to read a sign at the city limits that, to me, said it all: 'Welcome to Henniker—the only Henniker on Earth.' The problem is, you've got the other side of the American population. They'll stand up in public meetings and insist they have a God-given right to cheap underwear and whipping cream. It seems like their sense of community is no bigger than their own shopping cart."

FORTRESS AMERICA

What happens when affluenza causes communities to be pulled apart (for example, when a company leaves town and lays off hundreds of people), or crippled by bad design? We "cocoon," retreating further and further inward, and closing the gate behind us. Including secured apartment dwellers, residents of gated communities, prison inmates, and residential security system zealots, at least a fifth of the country now lives behind bars. "Socially, the house fortress represents a self-fulfilling prophecy," says community designer Peter Calthorpe. "The more isolated people become and the less they share with others unlike themselves, the more they do have to fear."[10]

Sociologist Edward Blakely would agree. "We are a society whose purported goal is to bring people of all income levels and races together, but gated communities are the direct opposite of that," he writes in the book *Fortress America*. "How can the nation have a social contract without having social contact?"[11] If gated enclaves are the final act of secession from the wider community and a retreat from the civic system, 20,000 such communities, housing almost nine million people, have already seceded. Why have so many retreated from the wider community? Don't we trust each other? In 1958, trust was sky-high. Seventy-three percent of Americans surveyed said they trusted the federal government to do what is right either "most of the time" or "just about always." By 1996–1997, that percentage had fallen to less than thirty percent. It's the same with trust among individuals. Sixty percent now believe "you can't be too careful in dealing with people."[12] It's the same story in the workplace, where the lack of trust is costly. "When we can't trust our employees or other market players," writes Robert Putnam, "we end up squandering our wealth on surveillance equipment, compliance structures, insurance, legal services, and enforcement of government regulations."

A 2000 nationwide poll conducted by the Pew School of Journalism reflected a collective queasiness in America. Compared to the ninety-six percent who felt safe in their homes, twenty percent did *not* feel safe in their own neighborhoods and thirty percent did *not* feel safe at the mall. What do these results say about the world "out there?" Grab the take-out dinner, survive the commute, just get home. In the poll, a wide sampling of Americans was asked, "What do you think is the most important problem facing the community where you live?" Predictably, crime/violence scored the highest, but surprisingly, it shared top ranking with development/sprawl/traffic/roads. Both are problems that many Americans feel are "out of control." And in an effort to regain control, we revert to the primal responses of fight or flight.

We try to fight crime with judicial and enforcement industries that have become seven percent of the U.S. economy. In recent years we've expanded the number of men and women in police uniforms to control crime and hired three times as many "rent-a-cops" as real cops. And in prisons, taxpayers pick up the tab for costs per prisoner that are comparable to sending a student to Harvard.

In any densely populated area, you'll hear the sounds of insecurity. Car alarms, beeping electronic locks, and police sirens reveal our futile quest to control crime. In reality, despite popular perceptions, living in suburbia may be statistically riskier than living in the inner city, because suburban residents drive three times as much as residents of close-in urban neighborhoods, and three times as many of them die in car crashes. Still, millions continue to take flight to the perceived security of suburbia.

MISSING: TWO MILLION CHILDREN

If an eight-year-old girl can walk safely to the public library six blocks away, that's one good indicator of a healthy community. For starters, you have a public library worth walking to, and a sidewalk to walk on. But more importantly, you have neighbors who watch out for each other. You have social capital in the neighborhood— relationships, commitments, and networks that create an underlying sense of trust.

Yet in many American neighborhoods, trust is becoming a nostalgic memory. Seeing children at play is becoming as rare as sighting an endangered songbird. Not only are children missing from our streets and parks, but in our statistical data as well. According to the 1990 Census, two million have officially "disappeared." The equivalent of a Kansas City or Miami, filled with children that the census takers did not find. Comparing birth and death statistics, that many children were unaccounted for.

Where are they? According to demographer William O'Hare, half a million are in foster care, moving frequently from one home to another. Others are shuffled between the homes of separated parents, or are living with grandparents or friends. Some live in converted garages or outbuildings not recognized by the census. Some live in households with more members than can be listed on a census form. The bottom line for O'Hare is that "More of our kids are slipping between the cracks, and there's no evidence that it's improving."[13]

THE SOCIAL COSTS OF PROSPERITY

Since 1950, the amount of land in our communities devoted to public uses— parks, civic buildings, schools, churches, and so on—decreased by a fifth, while the percentage of income we spend for house mortgages and rental payments increased from a fifth to a full half, according to the American Planning Association. The evidence shows that as we've disinvested in the public areas and "privatized" our lifestyles, we've often left citizenship and care at the front door. So many services are now delivered for a profit by the private sector, we seem to have just gotten out of the habit of taking care of each other.

The 1990s were the most continuously prosperous years in the history of America, as measured in economic terms. Yet Marc Miringoff at Fordham University's Institute for Innovation in Social Policy believes that the trends in his Index of Social Health point to a nation in crisis.

"In 1977," Miringoff says, "social health started its long decline, while the GDP continued upward. Since then, the social health index declined forty-five percent while the GDP rose by seventy-nine percent."[14]

Far from being just abstract statistics, the trends he cites are about *real people* in your family and mine, who constitute the social wealth and vigor of our communities. More than three million children are reported abused every year—forty-seven cases for every 1,000 children. Miringoff asks, "What will be the impact on marriage, child rearing, education, and employment from all that abuse?" He also points to youth suicide as an unmistakable indicator of underlying discontent. In 1950, the suicide rate among youth aged fifteen to twenty-four was a relatively low 4.5 per 100,000. By 1970, suicides had almost doubled, and by 1996, the rate was up to twelve. Each suicide resonates far beyond an individual's family, causing serious depression among the victim's friends, schoolmates, and neighbors—not to mention the lost potential of the youth.[15]

A GEOGRAPHY OF NOWHERE?

When affluenza infects our communities it starts a vicious cycle. We begin to choose things over people, a choice that disconnects us from community life and causes even more consumption, and more disconnection. Health scientists have documented that people in relationships outlive single people, and that people who feel the friendship and support of neighbors need less health care. One study also found that residents of neighborhoods in crisis tend to be clinically "socially" depressed, with lower levels of serotonin—what anti-depressants stimulate—in blood samples.

Have we become a nation too distracted to care? Like the medium-sized fish that ate a small fish, we consume franchise products in the privacy of our homes, then watch helplessly as the big-fish franchise companies bite huge chunks out of our public places, swallowing jobs, traditions, and open space. We assume that someone else is taking care of things—we pay them to take care of things so we can concentrate on working and spending. But to our horror, we discover that many of the service providers, merchandise retailers, and caretakers are not really taking care of us anymore. It might be more appropriate to say they're *consuming* us.

CHAPTER 9

An ache for meaning

*Man does not live by cheap
vacuum cleaners alone.*

—CONSERVATIVE ECONOMIST WILHELM ROPKE

We are the hollow men. We are the stuffed men.

—T.S. ELIOT

The road switchbacks up, down, and around precipitous canyons, crosses raging streams, and winds by glassy lakes offering mirror images of an immense snow-covered volcano, the main attraction in Washington state's Mount Rainier National Park. Each year, two million people drive the road. More than a few stop to admire the beautiful stone masonry, so perfectly in harmony with the natural setting, that forms the guardrails for the road or the graceful arches of its many bridges. This is quality work, built to last, built for beauty as well as utility. Built by the Civilian Conservation Corps (CCC).

In the 1930s, during the depths of The Great Depression, hundreds of young men came to Mount Rainier—ordinary, unemployed working men, mostly from cities back east. Living together in tent camps or barracks, they built many of the marvelous facilities visitors to the park now take for granted. At a time when the dominant notion is that government never does anything well, the work of the CCC at Mount Rainier and many other national parks provides something of a corrective.

The men's work was laborious, performed in snow, sleet, or blazing sun, and their wages barely provided subsistence. Their accommodations were anything but plush, and they had little to entertain them except story-telling and card games. Most could carry all the possessions they owned in a single suitcase. Yet when author Harry Boyte interviewed veterans of the CCC, he found that many looked back on those days as the best of their lives.

They'd forgotten the dirt, the strained muscles, the bite of the mosquitoes. But they remembered with deep fondness the camaraderie and the feeling they had that they were "building America," creating public works of true and lasting value that would be enjoyed by generations yet unborn. Their sense of pride in their CCC accomplishments was still palpable sixty years later.[1]

THE MAN WHO PLANTED TREES

Twenty years ago, John Beal was working as an engineer with the Boeing Company when heart problems forced him to take some time off work. To improve his health, he walked frequently near his home. His strolls took him past a stream called Hamm Creek, a tiny rivulet that descends from the hills of southwest Seattle and joins the Duwamish River, an industrial waterway emptying into Puget Sound. Beal knew that in years past, schools of salmon came up the Duwamish to spawning grounds on Hamm Creek.

But in 1980 the creek was barren of fish. The evergreen forests that once lined its banks had all been stripped away. Industries dumped waste into the creek and garbage lined its banks. John Beal set out to change that. "If we could restore Hamm Creek, in the most polluted part of the city of Seattle," he says he felt at the time, "we could demonstrate that it could be done anywhere."[2]

He worked actively, and successfully, to stop companies from polluting the creek, and hauled out tons of garbage. Then, over the next decade and a half, he planted trees, thousands of them. He restored natural ponds and waterfalls and spawning beds. At first he worked alone, but in time other people began to help. Some newspaper articles and a couple of TV reports attracted more. Beal showed them how to restore the watershed.

The salmon came back, each year a few more until the run is now nearly healthy again. Beal has never been paid for his efforts, though public donations cover his expenses. But he has, he says, been richly compensated by the personal satisfaction he feels from having made a real difference for Hamm Creek and his community. "That's my reward, that's how I get paid," Beal concludes.

What John Beal, the men of the CCC, and the countless people who give to their communities have in common is the understanding that meaningful activity matters more than money and that, indeed, it is better to give than receive. They've learned that fulfillment comes from such efforts. But in our consumer society they are becoming exceptions.

The more Americans fill their lives with things, the more they tell psychiatrists, pastors, friends, and family members that they feel "empty" inside. The more toys our kids have to play with, the more they complain of boredom. Two thousand years ago, Jesus Christ predicted they would feel that way. What profit would it bring a person, he asked his followers (Matthew 16:26), were that person to gain the whole world, but lose his soul? In the Age of Affluenza, that question is seldom asked, at least not publicly. It should be.

POVERTY OF THE SOUL

When Mother Teresa came to the United States to receive an honorary degree, she said, "this is the poorest place I've ever been in my life," recounts Robert Seiple, director of World Vision, the Christian charity organization. "She wasn't talking about economics, mutual funds, Wall Street, the ability to consume," he adds. "She was talking about poverty of the soul."[3]

Shortly before he died of a brain tumor, Republican campaign strategist Lee Atwater made a confession. "The '80s," he said, "were about acquiring—acquiring wealth, power, prestige. I know. I acquired more wealth, power and prestige than most. But you can acquire all you want and still feel empty." He warned that there was "a spiritual vacuum at the heart of American society, a tumor of the soul."[4]

In all the great religious traditions, human beings are seen as having a purpose in life. Stripped to its essentials, it is to serve God by caring for God's creations and our fellow human beings. Happy is the man or woman whose work and life energies serve those ends, who finds a "calling" or "right livelihood" that allows his or her talents to serve the common good. In none of those traditions is purpose to be found in simply accumulating things, or power, or pleasure—or in "looking out for Number One."

One seldom hears work described as a calling anymore. Work may be "interest-ing" and "creative" or dull and boring. It may bring status or indifference—and not in any sense in relation to its real value. Our lives are disrupted far more severely when garbage collectors stop working than when ball players do, for example. Work may bring great monetary rewards or bare subsistence. But we almost never ask what it means and what it serves. For most, though certainly not all of us, if it makes money, that's reason enough. Why do it? Simple. It pays.

Consider, for example, the handsomely compensated professionals who design the hyper-violent video game advertisements that so alarmed Caroline Sawe (described in Chapter 7). Undoubtedly, most would describe their jobs as "fun" and certainly "creative," allowing them to continually imagine new ideas for effective promotions (double-entendre intended). Nothing rote about such work. Comfort-able surroundings? No doubt. Flexible hours? Probably, if long ones. A certain smug self-satisfaction at being smart, effective manipulators, able to come up with oh-so-clever copy like "More fun than shooting your neighbor's cat." "I love my job," they'd be likely to tell you if you asked them.

Then consider the designers of the games themselves. All the same satisfactions apply, plus even higher levels of financial remuneration—enough to purchase Fer-raris, Porsches, and mansions. A few admit they would never let their *own* children use the products (or, in the case of purveyors of movie violence, see the films) that they make and market to other people's children. But stop making them? Not when the rewards are what they are.

Gain the world, lose the soul.

That such professionals can "enjoy" their work without the slightest qualms about its ultimate value or consequences surely testifies to the effective repression of questions about meaning and purpose in our modern economy. They do not ache—not outwardly, at least. Or perhaps the rewards—money, stimulation, power, status—they receive for their morally dubious products act like morphine to deaden any pangs of regret.

UNDER THE SMILE BUTTONS

But millions of other Americans do hunger for meaning. That's what Dr. Michael Lerner, a rabbi and writer, found when he worked in a "stress clinic" for working families in Oakland, California. Along with his coworkers, Lerner originally "imagined that most Americans are motivated primarily by material self-interest. So we were surprised that these middle Americans often experience more stress from feeling that they are wasting their lives doing meaningless work than from feeling that they are not making enough money."[5]

Lerner and his colleagues brought groups of working people from various occupations together to talk with each other about their lives. "At first, most of the people we talked to wanted to reassure us, as they assured their coworkers and friends, that everything was fine, that they were handling things well, that they never let stress get to them, and that their lives were good." It was, he says, the kind of response that pollsters usually get when they ask people superficial questions about life satisfaction. But in time, as participants in the groups felt more comfortable being honest about their emotions, a different pattern of responses emerged.

"We found middle-income people deeply unhappy because they hunger to serve the common good and to contribute something with their talents and energies, yet find that their actual work gives them little opportunity to do so," Lerner writes. "They often turn to demands for more money as a compensation for a life that otherwise feels frustrating and empty."

"It is perhaps this fear of no longer being needed in a world of needless things that most clearly spells out the unnaturalness, the surreality, of much that is called work today," wrote Studs Terkel in his best-seller *Working*. Perhaps it's feelings such as those described by Lerner and Terkel that have led to one of the most disturbing of contemporary American statistics: The rate of clinical depression in the United States today is *ten* times what it was before 1945. Millions of Americans dull their psychic pain with Prozac and other drugs.[6]

As Americans increasingly fall victim to affluenza, feelings of depression, anxiety, and lowered self-esteem are likely to become even more prevalent. Such a prediction finds scientific support in a series of recent studies carried out by two professors of psychology, Tim Kasser and Richard Ryan. They compared individuals whose primary aspirations were financial with others who were oriented toward lives of community service and strong relationships with other people.

Their conclusions were unequivocal: Those individuals for whom accumulating wealth was a primary aspiration "were associated with less self-actualization, less vitality, more depression and more anxiety." Their studies, they wrote, "demonstrated the deleterious consequences of having money as an important guiding principle in life."[7]

CHANGING STUDENT VALUES

Kasser and Ryan's studies confirm the wisdom of religious traditions that warn about the dangers of preoccupation with wealth. But such wisdom has been falling on deaf ears for quite some time now. In 1962, when Tom Hayden, now a California state senator, penned the Port Huron Statement, the founding manifesto of Students for a Democratic Society (SDS), he declared, "The main and transcending concern of the university must be the unfolding and refinement of the moral, aesthetic and logical capacities" to help students find "a moral meaning in life."[8]

"Loneliness, estrangement and isolation describe the vast distance between man and man today," Hayden wrote. "These dominant tendencies cannot be overcome by better personnel management, nor by improved gadgets, but only when a love of man overcomes the idolatrous worship of things by man."

During the '60s, calls such as Hayden's for a meaningful life of service to the world —responding in part to John F. Kennedy's inaugural admonition to "ask not what your country can do for you; ask, rather, what you can do for your country"— inspired tens of thousands of students. Oral historian Studs Terkel, while acknowledging some of the youthful excesses of the '60s (the drugs, the foul language, the casual sex), says that what he remembers most about that decade was symbolized by an episode during the 1968 Democratic Convention in Chicago, when police chased antiwar demonstrators through Grant and Lincoln parks, clubbing and gassing them.

Terkel was observing the demonstration with James Cameron, a British journalist, when all of a sudden the police sent a volley of tear gas their way. "We were scurrying away, the tears running down, and as I was stumbling, a canister of tear gas fell at my feet," Terkel recalls. "And I'll never forget this little goofy hippie kid with long blond locks. He kicks the tear gas away from Cameron and me and toward himself. Toward himself. He saves us from the gas! That kid's gesture was really what the sixties was all about. They had causes outside themselves. Civil rights. Vietnam. That's what the sixties was all about."[9]

The dreams of college students have changed markedly since then.

Not long ago, when Thomas taught at Duke University, he asked students to outline their goals. Above all, they wanted money, power, and things—very big things, including vacation homes, expensive foreign automobiles, yachts, and even airplanes. Their request of faculty members like himself: "Teach me to be a money-making, money-spending machine." The most common thing he remembers Duke students saying to each other was, "I can't believe how drunk I got last night." Alcohol abuse—and particularly binge drinking—is an increasing problem on American campuses. Alcohol-related deaths, injuries, and poisoning are common. Students now spend nearly six billion dollars a year on booze, more than they spend on all other beverages and their books combined.[10]

Apparently, it takes a lot of alcohol to fill an empty soul.

WHEN LEFT AND RIGHT AGREED

These days, critics of the emptiness of the consumer lifestyle come most often from the political Left. But that wasn't always so. Before Reagan, many conservatives hadn't yet hitched their star completely to libertarian, free-market worship. Prominent conservative philosophers and economists were often as critical of consumerism as were their leftist counterparts, suggesting that it leads to lives without meaning.

Wilhelm Ropke was one of the giants of traditional conservative economic thought. "*Homo sapiens consumens* loses sight of everything that goes to make up human happiness apart from money income and its transformation into goods," Ropke wrote in 1957. Those who fall into the "keeping up with the Joneses" lifestyle, he argued, "lack the genuine and essentially non-material conditions of simple human happiness. Their existence is empty, and they try to fill this emptiness somehow."[11]

In his book *A Humane Economy: The Social Framework of the Free Market*, Ropke posed powerful questions about the moral direction of consumer society:

> Are we not living in an economic world, or as R. H. Tawney says, in an "acquisitive society" which unleashes naked greed, fosters Machiavellian business methods and, indeed allows them to become the rule, drowns all higher motives in the "icy water of egotistical calculation" (to borrow from *The Communist Manifesto*), and lets people gain the world but lose their souls? Is there any more certain way of dessicating the soul of man than the habit of constantly thinking about money and what it can buy? Is there a more potent poison than our economic system's all-pervasive commercialism?"[12]

Ropke pointed out that in a capitalist society (which, as a conservative, he strongly supported), it is all the more important for each individual to ask questions about the moral value of his or her activities, and not merely be carried along by market currents. Without such vigilance, he suggested, life would become hollow. "Life is not worth living," he wrote, "if we exercise our profession only for the sake of material success and do not find in our calling an inner necessity and a meaning that transcends the mere earning of money, a meaning which gives our life dignity and strength."[13]

STANDARDIZED PEOPLE

Perhaps the best explanation of how the pursuit of material aims leads to meaningless, perpetually bored lives was provided by another conservative, the philosopher Ernest van den Haag.

First, he pointed out, mass production, which makes the universal consumer lifestyle possible, drives large numbers of people out of more varied occupations as artisans and small farmers, and agglomerates them in factories, where the division of labor reduces the scope of their activities to a few repetitive motions. Their work offers neither variety nor control.

In time, their output is sufficient enough, and their organized demands effective enough, that they begin to share in the material fruits of their labor. But to provide the quantity of goods that makes that possible, they must accept mass-produced, and therefore standardized, products. "The benefits of mass production," van den Haag wrote, "are reaped only by matching de-individualizing work with equally de-individualizing consumption." Therefore, he argued, "Failure to repress individual personality in or after working hours is costly; in the end, *the production of standardized things by persons also demands the production of standardized persons* [emphasis ours]."[14]

De-individualization, the result of material progress itself, cannot help but strip life of both meaning and inherent interest. The worker/consumer is vaguely dissatisfied, restlesss, and bored, and these feelings are reinforced and enhanced by advertising, which deliberately attempts to exploit them by offering new products as a way out. Consumer products and mass media—itself made possible only by ads for consumer products—"drown the shriek of unused capacities, of repressed individuality," leaving us either "listless or perpetually restless," declared van den Haag. The products and the media distract us from the soul's cry for truly meaningful activities.

The individual who finds no opportunity for self-chosen, meaningful expression of inner resources and personality suffers, said van den Haag, "an insatiable longing for things to happen. The external world is to supply these events to fill the emptiness. The popular demand for 'inside' stories, for vicarious sharing of the private lives of 'personalities' rests on the craving for private life—even someone else's—of those who are dimly aware of having none whatever, or at least no life that holds their interest."[15]

What the bored person really craves is a meaningful, authentic life. The ads suggest that such a life comes in products or packaged commercial experiences. But religion *and* the science of psychology say it's more likely to be found in such things as service to others, relationships with friends and family, connection with nature, and work of intrinsic moral value.

AFTER AFFLUENZA

Our technologically advanced culture offers opportunities for much more meaningful and creative lives than most of us lead. Our amazingly productive technologies could allow all of us to spend less time doing repetitive, standardized work, or work whose products bring us little pride, by allowing us to trade increased wages for reduced working hours.

Such choices would allow more time for freely chosen, voluntary, often unpaid work that enhances our relationships and communities and/or allows us to express more fully our talents and creativity (like the restoration work of John Beal, for example). And such choices would allow us more time to find meaning and joy in the beauty and wonders of nature, in the delightful play of children, or in the restoration of our damaged environment. They would give us time to think about what really matters to us, and how we really want to use the remaining years of our lives.

CHAPTER 10

Social scars

Today's unfettered celebration of wealth and the things money can buy has created an in-your-face, "I'm rich and you're not" attitude that pigeonholes people as winners or losers, princes or paupers.

—TREND-SPOTTER GERALD CELENTE

I go to Bloomingdale's, to the fourth floor, and I buy 2,000 of the black bras, 2,000 of the beige, 2,000 of the white. And I ship them around between the homes and the boat and that's the end of it for maybe half a year when I have to do it all over again.

—IVANA TRUMP

ew Americans saw the pictures from Thailand (we have little interest in "foreign" news, after all), but they were horrifying. In 1993, a Thai toy factory burned to the ground. Unable to escape, hundreds of female workers perished in the flames and smoke. Their charred bodies lay among the ruins of the building, a firetrap similar to many throughout the developing world where millions of plastic toys are made for American children. Here and there amid the blackened rubble were the toys themselves—Bart Simpson dolls, for example.

Many of the women were mothers, whose meager incomes would not even allow them to buy for their own children the toys they were making for export. The grisly images from that factory fire, and the facts that lay behind them, speak volumes about the widening canyon that separates the haves and have-nots in the Age of Affluenza.

One fact is simply undeniable: there is no economic system even remotely capable of producing consumer goods as cheaply as the unfettered, deregulated free market, backed of course, by the military and police powers of the state. It can, for example (especially with the help of regimes that allow workers little freedom to organize), produce children's toys so cheaply that they can be shipped halfway around the world and still be given away with two-dollar meals at fast-food restaurants like McDonald's and Burger King.

Deregulation of the American economy, which began in the 1980s under Ronald Reagan, coupled with a precipitous decline in the influence of organized labor, has increased domestic productivity. It delivers the goods, but in a manner far less equitable than before.

In contrast to other societies, Americans have long considered theirs a "classless" one, with few citizens who were either very rich or very poor. This notion of a "classless" America was always suspect. Even in 1981, when all political efforts to counteract or quarantine affluenza were abruptly abandoned, the United States ranked thirteenth among twenty-two leading industrial nations in income equality.

But today, we're dead last.[1]

THE OTHER AMERICA

The rising tide of American affluence hasn't lifted all boats but it has drowned a lot of dreams. A titanic gulf now separates rich and poor in America. "If you look at the big consumer boom since the '80s," says Harvard's Juliet Schor, "one of the things you'll find is that it's fairly heavily concentrated in the upper part of the middle-class and above."[2]

Indeed, during the '80s, three-quarters of the increase in pretax real income went to the wealthiest one percent of families, who gained an average of seventy-seven percent. Median-income families saw only a four percent gain, while the bottom forty percent of families actually lost ground. Some might argue that these figures reflect overstated inflation estimates, and that, therefore, all sectors actually gained more than official figures suggest. But what is uncontestable is the astoundingly unequal distribution of the gains.[3]

As the super-rich increased their share of national income during the '80s, they also became stingier. They gave a far smaller share of their incomes to charity than was previously the case. In 1979, people who earned incomes of more than $1 million (in 1991 dollars) gave seven percent of their after-tax incomes away. Twelve years later, that figure had dropped to less than four percent.[4] This, at a time when advocates of sharp cuts in government welfare programs suggested that private charity would make up much of the difference.

Instead, not surprisingly, the percentages of families in poverty, which had been declining, began once again to rise. The number of people who were actually working (not on welfare) but earning below-poverty wages nearly doubled during the '80s, while, from 1979 to 1994, the rate of child poverty increased from eighteen to twenty-five percent.[5]

In spite of America's image as a cornucopia of plenty, where the shelves of supermarkets are always fully-stocked, ten million Americans go hungry each day, forty percent of them children, and the majority, members of working families. Twenty-one million other Americans keep hunger from the door by turning frequently to emergency feeding programs such as food banks and soup kitchens. On any given night at least 750,000 Americans are without shelter, and nearly two million experience homelessness during the course of the year. That's the bad news. The good news is that nine million Americans own second homes. America's housing shortage might really be a distribution problem.[6]

Increasing concentration of income has continued throughout the Clinton economic boom. The top twenty percent of American households now earn nearly as much as the bottom eighty percent (forty-nine versus fifty-one percent of national income), a record high rate of inequality. The distribution of wealth is even more skewed. By 1999, ninety-two percent of all financial wealth (stocks, bonds, and commercial real estate) in America was owned by the top twenty percent of families (and eighty-three percent of stock was owned by the top ten percent). Many of the richest Americans find ways to pay little or nothing in the way of taxes. A recent article, "Tax Cheater's Paradise," in *Mother Jones* magazine (December 2000) shows how the rich evade billions in taxes by sheltering their money in offshore accounts in the Caribbean and elsewhere.

THE BIG WINNERS . . .

At one point, before a drop in Microsoft stock prices halved his net worth, Bill Gates held assets worth about $90 billion, nearly as much as the bottom half of the American population (and greater than the gross national products of 119 of the world's 156 nations). But Bill is now estimated to be worth only a paltry $45 billion. By contrast, forty percent of all Americans own no assets at all.

Nothing better illustrates the extent to which affluenza has been embraced in America than the compensation awarded senior executives of large companies. In a cover story entitled "Is Greed Good?" *Business Week,* which seems to think so, reported that in 1998, average total compensation for CEOs of the 365 largest American companies increased by a whopping thirty-six percent to $10.6 million each. By contrast, blue-collar workers got a 2.7-percent raise.

Average total CEO compensation has increased by 442 percent since 1990, when the poor fellows averaged only $2 million a year. They now earn more than 400 times what their average workers make, up from 40 times as much in 1980.[7] By contrast, until recently, when they began to feel a need to keep up with their American counterparts, Japanese and German CEOS earned only about twenty times as much as average workers.

AND THE LOSERS

Meanwhile, columnist David Broder reports that the people who clean the bathrooms and offices of "the masters of the universe" (as he calls high-tech millionaires) earn poverty-level wages. In Los Angeles, he found janitors picketing for a pay raise that would bring them $21,000 a year by 2003. Even at that pay scale, it would take 27,380 such janitors to earn as much as a single Los Angeles CEO, Michael Eisner of Disney, made in 1998 ($575 million).

To the affluent, the poor have become invisible. "There are millions of people whose work makes our life easier, from busboys in the restaurants we patronize to orderlies in the hospitals we visit, but whose own lives are lived on the ragged edge of poverty," writes David Broder. "Most of us never exchange a sentence with these workers."[8] In sight, but out of mind.

One fact Americans used to point to as evidence of a "classless" society was that (compared to the wealthy of Latin America, for example) few American families employed servants to do cleaning and housework. But as we become increasingly a two-tiered class society, that's changing. Upper-middle-income Americans are turning to domestic servants in a big way. In 1999, between fourteen and eighteen percent of American households employed an outsider to do their cleaning, a fifty-three-percent increase from 1995. Fulltime house cleaners and servants earned an average of $12,220 in 1998, $1,092 below the poverty line for three-person families.[9]

"This sudden emergence of a servant class is consistent with what some economists call the 'Brazilianization' of the American economy," writes Barbara Ehrenreich in *Harpers*. "In line with growing class polarization, the classic posture of submission is making a stealthy comeback," charges Ehrenreich, who worked as a maid for $6.63 an hour to research the story. She points out that one franchise, Merry Maids, even advertises its maid services with a brochure boasting that "we scrub your floors the old fashioned way—on our hands and knees."[10]

Ehrenreich went a-scrubbing from McMansion to McMansion in Portland, Maine, working under rules that even prohibited her from taking a drink of water while cleaning a house. She discovered that some homes had hidden video cameras to be sure she stayed on track. She was amazed at what messes people left for her. Especially the children, one of whom exclaimed "Look Mommy, a white maid!" upon seeing Ehrenreich.

Having "cleaned the rooms of many overprivileged teenagers," as she worked as a maid, Ehrenreich concluded that "the American overclass is raising a generation of young people who will, without constant assistance, suffocate in their own detritus."

Whether or not they are literate enough to know what that means.

THE POOR PAY TWICE—AND THEN SOME

Affluenza affects Americans across all income barriers, but its impacts are more destructive for the poor. In the first place, the poor are often the original victims of the environmental consequences of cost-cutting production strategies. They live disproportionately in areas where environmental contaminants and patterns of pollution are most severe—for example, Louisiana's notorious "Cancer Alley," where petrochemical companies unleash a frightening barrage of carcinogens into the air and water.

At the same time, vastly inflated wage scales paid to winners in the new "information economy" lead to competitive bidding on housing stock that drives the cost of shelter beyond reach of even average earners. Many are forced to leave communities where they and their families have spent their entire lives.

Finally, the poor are taunted by television programs and commercials that flash before them images of consumption standards that are considered typical of the average American, but which they have no possibility of achieving—except perhaps by robbing a bank or winning the lottery.

Felicia Edwards, an African-American mother of two, who lives in a small apartment in a Hartford, Connecticut housing project, worries about the pressures her children feel to wear the designer-label clothes they see on other children in their school. "These schools tend to be like fashion shows," she says with a shake of her head. "There's a lot of peer pressure that can lead to crime. Kids in school have killed other kids over a pair of sneakers. Parents work two and three jobs to clothe their kids." Felicia's own children rarely pester her for stuff, but when her oldest son begged for a pair of Air Jordans he saw on sale for $90 instead of $120, she relented, after first telling him she couldn't afford them. "Me and his aunt came to a decision that we was going to go half on them," she says. "So he got the sneakers."[11]

In our poorest communities, the sense of deprivation is intense. Trend-spotter Gerald Celente tells of a conversation he had with a man who works with youthful gang members. "I asked him 'what's the one thing that you see that's causing a lot of these problems?'" Celente says. "Without skipping a beat, he said, 'greed and materialism. These kids don't feel like their lives would be worth anything unless they have the hottest product that's being sold in the marketplace.'"[12]

Margaret Norris, codirector of the Omega Boys Club in San Francisco, agrees. She says the ethic among the low-income youths she works with is "Thou Shalt Get Thy Money On," and by any means necessary. Such desperation often leads to crime.

"Never mind, just lock em up" seems to be our social response to this situation. Overall crime rates have been falling in the past few years, a trend generally attributed to better availability of jobs in the current booming economy. But the United States already has locked two million of its people behind prison bars, the largest percentage of any nation in the world, ten times the rate of most industrial countries. California alone now has more inmates than France, Germany, Great Britain, Japan, Singapore, and Holland combined. In some dying "Rust Belt" industrial cities, like Youngstown, Ohio, prisons have become the biggest source of jobs. Private companies like the Corrections Corporation of America now make millions running lockup facilities. Smart Wall Street brokers play "dungeons for dollars," investing heavily in the newly privatized prison industry.[13]

GLOBAL INFECTION

The social scars left by affluenza are now being replicated throughout the entire world, as more and more cultures copy the American lifestyle. Every day, television exposes millions of people in the developing world to the Western consumer lifestyle (without showing them its warts), and they are eager to be included. David Korten, author of *When Corporations Rule the World,* once believed they could and should be included. Korten taught business management at Stanford and Harvard, then worked in Africa, Asia, and Central America for the Harvard Business School, the Ford Foundation, and the U.S. Agency for International Development.

"My career was focused on training business executives to create the equivalent of our high-consumption economy in countries throughout the world," Korten says now. "The whole corporate system in the course of globalization is increasingly geared up to bring every country into the consumer society. And there is a very strong emphasis on trying to reach children, to reshape their values from the very beginning to convince them that progress is defined by what they consume."[14]

Korten now believes that, by pushing consumer values in developing countries, he was actually spreading the affluenza virus. As he continued to work in the "development" field, the symptoms of that virus became increasingly apparent. He gradually came to realize that his efforts were causing more harm than good. "I came to see that what I was promoting didn't work and couldn't work," he reflects. "Many people's lives were actually worse off. We were seeing the environment trashed, and we were seeing the breakdown of cultures and the social fabric."

As affluenza, the disease of unbridled consumerism, spreads throughout the world, the gap between rich and poor grows ever wider, and the social scars that still remain somewhat hidden in the United States fester as open sores elsewhere. The grim shantytowns of Rio push to the golden sands of Copacabana and Ipanema. The luxurious malls of Manila stand alongside the Smoky Mountain, a massive garbage dump where thousands of people live right in the refuse, dependent for their survival on what they can scavenge.

The virus passes easily from Sheraton to slum.

One-fifth of the world's people—a billion human beings—live in abject poverty, slowly dying of hunger and disease. Millions of others also desperately need *more* material goods. Yet, were they to begin consuming as we do, the result would be an environmental catastrophe.

It is critical that we begin to set another example for the world, and quickly.

CHAPTER 11

Resource exhaustion

We buy a wastebasket and take it home in a
plastic bag. Then we take the wastebasket out of
the bag, and put the bag in the wastebasket.

—LILY TOMLIN,
comedian

This just in:

WASHINGTON, D.C. –According to an EPA study conducted in con-
junction with the U.N. Task Force on Global Developmental Impact,
consumer-product diversity now exceeds biodiversity. According to the
study, for the first time in history, the rich array of consumer products
available in malls and supermarkets surpasses the number of living
species populating the planet.

Last year's introduction of Dentyne Ice Cinnamint gum, right on the
heels of the extinction of the Carolina tufted hen, put product diversity
on top for the first time," study chair Donald Hargrove said. "Today, the
Procter & Gamble subphylum alone outnumbers insects two to one." The
sharp rise in consumer-product diversity —with more than 200 million

new purchasing options generated since 1993—comes as welcome news for those upset over the dwindling number of plant and animal species.

"Though flora and fauna are dwindling, the spectrum of goods available to consumers is wider than at any time in planetary history. And that's something we can all be happy about," Hargrove said. University of Chicago biologist Jonathan Grogan said, "Any complex system, whether we are talking the Amazon rainforest or the Mall of America, needs a rich array of species/products if it is to survive. That is why, in light of the crumbling global ecosystem, it is increasingly vital that we foster the diversification of the global marketplace by buying the widest range of consumer products possible."

Parody, yes. But this anonymous Internet joke is painfully close to the truth. The more we buy, the faster natural species disappear. And the damages accelerate every minute. As you read this chapter, at least thirty acres of farmland and open space are being bulldozed to meet a still-burning demand for suburban "starter castles." Each one of these homes typically requires an acre's worth of trees, as well as the equivalent of a house-sized hole to provide minerals for concrete, steel, and other construction materials.

Our demand for buildings, fuel, and consumer products sends huge draglines, combines, chainsaws, bulldozers, and oil rigs blindly into pristine wilderness.

"Industry moves, mines, extracts, shovels, burns, wastes, pumps, and disposes of *four million pounds* of material in order to provide one average middle-class family's needs for a year," write Paul Hawken, and Amory and Hunter Lovins in *Natural Capitalism.*[1] According to the United Nations Environment Program, Americans spend more for trash bags than ninety of the world's 210 countries spend for everything! In an average lifetime, each American consumes a reservoir of water (forty-three million gallons, including personal, industrial, and agricultural uses)[2] and a small tanker full of oil (2,500 barrels).[3] Experts at the U.S. Geological Survey predict that world oil production will peak within ten to twenty years, then begin its final decline.

Depressed yet? Facts like these hit us like urgent, middle-of-the-night phone calls. Nature, our mother, is not looking well at all. Virtually unreported by the media, she's been admitted to the emergency room, with a critically elevated temperature and hemorrhaging chest wounds. Hours later, distant relatives of Nature (we typical Americans) wait in chilly air-conditioned rooms for news of her condition (or a *Married With Children* rerun, whichever comes first). Compulsively, we consume snacks, cigarettes, and electronic games as we wait, somehow oblivious

"HELP! THIS IS *MOTHER NATURE*...
I THINK I'M BEING *STALKED!*"

that we are carriers of affluenza—the human disease that strikes Nature like a dozen ongoing hurricanes.

ON THE PAPER TRAIL

Most weeklong backpack trips eventually include a weight-comparison of the stuff in each pack. On a sixty-mile hike on Vancouver Island's West Coast Trail, Dave's sixteen-year-old son Colin insisted his pack was heavier than his father's, because it contained more of the shared food supplies. Dave maintained that anyone whose pack contained the tent, ground cloth, and cook stove was carrying the lion's share. When the sum total of your stuff weighs heavily on your back, you tend to perform cost/benefit analyses on each object. As they slowly made their way up the coast of Vancouver Island, across suspension bridges and moss-covered logs, the debate about the relative value of the stuff was a recurring topic of conversation. "You shouldn't have brought so many snacks." Colin needled (Each carried their own energy bars, powdered drinks, and nuts.) Dave countered, "What if the Park provided a trailside scale so hikers could settle these differences of opinion? Then we'd find out who's doing the work."

"Next time pack a scale," Colin suggested, shrugging his shoulders.

That hike was a pivotal experience for both father and son. They "got" the value inherent in unmarketed, pristine nature—in their lungs, and in their senses—especially the sense of being alive. They reaffirmed a lesson that brought Dave to this book and Colin to a first stop as an Outward Bound instructor: *You don't need as much stuff when you genuinely appreciate the value of what's already here.* As their heads cleared out, other forms of wealth besides money came into focus: the biological abundance of the rainforest and ocean around them; the social and cultural wealth of indigenous inhabitants of Vancouver Island; and wellness, surely the most valuable wealth of all.

Originally constructed as a survival route for shipwrecked sailors, the West Coast Trail provides spectacular vistas of bright blue ocean and white, pounding surf, often through dark silhouettes of shady rainforest. Tide pools filled with starfish and crabs, families of bald eagles soaring silently overhead, and the breathing spouts of hundreds of humpback whales all speak of nature's abundance.

Yet the beaches were littered with the trunks of dead spruce and fir trees, river-borne escapees from a logging industry that has transformed much of the island's natural capital into barren terrain. One photograph from that trip shows Colin standing on a sawed-off trunk the size of a small stage. He and his father were graphically reminded that many of the products they consumed back home had their beginnings in this particular bioregion, where ten percent of the world's newsprint comes from.

If asked that week what Vancouver Island was good for, they probably would have said in exhilaration, "Wilderness. Let it regenerate." If the logger whose flatbed-semi transports three eighty-foot tree trunks had been asked the same question, he'd have said, "Timber. Let me harvest it." The issue isn't a simple one, especially since Americans consume a third of the world's wood. After returning home from their travels in Canada, Dave resumed his higher-than-average consumption of paper, being a writer, while the logger probably looked for a great, convenient place to take his kids, being also a father.

Although logging companies leave curtains of trees along the road to hide the damages, Dave and Colin caught glimpses of barren patches of land through the trees, spotlighted by afternoon sun. But less obvious was the fact that operations like these force society to work harder. Though hard to track directly, water utility bills go up when logging sediments pollute rivers that supply drinking water. Taxes go up when roads and bridges are washed out by floodwaters that run off clear-cut land. The price of lumber and paper goes up as companies feel compelled to advertise how "green" their practices are. In short, we each write checks and work extra hours to smooth over the *"out of sight, out of mind"* sloppiness.

OUT OF MIND

In the Middle Ages, people carried sticks of burning incense, hoping to ward off the plague, which they believed was caused by foul smells. Seven hundred years later, we still fail to make critical connections, for example, between what we consume and what's happening to the world. We buy plantation-grown coffee, not realizing that each cup of coffee exposes another migratory songbird to potentially lethal pesticides in coffee plantations. Like Rachel Carson, we no longer hear chirps in our own backyards, but we don't make the connection as we take another sip of coffee. The songbirds no longer fly thousands of miles each year from Central or South America to our backyards because they're dead. And if they do survive to return home, chances are good their northern habitats are covered with roads, houses, driving ranges, and parking lots.

When we buy a computer, it doesn't occur to us that 700 or more different materials went into it, converging from mines, oil derricks, and chemical factories all over the world. The sleek, colorful machine purring on each desktop generated 140 pounds of solid and hazardous waste in its manufacture, along with 7,000 gallons of wastewater, and about a fourth of its lifetime energy consumption. Every year, more than twelve million computers—amounting to more than 300,000 tons of electronic junk—are disposed of.[4] The point is, when we buy a computer, all the rest comes with it, even if it's *out of sight, out of mind.*

What about junk mail? Most of it comes as commercial advertising, but even the nonprofits are guilty on that one. According to Donella Meadows, it takes 150,000 direct-mail appeals to garner 1,500 memberships in a given organization. "That means 148,500 are just pollution. Made from trees, printed with inks by fuel-consuming machines, collated, labeled, sorted by other machines, loaded into pollution-spewing trucks, delivered to mailboxes, loaded into other vehicles headed for (twenty percent) recycling stations or (eighty percent) landfills."[5] When we toss a piece of junk mail without complaining, we encourage junk mailing.

Every time we eat a fast-food burger, an unseen 600-gallon tank of water comes with it, counting both what the cow and the feed crops drank.[6] And when we ceremoniously open the little jewelry boxes with the glittering gold wedding rings in them, six tons of very drab ore are invisibly connected to the rings—lying in a tailings heap back at the mine, often polluting a stream.[7]

REAL PRICE TAGS

The distinction of being the mother of unseen impacts and hidden costs goes to the automobile. Imagine your sticker shock if the price tag on your new SUV included not only the car's FOB price, but also the full environmental and social costs of the vehicle. The sticker would cover most of the vehicle's windows to list those hidden costs, but here's an executive summary:

THE REAL COST OF YOUR SHINY NEW LIGHT TRUCK

Congratulations! You've just purchased a vehicle that will cost $130,000 by the time it's paid for! (In fact, if you're in your 20's, financing new vehicles like this one every five years for the rest of your life, you'll spend more than a half a million dollars in interest and payments.) That's impressive. As an average American, you'll use your vehicle for eighty-two percent of your trips compared to forty-eight percent for Germans, forty-seven for the French, and forty-five for the British.

The cost of a thirty-mile round-trip commute in this vehicle will be about $15 a day, assuming gas prices remain at current levels. At that rate, you'll spend on average more than $3,500 annually to get to and from work. When insurance, car payments, maintenance, registration, fuel, and other costs are added together, you'll spend more than $8,000 a year to park this vehicle for 22 hours a day and drive it for two.

Your vehicle generated 700 pounds of air pollution in its manufacture, and four tons of carbon. It will burn at least 450 gallons of gas every year, requiring more than thirty-five gas station fill-ups. You'll spend three full days every year vacuuming, polishing, and cleaning the windows of the vehicle, and waiting anxiously for it at the auto shop. When you divide the miles driven by the time spent to buy and maintain your car, you'll be going about five miles an hour—even slower than rush hour in L.A.

Your new vehicle will contribute its fair share to the following national costs:

- 155 billion gallons of gasoline burned annually
- $60 billion spent annually to ensure Middle Eastern oil supply
- 40,000 fatal car crashes annually, and 6,000 pedestrian deaths
- 250 million people maimed or injured since the days of Charles Olds (1905), and more killed than all the wars in America's history
- 50 million animals killed annually, including at least a quarter million of "extended family": cats, dogs, and horses

- Noise and pollution that inhibit sleep and contribute to radical increases in asthma, emphysema, heart disease, and bronchial infections
- One-fourth of U.S. greenhouse gases, which increase drought, hurricanes, and crop failures
- 7 billion pounds of unrecycled scrap and waste annually
- More than $200 billion annually in taxes for road construction and maintenance, snow plowing, subsidized parking, public health expenditures, and other costs that come directly out of pocket
- A total of more than $1 trillion a year in social costs

Sources: *Natural Capitalism,* by Paul Hawken, Amory Lovins and L. Hunter Lovins; Consumers Union website, "How Green Is Your Pleasure Machine?" 09/17/99; *The Roads Aren't Free,* by Clifford W. Cobb, Redefining Progress

Happy motoring!

THE COST OF HIGH LIVING

Alan Durning of Northwest Environment Watch observes, "Everything we use in our daily lives has an ecological wake that ripples out across the ecosystems of the planet." Durning and colleague John Ryan traced the impacts of everyday products in a book titled *Stuff: The Secret Lives of Everyday Things.* Their coffee, for example, came from the highlands of Columbia, where 100 beans were picked for each cup. The beans were packed in 130-pound sacks and shipped in a huge ocean freighter to roasting factory, warehouse, supermarket, and coffee cup. At each stage, energy and materials were expended to add value to their morning coffee. The beginning of the story is especially troubling:

> Colombia's forests make it a biological superpower. Though the country covers less than 1 percent of the Earth's land surface, it is home to eighteen percent of the world's plant species and more types of birds than any other nation. . . . In the late 1980s, farm owners sawed down most of the shade trees surrounding the coffee trees and planted high-yielding varieties, increasing their harvests, and also increasing soil erosion and bird fatalities. Biologists report finding just five percent as many bird species in these new, sunny coffee fields as in the traditional shaded coffee plantations. With the habitats of birds and other insect

eaters removed, pests proliferated and the growers stepped up their pesticide use. Some of the chemicals they sprayed entered the farm-workers' lungs; others washed or wafted away, to be absorbed by plants and animals. . . . For each pound of beans, about two pounds of pulp was dumped into the river. As the pulp decomposed, it consumed oxygen needed by fish in the river...[8]

"When I first started looking at the real costs of stuff," said Durning, "a friend read my manuscript and said, 'Oh I get it, what you're talking about is guilt trips, not shopping trips.' But it's not really about guilt. It's about creating a lifestyle that doesn't require as much stuff to make us even happier than we are now. Simple things, like buying shade-grown coffee that reduces the use of pesticides. We need to be thinking about what we get, not what we give up."[9]

Because few of us supply our own materials for daily life, almost everything we consume, from potatoes to petroleum to pencils, comes from somewhere else. "The problem is that we're running out of 'somewhere elses,' especially if developing countries try to achieve a Western style of life," says engineer Mathis Wackernagel, a staffer at Redefining Progress.[10] Dividing Earth's biologically productive land and sea by the number of humans, Wackernagel and colleague William Rees come up with 5.5 acres per person. That's if we put *nothing* aside for all the other species on the planet. "In contrast," says Wackernagel, "the average world citizen used seven acres in 1996—what we call his or her "ecological footprint."

"That's over thirty percent more than what nature can regenerate. Or in other words, it would take 1.3 years to regenerate what humanity uses in one year." He continues, "If all people lived like the average American, with thirty-acre footprints, we'd need five more planets."

Wackernagel observes, "We can't use all the planet's resources, because we're only one species out of ten million or more. Yet if we leave half of the biological capacity for other species (or if the human population doubles in size), human needs must come from less than three acres per capita, only about *one-tenth* of the capacity now used by Americans."

The solution? No sweat, we'll use the market. We'll just go out and buy another five planets.

DARWIN IN REVERSE

It's bad enough that resource supplies, along with recreational and aesthetic opportunities, are wearing thin as the affluenza-encouraged plundering of the planet continues. But even more distressing is the fact that life on Earth becomes far less diverse as habitats disappear. The loss of a key species from an ecosystem is like pulling out the wrong melon from a supermarket display. You create an avalanche of melons thunking to the floor, because each melon was supported by another. To give just one example, when sun heats up a mountain stream because clear-cutting has removed natural shade along the banks, it's a holocaust for the trout population

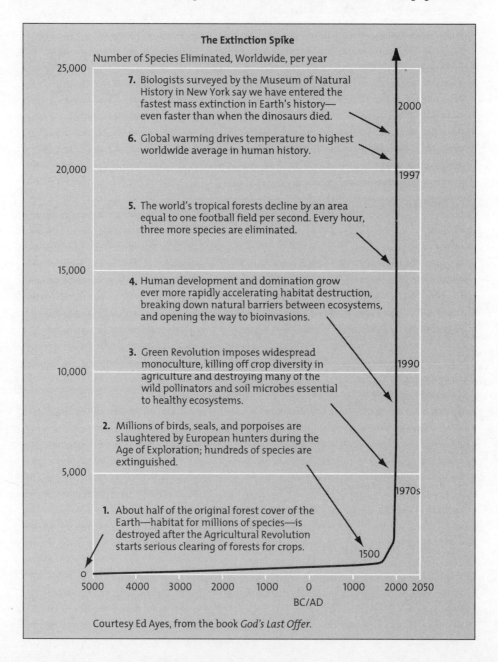

The Extinction Spike

Number of Species Eliminated, Worldwide, per year

7. Biologists surveyed by the Museum of Natural History in New York say we have entered the fastest mass extinction in Earth's history— even faster than when the dinosaurs died.

6. Global warming drives temperature to highest worldwide average in human history.

5. The world's tropical forests decline by an area equal to one football field per second. Every hour, three more species are eliminated.

4. Human development and domination grow ever more rapidly accelerating habitat destruction, breaking down natural barriers between ecosystems, and opening the way to bioinvasions.

3. Green Revolution imposes widespread monoculture, killing off crop diversity in agriculture and destroying many of the wild pollinators and soil microbes essential to healthy ecosystems.

2. Millions of birds, seals, and porpoises are slaughtered by European hunters during the Age of Exploration; hundreds of species are extinguished.

1. About half of the original forest cover of the Earth—habitat for millions of species—is destroyed after the Agricultural Revolution starts serious clearing of forests for crops.

Courtesy Ed Ayes, from the book *God's Last Offer*.

ENDANGERED SPECIES	
Species	**Observation**
Plants	A quarter of the world's plants are threatened with extinction by the year 2010
Amphibians	More than 38% of US amphibians are endangered
Birds	Three-quarters of all bird species are declining; 11% are threatened with extinction
Carnivores	Almost all species of cats and bears are declining in numbers
Fish	One-third of North American freshwater fish are rare or endangered
Invertebrates	About 100 species are lost each day due to deforestation
Mammals	25% of species are threatened with extinction
Reptiles	Over 40% of reptile species are threatened, 20% with extinction

Source: Hutchinson Encyclopedia, Published by Helicon, 1999 www.helican.co.uk

because trout thrive in *cold* water. And when sediment washes off the naked land into that stream, it plugs up the cobbled spaces in rocks that are hiding places for the baby fish. In turn, mammals whose diet includes trout lose an important protein source, so ecological services provided by those mammals are diminished . . .

Eons of ecological work are instantly undone. The alarming truth is that hundreds of "melon avalanches" occur every day on the battlefields of resource extraction. Far from being just a rainforest phenomenon, habitat destruction and accompanying extinction are happening right under our noses. "A silent mass extinction is occurring in America's lakes and rivers," says biologist Anthony Ricciardi.[11] His research indicates that freshwater species from snails to fish to amphibians are dying out five times faster than terrestrial species—as fast as rainforest species, which are generally considered to be the most imperiled on Earth. Half of America's wetlands are gone, and ninety-nine percent of its tall-grass prairies. As these systems are being destroyed for development, agriculture, and other uses, 935 species in the United States (356 animals, 579 plants) are fighting for their lives.[12]

Before nature's health began to slide, we rarely thought about how a product got to us, and what came with it; we just consumed it and threw the leftovers away. We didn't think about the plants, animals, and even human cultures that

were displaced or destroyed when the materials were mined. Now, when biologists like Norman Myers and E.O. Wilson tell us we may be in the middle of the
most severe extinction since the fall of the dinosaur sixty-five million years ago,
many people are finally moving beyond denial. We are losing species 1,000 times
faster than the natural rate of extinction.

What will civilizations of the far future say about our era? Will they somehow
deduce the causes of the calamitous decline in species diversity? Or will they shrug
their shoulders (if they have shoulders to shrug) the way our scientists do when they
ponder extinctions of the past? "It was global warming," the future scientists might
conclude. "Inefficient use of land," others will hypothesize. But for the sake of our
civilization's dignity, let's hope and pray that none of them uncovers humiliating evidence of our obsessive need for cheap coffee, gasoline, and underwear.

CHAPTER 12

Industrial diarrhea

DDT is good for me!

—1950s jingle

The chemical age has created products, institutions and cultural attitudes that require synthetic chemicals to sustain them.

—THEO COLBURN ET AL,
Our Stolen Future

Imagine spotting them through binoculars at a baseball game—the all-stars of advertising, sitting together in front row seats behind home plate. There's the Marlboro Man and Joe Camel, signing autographs and passing out smokes to the kids. The Energizer Bunny flings handfuls of potentially toxic batteries into the crowd like Tootsie Rolls, while Ronald McDonald argues defensively with an environmentalist about hormones, antibiotics, and pesticide residues now being detected in the Big Mac. The Green Giant looks down on the game from the parking lot, ho-hoing every time the home team scores. No one messes with a guy that size, even though chunks of pesticide slough off his green body like gigantic flakes of dry skin. (Look out, here comes another one!)

They all seem so innocent, don't they—so American? We grew up with these guys, and we love their optimism, their goofiness, and their cool. Our demand for their products keeps the U.S. economy cranking at a feverishly giddy pace, and it can't be denied that America's dazzling products make life seem bright, shiny, and convenient. But with a steady diet of this stuff, we risk serious damage to our environment and to our health. Many of the goods we buy contain toxic "bads" such as dangerous chemicals hidden from plain view, but for some reason, we don't want to believe that.

THE GENERATION OF SURPRISES

We don't want to believe that cigarettes now kill more than 430,000 Americans annually, wiping out *five million years of potential life each year*. That radiation from nuclear power—once thought to be "too cheap to meter"—really does destroy DNA and cause cancer, and has obliterated a handful of bioregions, effectively forever. That one tiny particle of dioxin transmitted to a fetus at the wrong time could permanently disrupt the unborn child's reproductive system. That between 1940 and 1995 the production of synthetic chemicals increased 600 times—we now produce 1,600 pounds a year per capita. And that two out of every five Americans will contract cancer at some point in their lives, including increasing percentages of children.[1]

"Americans have a tradition of trusting manufacturers," said Dr. Suzanne Wuerthele, a toxicologist in EPA's Denver office. "Ever since the days of the flour mill, the small leather-tanning company, and the blacksmith, products have been assumed innocent until proven guilty—just the opposite of the way it should be. We've worked within an "acceptable risk" strategy. Industry's stance is, 'Show me the dead bodies, or else let me make my product the way I want to.' When a disaster happens, industry begins to respond, and sometimes not even then."

As Wuerthele points out, the track record for synthetic chemicals is laced with unpleasant surprises. "From nuclear radiation and CFCs to the various chlorinated hydrocarbon pesticides, we're always playing catch up, finding out about health and ecological effects after it's too late. The most recent surprise is that genetically engineered organisms can migrate into the environment, even when they're engineered into the cells of plants. For example, pollen from genetically engineered corn plants migrates to plants like milkweed, where it has been shown to kill the "Bambis" of the insect world—Monarch butterflies. That shouldn't have caught the corporate and government scientists by surprise—with hundreds of thousands of acres of genetically engineered corn already planted—but it did."[2]

We typically assume that somebody else is minding the shop, making sure all these chemicals are safe. Yet the truth is that out of 75,000 chemicals now in common commercial use, only about 1,200 to 1,500 have been tested for carcinogenicity. Dr. Sandra Steingraber writes in her book *Living Downstream*, "The vast majority of commercially used chemicals were brought to market before 1979, when federal

legislation mandated the review of new chemicals. Thus many carcinogenic environmental contaminants likely remain unidentified, unmonitored, and unregulated."[3]

Steingraber, herself a victim of bladder cancer, recalls the advertising blitz for
DDT, a product that returned home victorious from World War II after protecting
American soldiers from malaria and other diseases overseas. "In one ad," writes Steingraber, "children splash in a swimming pool while DDT is sprayed above the water.
In another, an aproned housewife in stiletto heels and a pith helmet aims a spray
gun at two giant cockroaches standing on her kitchen counter. They raise their front
legs in surrender. The caption reads, 'Super Ammunition for the Continued Battle
on the Home Front.'"[4]

DDT was seen as a harmless pal, despite the fact that by the time those ads
appeared, biologists had already documented that the chemical killed birds and fish,
disrupted the reproductive systems of laboratory animals, created population explo-
sions of pests with newly evolved resistance, and showed strong signs of causing
cancer. By 1951, DDT had become a contaminant of human breast milk and was
known to pass from mother to child.

Yet DDT continued to be seen as an "elixir" until Rachel Carson's book *Silent
Spring* put the spotlight on birds with convulsions, twitching to death under the
elm tree. Since the time of those DDT ads, cancer has become an epidemic in slow
motion. Cancers of the brain, liver, breast, kidney, prostate, esophagus, skin, bone
marrow, and lymph have all escalated in the past fifty years, while the incidence of
cancer increased by more than fifty percent.

The use of chemicals like DDT seemed justified at first. After all, the use of
other pesticides has played a role in the low prices Americans pay for food. (As a
percentage of income, we have the world's cheapest food). But what hidden costs
do we pay?

ACCIDENTAL CONCOCTIONS

Ever since the days of alchemy, the field of chemistry has suffered from a tragic
flaw: its isolation from the field of biology. Humans were deploying technology long
before they understood what causes disease, or how living things interrelate. Sir
Isaac Newton may have discovered gravity, but he didn't seem to have a clue that
the heavy metals he experimented with could kill him. In a 1692 letter to colleague
John Locke, he blamed insomnia, depression, poor digestion, amnesia, and paranoia
on "sleeping too often by my fire." We found out otherwise 300 years later, when
scientists analyzed a lock of his hair, passed along as a family heirloom. The hair was
a repository of lead, arsenic, antimony, and mercury molecules from his alchemy

experiments. Carefully recorded in his logs were descriptions of the *taste* of each chemical. Little did he know the gravity of his actions.

Even when a toxic cause-and-effect connection was made, our ancestors often adopted a policy of "acceptable risk." Mercury was mined in Spain as far back as 400 B.C., despite severe health effects like chronically bleeding gums, dementia, and eventual death. In that case, the risks were deemed acceptable because convicts and slaves did the mining.

While the benefits accrue only to those who sell or use the products, the risks are often spread among the whole population. Chemicals, if profitable, are deemed innocent until alarming evidence proves otherwise. For example, workers in a pesticide factory didn't realize that their exposure to Kepone was sterilizing them until they sat around the lunch table talking about a common inability to start a family.

BETTER LIVING THROUGH CHEMISTRY?

As America's economy grew at rates never seen in human history, millions of chemical compounds were brought into the world. Most did not find immediate uses, but a century's worth of tinkering created an alphabet soup of persistent molecules that hang around in our world like uninvited guests. Many of these ingredients are incorporated into familiar products like detergents, varnishes, plastics, fingernail polish, bug spray, and pharmaceuticals, as well as behind-the-scenes industrial products like degreasers and plasticizers.

A new chemical substance is discovered every nine seconds of the working day, as the "invisible hand of the market" continues to call forth legions of them, like a throng of marching broomsticks straight out of "The Sorcerer's Apprentice." It's become impossible to call them off and, as a consequence, we're living in a sea of our own waste products. Scientists call them PBTs—Persistant Bioaccumulative Toxins. We're exposed to chemicals in consumer products and in the workplace. We're also bombarded by invisible particles that escape into our water, the air in our houses, and the living tissue in our bodies. There is no place on Earth that does not contain runaway molecules. "Tree bark sampled from more than ninety sites around the world found that DDT, chlordane and dieldrin were present no matter how remote the area," writes Ann Platt McGinn in *State of the World 2000*.[5]

If we had microscopic vision, we might get outdoors a bit more—where the air is cleaner—because the horrors we'd see in our own houses would send us running. We'd see microscopic bits of plastics, carpet fibers, and pesticides disappear into the nostrils of family members, and never come back out! Because of all the chemicals contained in our everyday products, indoor pollution levels can be two to 100 times higher than those found outdoors, especially now that homes are more tightly sealed for energy efficiency and air-conditioning.

NOWHERE TO RUN

David and Mary Pinkerton were trusting souls. They were buying a "dream house" in Missouri, and they liked to walk through the construction site after work, to see the house taking shape. On one visit just before moving in, David noticed a health warning printed on the sub-flooring that had been put in their new house. Irritation of the eyes and upper respiratory system could result from exposure to the chemicals in the plywood. But David trusted the builder. "He makes a living building houses. He wouldn't put anything in there that would hurt anybody."

"Within a month," write the authors of *Toxic Deception*, "the three girls and their parents had grown quite ill. David would sit in an old overstuffed chair until supper was ready; after dinner he would usually go right to bed. . . . One night Mary tried to make dinner and David found her leaning against the wall with the skillet in her hand. . . . All five had bouts of vomiting and diarrhea that would wake them up, almost nightly. Brenda no longer wanted to go to dance classes, even though ballet had been 'her big thing in life,' Mary later recalled."[6]

After the family was forced to evacuate the house within six months of moving in, a state environmental inspector found ten parts per million of formaldehyde in the house, many times higher than the standard.

As many as forty million Americans may be allergic to their own homes, according to the American Lung Association. Fifteen million of us have become allergic just in the last five years, bombarded by chemicals in paint fumes, cleaning products, particleboard, plastics, glues, wallpaper, cosmetics, and a hundred other standard products of the twenty-first century.

DEAD ZONES

Scientists *do* have microscopic vision, and with new-millennium equipment they are now finding toxic chemicals wherever they look. The average American hosts up to 500 different chemicals in his or her body. Among the most exotic of the chemicals now being found in waterways are refugees from the American lifestyle: trace amounts of pain relievers, antibiotics, birth control pills, perfumes, codeine, antacids, cholesterol-lowering agents, antidepressants, estrogen replacement drugs, chemotherapy agents, sunscreen lotions, and hormones from animal feed lots.

These compounds survive the assault of sewage treatment's microbes, aeration, and chlorination, and eventually show up unannounced in drinking water.

With reports of pesticide, lead, and other industrial compounds gracing the front pages of newspapers across the country, it's no wonder per-capita consumption of bottled water increased by a whopping 900 percent between 1977 and 1997. Yet the Natural Resources Defense Council advises that bottled water, at up to 1,000 times the cost of tap water, is not only expensive but somewhat suspicious. At least a third of the bottled water on the market is just packaged tap water, and another twenty-five percent contains traces of chemical contaminants.

"In the past we looked for the really toxic actors that have immediate effects like death or cancer," said Edward Furlong, a chemist with the U.S. Geological Survey.[7] "Now we're starting to look more closely at compounds whose effects are more subtle and less easily identified." To his surprise, Furlong discovered what he calls "The Starbucks Effect," an indicator that caffeine may be giving aquatic life an unsolicited buzz. In addition to being a basic fuel of the American lifestyle (twenty-four gallons a year per capita), caffeine is a very persistent and detectable compound. Just as it often persists in our bloodstreams when we try to sleep, it also lingers in our rivers and streams. These findings are only the most recent in a series of aquatic conundrums presented by our affluent, often oblivious civilization. How long can an economy boom without adequate supplies of drinking water?

A decade or so ago, fishermen began reporting a "dead zone" in the Gulf of Mexico, where their nets always come up empty and their lines never record a strike. By the time the Mississippi River reaches the Gulf of Mexico, it contains enough pesticides, wasted nutrients (from eroded farm soil), and petrochemicals to poison a body of water the size of New Jersey. Luxury cruise ships in the Gulf add insult to critical injury by dumping raw sewage and other wastes into open waters. Because of regulatory loopholes, cruise ships can legally discharge "graywater" (used water that doesn't contain human wastes) anywhere, and can dump human waste and ground-up food when they're more than three miles from shore. On a weeklong voyage a typical Carnival or Royal Caribbean cruise ship with 3,000 passengers and crew members generates eight tons of garbage, one million gallons of gray water, 25,000 gallons of oil-contaminated water, and 200,000 gallons of sewage.[8] Scuba diving, anyone?

DEADLY MIMICRY

The surprises just keep coming, some of them involving other dead zones, in the Great Lakes, the Arctic, and, potentially, even the human womb. Like evidence in a gruesome criminal case, the mounting data tells us more than we really want to know. Scientist and author Theo Colburn compiled thousands of data sets spanning three decades. The data report chaos and dysfunction in the natural world: male alligators with stunted sex organs; roosters that didn't crow; eagles that didn't build nests to take care of their young; "gay" female seagulls that nested together because males weren't interested; whales with both male and female sex organs; and other cases of "sexual confusion."

Though she knew that chemicals were central evidence in the case, Colburn couldn't deduce the mechanism until she began to look beyond cancer, the standard disease of toxicology. She and her colleagues traced persistent chemicals like PCBs, DDT, dioxin, and other pollutants into the human body, where they are stored in fatty tissue, passing from prey to predator, and from mother to breastfed baby. The key finding was that these persistent chemicals fake their way into the endocrine system, masquerading as hormones like estrogen and androgen. It's a deadly case of miscommunication. When hormones, our chemical messengers, are released or suppressed at the wrong time in the wrong amounts, life gets bent out of shape.

For example, ecotoxicologist Pierre Béland began finding dead whales washed up on the shores of the St. Lawrence River in the early '90s, sometimes too toxic to be disposed of as hazardous waste. His autopsies typically reveal a devil's brew of breast tumors, stomach tumors, and cysts—all indicators of industrial production gone haywire.

It would be distressing enough if endocrine disruption was taking a toll on the planet's wildlife, but not on humans. However, research is now revealing what some scientists have suspected for years: Humans are by no means immune, since endocrine systems function similarly throughout the animal kingdom. One experiment studied the health of children whose mothers had eaten PCB-contaminated fish during pregnancy. As compared with a control population, the 200 exposed children, on average, were born sooner, weighed less, and had lower IQs.[8]

LET THEM EAT VIAGRA

Other research demonstrated that barely detectable molecules of a certain plastic unexpectedly leached off laboratory beakers, mimicked estrogen, and initiated cancerous growth in lab experiments with human breast cells. Perhaps most startling of all is the 1992 study involving 15,000 men in twenty countries, indicating up to a fifty-percent decline in human sperm production since 1938. "Consider what it might mean for our society if synthetic chemicals are undermining human intelligence in the same way they have apparently undermined human male sperm count," write the authors of *Our Stolen Future,*[10] who also speculate on possible connections between chemicals and increased incidence of hyperactivity, aggression, and depression—all behaviors regulated by hormones.

The products that cause industrial diarrhea are innocent enough on the surface: plastic packaging, toys, cars, and computer circuit boards. But when we track hazardous chemicals to their sources and endpoints, we slosh through muck every step of the way. Even the familiar bacon on our plates literally results in industrial diarrhea, as writer Webster Donovan describes:

> Raising hogs used to be a family business, until one enterprising North Carolina farmer made it big business. But this booming national industry is churning out at least one unwelcome by-product—millions of gallons of pig waste that soil the water and foul the air.

> The smell is what hits you first. Like a hammer, it clamps against the nerve endings of your nose, then works its way inside your head and rattles your brain. Imagine a filthy dog run on a humid day; a long-unwashed diaper in a sealed plastic bag; a puffed roadkill beneath the hottest summer sun. This is that smell: equal parts outhouse and musk, with a jaw-tightening jolt of ammonia tossed in.

In recent years, this potent mix of acrid ammonia, rotting-meat ketones, and spoiled-egg hydrogen sulfide has invaded tens of thousands of houses—and millions of acres—across rural America. The vapor billows invisibly, occasionally lifting off and disappearing for hours or weeks, only to return while the neighbors are raking leaves, scraping the ice off their windshield, or setting the table for a family cookout.[11]

Isn't it time to say good-bye to the Industrial Revolution—plagued from the start with diarrhea—and bring in a new Era of Ecological Design and Caution?

CHAPTER 13

The addictive virus

The urge sweeps over them like a tidal wave.
They go into a kind of trance, an addictive high,
where what they buy almost doesn't matter.

—PSYCHOTHERAPIST OLIVIA MELLAN

In my family, money was used to express love,
so I later spent money to show myself love.

–Participant in Debtors Anonymous,
a 12-step program

You suspect you may be a coffee addict when you start answering the front door *before* the doorbell rings! But when you can't resist buying a coffee mug with a picture of a coffee mug on it . . . it's official. You're hooked. For you and at least thirty-five million other javaholics (four to five cups a day), coffee is life, the rest is only waiting.

But coffee's not the worst of our addictions, not by a long shot. Fourteen million Americans use illegal drugs, twelve million Americans are heavy drinkers, and sixty million are hooked on tobacco. Five million Americans can't stop gambling away incomes and savings. And at least ten million can't stop buying more and more stuff—an addiction that in the long run may be the most destructive of all.[1]

Lianne, a department store publicist in New York City, is a problem shopper. Every year, she uses her employee discount to rack up more than $20,000 in clothing and accessory bills. She finally suspected she might be addicted when she broke up with her boyfriend and moved her stuff out of his apartment. "Some women tend to shop a lot because they live out of two apartments, theirs and their boyfriend's," she explains. "You never look at your wardrobe as one wardrobe. But when I saw how many things I had that were identical, I began to see that maybe I did have a problem."[2]

Addiction to stuff is not easily understood. It's a bubbling cauldron of such traits as anxiety, loneliness, and low self-esteem. "I'd like to think I shop because I don't want to look like everybody else," Lianne confides anonymously, "but the real reason is because I don't want to look like myself. It's easier to buy something new and feel good about yourself than it is to change yourself."

Addicts need to go back for more in order to feel good again. The addictive substance or activity takes away the emotional discomfort of everyday life, and also releases the built-up tensions of craving. The goal is to get back to a place of perceived power and carefree abandonment. The drinker suddenly becomes loose and uninhibited, certain he's the funniest man in the world. The gambler feels the elation of risk and possibility—putting it all on the line so Lady Luck can find him. The addicted shopper seeks the high she felt a few days earlier, when she bought a dress she still hasn't taken out of the box.

According to Dr. Ronald Faber, compulsive buyers often report feeling heightened sensations when they shop. Colors and textures are more intense, and extreme levels of focus and concentration are often achieved—literally, altered states of consciousness. Some extreme shoppers compare their highs to drug experiences, while others have compared the moment of purchase to an orgasm.[3]

"I'm addicted to the smell of suede, the smooth texture of silk, and the rustle of tissue paper," admits one shopping addict. She also loves the captive attention she commands from shopkeepers. And because her credit card is always ready for use, she can shop whenever she wants. Now that's power.

NEVER ENOUGH

The thrill of shopping is only one aspect of the addiction to stuff. Many Americans are also hooked on building personal fortresses out of their purchases. Whether it's a new set of golf clubs or a walk-in closet full of sweaters and shoes, having the right stuff and sending the right signal somehow reassures addictive buyers. The problem is that the world's signals keep changing, so addicts never reach a point of having enough. The computer never has enough memory, and is never as fast as it should be. The SUV doesn't have a satellite-linked Global Positioning System, so how do we know where we are? The phone system is obsolete without call waiting and caller ID; the refrigerator doesn't dispense ice cubes; and the big-screen TV is a good six feet narrower than the living-room wall. Deficiencies like these become unacceptable when affluenza sets in.

Economists call it "the law of diminishing marginal utility," jargon that simply means we have to run faster just to stay in place. As social psychologist David Myers phrases it, "The second piece of pie, or the second $100,000, never tastes as good as the first."[4]

Yet, despite diminishing returns that are plain to see, affluenza victims get stuck in the more mode, not knowing when or how to stop. If eating pie ultimately fails to satisfy, we think we need *more* pie to become satisfied. At this point, the affluenza virus has become an addiction. "Consuming becomes pathological because its importance grows larger and larger in direct proportion to our decreasing satisfaction," says economist Herman Daly.[5]

In terms of the social factors that trigger the addictive virus, our thanks go first to the "pusher men" on the supply side. For example, when the highways to which we are addicted become clogged, dealers push *more* highways, which very soon become clogged as well. When we get used to a certain level of sexually explicit advertising, the pusher men push it a step further, and then further, until preteens pose suggestively on network TV ads, in their underwear.

It's the same in restaurants, fast-food outlets, and movie theaters, where portions get bigger, and then get huge. Plates of food become platters, Biggie burgers become Dino-Burgers, and boxes of popcorn become buckets. What's next, barrels requiring hand trucks? Our stomachs expand to accommodate the larger portions, which we soon regard as normal (sixty-four-ounce soft drinks, normal?!).

Sometimes more and bigger are not enough. When we can't maintain our consumer highs with familiar products and activities, we search for new highs. Sports become extreme sports or fantasy sports in which thrill-seekers bungee jump off skyscrapers or gamble in Internet fantasy sports leagues. Even real professional athletes, with fantasy salaries, can never get enough. When a bright young baseball prospect signs for $10 million a year, a veteran who makes only $7 million suddenly feels dissatisfied. This is the plight of the affluenza addict: even too much is never enough.

SHOPPING TO FILL THE VOID

Similarities among addictions are alarming. When pathological becomes normal, an addict will do whatever is necessary to maintain the habit. Gamblers and overspenders alike bounce checks, borrow from friends, and go deeply in debt to support their habit, often lying to loved ones about their actions. It's not hard to see the connection between addictive behavior and the huge craters in our culture and environment. Just as gamblers sell family heirlooms to continue gambling, addicted consumers sacrifice priceless natural areas, contentment, and tradition to maintain a steady stream of goods.

Psychologists tell us pathological buying is typically related to a quest for greater recognition and acceptance, an expression of anger, or an escape through fantasy—all connected to shaky self-images. Writes Dr. Ronald Faber,

> One compulsive buyer bought predominantly expensive stereo and television equipment but demonstrated little interest when discussing the types of music or programs he liked. Eventually, it came out that his motivation for buying came mainly from the fact that neighbors recognized him as an expert in electronic equipment and came to him for advice when making their purchases.[6]

Faber reports that anger is often encoded in pathological buying—debt becomes a mechanism for getting back at one's spouse or parent. Or in other cases, extreme shopping is a fleeting getaway from reality:

> Buying provides a way of escaping into a fantasy where the individual can be seen as important and respected. Some people indicated that the possession and use of a charge card made them feel powerful; others found that the attention provided by sales personnel and being known by name at exclusive stores provided feelings of importance and status.[7]

WHAT ARE WE THINKING?

If we could read the minds of the busy, intent shoppers at the region's largest mall, wouldn't we be amazed? Certainly we'd feel a little less abnormal, because we'd see that the mall is packed with shoppers-in-therapy. (We're all crazy!) At least three in ten flee to the mall when things get out of control at home or work. Others come without a particular purchase in mind, just wanting to be around people, to feel less lonely. One woman resents having to buy a present for her son, who recently stole money from her purse. Several teenagers are desperately hoping their new clothes will facilitate sexual conquests that evening. At least six in ten of the shoppers feel a sense of euphoria from all the stimulation, but it's euphoria with a twist of anxiety. Each shopper knows from past experience that guilt, shame, and confusion—consumer regret—lurk right outside the door.

Still, they'll keep coming back, because they're addicted.

That is, unless they find a way to beat the all-consuming bug, as Thomas Monaghan did. In 1991 the founder of Domino's Pizza suddenly began to sell off many of his prized possessions, including three houses designed by Frank Lloyd Wright and thirty antique automobiles, one of which was an $8 million Bugatti Royale. Construction was halted on his multimillion-dollar home, and he even sold his Detroit Tigers baseball team because it was just a "source of excessive pride." He was quoted as saying, "None of the things I've bought, and I mean none of them, have ever really made me happy."[8]

CHAPTER 14

Dissatisfaction guaranteed

The only chance of satisfaction we can imagine is getting more of what we have now. But what we have now makes everybody dissatisfied. So what will more of it do—make us more satisfied, or more dissatisfied?

—PSYCHOLOGIST JEREMY SEABROOK
INTERVIEWEE

More than ever, we have big houses and broken homes, high incomes and low morale, secured rights and diminished civility. We excel at making a living but often fail at making a life. We celebrate our prosperity but yearn for purpose. We cherish our freedoms but long for connection. In an age of plenty, we feel spiritual hunger.

—PSYCHOLOGIST DAVID MEYER

It's like going into a room and forgetting what you came for, except in this case it's the whole culture, forgetting. We forget to ask, "What's an economy *for?*"

En route to a brand new American millennium, we got detoured. Price tags and bar codes began to coat the surfaces of our lives, as every single activity became a transaction. Eating, entertainment, socializing, health, even religion—all became marketable commodities. To sleep or to jumpstart sex, take a pill. To eat, grab some fast food, or order "room service" from a three-course, store-to-door caterer. To exercise, join a health club. For fun, buy e-products on the Internet. To quit smoking, buy a nicotine patch, or ask your doctor for clinical doses of laughing gas! (No joke).

To live, we buy. Everything (except, of course, "free air" at the gas stations). But this way of life is not sustainable. You can withdraw only so much money from a trust fund (or fossil fuel and fossil water from underground). You get only so many miles out of a vehicle—even a high-end racecar. The American racecar lifestyle is fast approaching burnout because it requires long, stressful workweeks that eat up chunks of life, natural resources, and health. It programs us to substitute consumption for both citizenship and companionship. And it tries to meet nonmaterial needs with material goods, a losing strategy.

GAME OVER

Psychologist Richard Ryan points to scores of studies—his own among them— showing that material wealth does *not* create happiness. "We keep looking outside ourselves for satisfactions that can only come from within," he explains.[1] In the human species, happiness comes from achieving intrinsic goals like giving and receiving love. *Extrinsic* goals like monetary wealth, fame, and appearance are surrogate goals, often pursued as people try to fill themselves up with "outside-in" rewards. Says Ryan, "People with extrinsic goals sharpen their egos to conquer outer space, but they don't have a clue how to navigate inner space."

"We've documented that unhappiness and insecurity often *initiate* the quest for wealth," he continues. Is this surprising, given other evidence that addiction often springs from childhood abuse? In three studies with 140 adolescents, Ryan and colleague Tim Kasser showed that those with aspirations for wealth and fame were more depressed and had lower self-esteem than other adolescents whose aspirations centered on self-acceptance, family and friends, and community feeling.

"The wealth-seekers also had a higher incidence of headaches, stomach aches, and runny noses," Ryan says. He believes that while people are born with intrinsic curiosity, self-motivation, and playfulness, too often these qualities are squelched by "deadlines, regulations, threats, directives, pressured evaluations and imposed goals" that come from external sources of control rather than self-motivated choices and goals. Curious about the origins of extrinsic goals, the psychologists looked at family influences. "When mothers were controlling and cold (based on perceptions of family and friends), individuals were more likely to base their self-worth and security on external sources like money."

Their findings do not prove that rich people are always unhappy (some are, some aren't, depending on how they use their money). But they do point out that seeking

extrinsic goals can dislodge us from vital connections with people, nature, and community—and *that* can make us unhappy.

Dysfunctions and disconnects seem to detour everyone's life these days, rich and
poor alike. Donella Meadows cut to the heart of it in *Beyond the Limits:*

> People don't need enormous cars, they need respect. They don't need
> closets full of clothes, they need to feel attractive and they need excite-
> ment and variety and beauty. People don't need electronic equipment;
> they need something worthwhile to do with their lives. People need
> identity, community, challenge, acknowledgement, love, and joy. To try
> to fill these needs with material things is to set up an unquenchable
> appetite for false solutions to real and never-satisfied problems. The
> resulting psychological emptiness is one of the major forces behind the
> desire for material growth.[2]

Opinion polls reveal that Americans crave reconnection with the real sources of
satisfaction, but we can't find our way back through all the jingles, static, broken
gadgets, and credit card bills. We adopt a pattern clinically proven to lower our
resistance to affluenza when we ask, "How much?" rather than "How well?" The
inevitable result can only be dissatisfaction, guaranteed. Quantity can't satisfy like
quality can, and even an infinite supply of virtual reality will never actually be real.

ANOTHER VIEW OF WEALTH

The more real wealth we have—such as friends, skills, libraries, wilderness, and afternoon naps—the less money we need in order to be happy. Throughout history, many civilizations have already discovered this truth, as author Taichi Sakaiya describes in *The Knowledge-Value Revolution*. As the cedars of Lebanon and the topsoil of Northern Africa disappeared, people in these areas finally wised up, learning to substitute knowledge, playfulness, ritual, and community for material goods. Their cultures became richer. "Circumstances had changed, and they moved away from a guiding principle that happiness comes from consuming more things. . . . Working oneself into the ground simply to produce and consume more things was not the thing to do. . . . The truly high-class lifestyle was one that allowed free time in which to enrich one's heart and soul—and this led to a groundswell of interest in religion. The people of the medieval era stressed the importance of loyalty to and faith in a communally held vision."[3]

During resource-scarce periods, the Japanese culture developed kenjutsu (fencing), jujitsu (martial arts), saka (tea ceremony and flower arrangement), go (Japanese "chess"), and many other cultural refinements. Their culture became so highly evolved, according to Sakaiya, that the firearm was banned as too crude and destructive a method of settling differences.

When humanist psychologist Abraham Maslow observed the Canadian Blackfoot Indian culture in the 1930s, he too found evidence that the concept of wealth is a social construct, based partly on instinct and partly on the strategic pursuit of such socially laudable goals as equity, diversity, and resourcefulness. "The rich men of the tribe accumulated mounds of blankets, food, bundles of various sorts, and sometimes a case of Pepsi-Cola. . . . I remember the Sun Dance ceremony in which one man strutted and, we would say, boasted of his achievements. . . . And then, with a lordly gesture of great pride but without being humiliating, he gave his pile of wealth to the widows, to the orphaned children, and to the blind and diseased. At the end of the ceremony, he stood stripped of all possessions, owning nothing but the clothes he stood in."[4]

Maslow contends that this concept of wealth is based on higher values than material gratification. "It would seem that every human being comes at birth into society not as a lump of clay to be molded by society, but rather as a structure which society either suppresses or builds upon."

LOWER ON THE HIERARCHY?

Everyone knows a few unique individuals—usually elderly—who are healthy, wise, playful, relaxed, spontaneous, generous, open-minded, and loving: people who focus on problems outside of themselves and have a clear sense of what's authentic and what's not. They are people for whom life gets in the way of work, on purpose. For them, work is play, because they choose work they love. Abraham Maslow termed these people "self-actualized" individuals. He placed a lot of faith in human potential to meet basic needs and then progress—under one's own guidance—up a hierarchy of needs toward fulfillment. Before he died in 1969, Maslow concluded that most Americans had met the basic physical (the only ones that are primarily material) and security needs, and had progressed to at least the "love and belong-ingness" rung of the hierarchy. Many individuals were higher than that.

MASLOW'S HIERARCHY OF NEEDS

Self-actualization: becoming all we can be, doing what we are "born to do"

Aesthetic: beauty, balance, form

Cognitive: knowledge, meaning, order

Esteem: self-esteem and the respect and admiration of others

Love and belongingness: giving/receiving love and affection

Safety: stability and security from crime, disease, poverty

Physiological: air, food, water, shelter, sex, sleep

The question is, has America—weakened by affluenza—slipped *down* the hier-archy in the last thirty years? It seems the rungs of Maslow's ladder have become coated with slippery oil, as in a cartoon. According to polls, we're more fearful now. We're more insecure about crime, the possible loss of our jobs, and catastrophic ill-ness. More than 50,000 Americans die every year from medical malpractice, mak-ing us all the more insecure about our health.

How can we meet intrinsic community needs when sprawl creates distances between people? How can we feel a sense of beauty, security, and balance if beauti-ful open spaces in our communities are being smothered by new shopping malls and rows of identical houses? (Sometimes the only way to find your new house is to push the "housefinder" button on your garage door opener, and watch which door opens). How can we have self-respect in our work if it contributes to environmental destruction, social inequity, and isolation from living things? (The highest incidence of heart attacks is on Monday morning; apparently some would rather die than go back to work.)

Since America became a nation of consumers spoon-fed by automated products, fewer of us are now able to use our hands, or a sense of craft, in our work. As a result, creative satisfaction gets lost in the shuffle, along with knowledge, meaning, beauty, and balance—all higher rungs on Maslow's ladder.

Psychologists, anthropologists, artists, and the distant voices in our own heads tell us that both the potential and the urgency exist for a new definition of wealth in America. If we enrich our own nonmaterial sources of wealth, how much less money—and less paid labor—will be necessary? If we "produce" our own entertainment, perhaps by learning to be musicians, master gardeners, or woodworkers; informed conversationalists; or sports participants rather than ticket-purchasing fans, we'll reduce our financial needs substantially. If we provide some of our own transportation (and exercise) needs on foot—by living closer to work, stores, and recreation—we carve a large chunk out of the $7,000 spent annually by the average car owner. In effect, instead of working from January 1 to March 10 just to cover transportation costs, we can knock off in February.

Good diet, satisfying work, and regular exercise will keep our shopping carts free of side-effects from expensive medicines we don't need, as well as preventing some of the 30,000 deaths in America annually from reactions to prescription drugs. Cooking with healthy ingredients can make our taste buds, synapses, and white blood cells happy enough for us to raise our health insurance deductibles and lower our premiums. Living in an energy-efficient home will shave at least $300 off utility bills, and make our homes more comfortable. Changes like these are not about deprivation but about *increases* in the richness of our lives—and decreases in bills, stress, and waste. Quality satisfies more deeply than mere quantity.

Maslow termed the basic physical needs *deficiency needs,* and assumed that as long as you ate, your food needs were being met. If you lived in a house or apartment (as opposed to the street), your shelter needs were being met, and so on. However, his concept of deficiency didn't explore the *quality* of the food or shelter, or whether the needs were being supplied in a way that preserved the systems— the farms, forests, and fisheries—that met those needs. Individual satisfaction ultimately banks on the stability of the system.

Maslow didn't consider *sufficiency* and the implications of *over*consumption of the basic needs. Nor did he really get into *efficiency* in meeting needs—the technologies and pathways of production and use. If technologies are wasteful and destructive, they can't deliver overall satisfaction, because they leave scars in nature. In our free market, waste itself has become an important product, and it's hard to feel proud of that. Loans and incentives offered by bankers, tax policy-makers, and regulators guide us toward wasteful designs and approaches, further frustrating our search for self-actualization. In summary, our economic system is programmed for dissatisfaction!

"MAY THE FORK BE WITH YOU"

Even with its shortcomings, Maslow's hierarchy is still widely used as a tool to explore personal and cultural growth. We use it here to look at how affluenza gets in the way of satisfaction. Imagine carrying a bulging sack of groceries from the supermarket to your car. What kind of value does the sack contain? What kind of health does the food provide? Between 1950 and 2000, America attained the lowest cost per unit of food in the world, as a percentage of income, but also the highest health care costs per capita. What's the connection? Are the items in our grocery sacks toxic? Are our habits—and the habits of industry—also toxic?

In America, obesity is a greater health threat than starvation. Because the typical diet is too high in fats and sugars and too low in unrefined, slow-release carbohydrates, seventy-one percent of Americans are overweight by an average of ten pounds. An estimated 300,000 Americans die each year from unhealthy diets in combination with chronic inactivity. The GDP swells in proportion to our waistlines, since at least $150 billion is spent to control obesity and treat related diseases. While we continue to gorge, the contents of our grocery sacks deliver diabetes, gallbladder disease, hypertension, cancer, and higher risks of stroke.

The weight-control and health care industries in particular grow large as America tries, unsuccessfully, to grow lean. Our grocery sacks are filled with brightly-packaged frustration! On average, we gulp about a fifty-five-gallon drum of soft drinks every year, eat 250 fatty pounds of meat annually, and ingest the equivalent of fifty-three teaspoons of sugar *every day*.

Much of our dietary dissatisfaction comes from the lack of vitality that processed food delivers. The loss of control about food choice is also dissatisfying. Sugar is a good example. In 1997, Americans consumed three-fourths more sugar per capita than a hundred years ago, when most of the sugar produced went directly into our homes. In those days, we prepared most of our own meals, and determined the amount of sugar that went into them. In today's world, we've lost control, in many ways! More than three-quarters of the sugar produced today goes into the prepared, processed foods in our grocery sack.

Our high-protein diet is a prime example of meeting needs imprecisely. Livestock eat seventy percent of the grain produced in America, yet if humans ate more grain directly, our diet would be seven to eight times more efficient per pound.

Essentially, we wouldn't waste the grain's energy in the production of mountains of concentrated cow, hog, and chicken manure that pollute our waterways.

As Japan and China adopt a Western diet, previously rare Western diseases like arteriosclerosis and coronary heart disease come with it, explains health guru Andrew Weil. "Japanese women on traditional diets have one of the lowest rates of breast cancer in the world, but when they move to America and eat like Americans, their breast cancer risk quickly rises."[5]

Weil notes that there's far more to eating than the well-known consumer food groups (is that greasy, crunchy, sweet, and salty?). Food has always been a medium of social activity, he explains. The word "companion" means literally "with bread." High-quality food delivers satisfaction and contentedness, but low-quality food delivers poor health, irritability, pesticide residues, cancer, farm erosion, and the loss of rural communities as agribusiness giants take over. Simply put, junk food reduces our chances of reaching the top of Maslow's ladder. Sadly, our excessive diet too often produces lethargic and hyperactive humans who lack the energy and motivation to climb toward peak potential.

IS THE OBJECT SEX?

Monetary wealth is not a prerequisite for self-actualization, but authentic, vital connections are. In our culture, sex is another physical need that sometimes becomes an obstacle, rather than stepping stone, to self-actualization. Because sex is so instinctively compelling, it's become one of affluenza's most virulent carriers. Sex sells. But like food, it's also a fundamental social bond. Writes Erich Fromm, "The experience of sharing keeps the relation between two individuals alive. . . . Yet the sexual act—the prototype of shared enjoyment—is frequently so narcissistic, self-involved, and possessive that one can speak only of simultaneous, but not of shared pleasure."[6]

How much more self-involved can sex be than "cybersex," an emerging icon of isolation and unreality? "The affordability, accessibility and anonymity of the Internet have spawned a new psychological disorder among men and women who seek sexual stimulation from their computers. Some of these addicts spend hours each day masturbating to online pornographic images or having online sex with someone they have never seen, heard, touched, felt, or smelled."[7] We might call cybersex gratification, but in no way can it be termed satisfaction. It's pleasure without consequence. Think of these men and women as the son in a Woody Allen joke in which a mother catches her son in the act of fantasy sex. "Don't do that, you'll go blind!" she screams. Expressing the essence of our addicted consumer culture in a single phrase, he pleads, "Can I do it until I need glasses?"

CULTURE CRUNCH

An old story about a native Pacific Islander rings true in the Age of Affluenza. A healthy, self-motivated native relaxes in a hammock that swings gently in front of his seaside hut, as he plays a wooden flute for his family and himself. For dinner, he picks exotic fruits and spears fresh sunfish. He feels glad, and lucky to be alive. (Think of it—he's on "vacation" most of the time!) Suddenly, without warning, affluenza invades the island. Writes Jerry Mander, "A businessman arrives, buys all the land, cuts down the trees and builds a factory. He hires the native to work in it for money so that someday the native can afford canned fruit and fish from the mainland, a nice cinderblock house near the beach with a view of the water, and weekends off to enjoy it."[8]

Like Pacific Island natives, we've been cajoled into meeting most of our needs with products brought to us courtesy of multinational corporations—what you might call take-out satisfaction. "Almost every facet of American life has now been franchised," observes writer Eric Schlosser, "from the maternity ward at a Columbia/HCA hospital to an embalming room owned by the Houston-based Service Corporation International—which today handles the final remains of one of every nine Americans."[9]

What's good for America is good for the world—that's what the CEOs will tell you. One of the seven modern wonders of the world, the Golden Arches of McDonald's now grace 25,000 restaurants in 114 countries, an empire upon which the sun never sets. A friend of Dave's recently returned from China, where he observed a culture clash beneath the Arches. "McDonald's missionaries spread the gospel of high-volume, low-cost fast food," he says, "but the Chinese don't really seem to want fast food—although they're intrigued with American burgers. They want to sit and leisurely drink tea. They don't get that they're supposed to be in a hurry. And they can't go out and sit in their cars to eat, because they came on their bikes."[10]

Now that the Great Wall is showing signs of cracking, can the Taj Mahal be far behind? Will India's sacred cow become the sacred burger? Culture-crunchers have already scored a huge victory in Spain, with a surgical procedure to remove the siesta. In her lovely book *Leap,* Terry Tempest Williams describes a conversation she had on an airplane with a Procter and Gamble executive who boasted to her of his role in squeezing out the Spanish siesta. For a thousand years or more, the Spanish had enhanced their quality of life with a luxurious midday break that doesn't cost a single peseta. Yet in the eyes of commerce, siestas are a complete waste of time. What the world needs is more production, more consumption, less relaxation, and more money. Wake up, and get rich! An English friend informs us that the British afternoon tea is also vanishing, along with the traditional sit-down dinner.

However, commerce's most successful culture coup to date has taken place in the once-fertile frontiers of the American mind. Accounts of North America in the 1600s tell of a forest so vast that a squirrel could travel from Virginia to Illinois "without ever touching the ground." Today, by virtue of a media-happy free market, it may now be possible for a person to travel from one week to the next without thinking an original thought unshaped by manipulative messages! Much of the territory between our ears has now been commercially "colonized." The question is, if we get evicted from our own minds, who are we?

WANTING WHAT WE HAVE

Let's assume you've somehow satisfied physical, safety, and security needs, and even Maslow's "higher" needs for giving and receiving love. You've avoided junk food, the carelessness of the health care industry, and the battlefields of wounded relationships that stifle love and belongingness needs. Watch out, because the next rung, Esteem, is teeming with viruses. Better wear gloves when you get to the esteem trap. How much of our consumer behavior is dictated by needs for self-esteem and peer approval? In our search to fulfill these needs, we often contort ourselves into human doings rather than human beings.

We look outside ourselves for approval, talking loudly about what we have rather than what we know or what we believe in. Having what we want becomes a more important goal than *wanting what we have*. As we identify ourselves with the social species "consumer," our sense of confidence becomes dependent on things largely out of our control. We experience mood swings with the rising and falling of economic tides.

As of this writing, our "consumer confidence" is at record levels. ("We're in the money!") But are these real or simulated boom times? The same issue of the newspaper that reported our highest-ever level of consumer confidence featured an article explaining "Why the Ignorant Are Blissful."[11] David Dunning, a professor of psychology at Cornell, demonstrated that people who do things poorly usually appear more confident and self-assured than those who do things well. "Not only do they reach erroneous conclusions and make unfortunate choices," wrote Dunning, "but their incompetence robs them of the ability to realize it." The study documented that subjects who scored the lowest on logic, English grammar, and humor tests were also the most likely to overestimate how well they had done.

As a culture, aren't we blissfully ignorant? Aren't we erroneously confident we'll find peer approval, self-esteem, and meaning in material things, if we just keep looking?

PART TWO

Causes

CHAPTER 15

Original sin

Empty-handed we came into the world, and empty-handed, beyond question, we must leave it; if we have food and clothing to last us out, let us be content with that. Those who would be rich fall into temptation, the devil's trap for them; all those useless and dangerous appetites which sink men into ruin here and perdition hereafter. The love of money is a root from which every kind of evil springs.

—FIRST TIMOTHY 6:7–10

ow that you've been introduced to affluenza and its multiple symptoms, you may be asking yourself how we got to where we are today. What was the genesis of affluenza? Is it a bug that's always been there, just part of human nature? Is it culturally conditioned? Could it result from both nature and nurture? Those are the questions we'll attempt to answer in the next section of this book. We'll examine early efforts to contain or quarantine the disease, and attempt to understand how the virus mutated and grew more virulent over time in response to the forward march of history.

We believe it's necessary to understand the epidemiology of affluenza in order to begin to fight it effectively. As we researched this aspect of the issue, we became convinced that affluenza is not a new disease. But during the last half century, it has been spreading faster than ever before, as cultural values that once kept it in check have eroded under modern commercial pressures and technological changes.

THE SEARCH FOR PATIENT ZERO

When epidemiologists trace the evolution of a disease they look for the first individual known to have contracted it, who is given the inglorious label "Patient Zero." For example, the official Patient Zero for the AIDS epidemic was a South African man who died in 1959 (though it is suspected that the disease originated as early as the 1920s).

So who was affluenza's Patient Zero? In the Judeo/Christian/Islamic tradition, there were two of them: Adam and Eve. While they had everything they needed in the Garden of Eden, they transgressed God's limits to eat the forbidden apple. So the first lesson in the Bible is an admonishment against coveting more than we need. Greed is, in fact, the Original Sin.

Some evolutionary biologists suggest that the uncertainties of primitive life meant that a hoarding orientation became part of human nature. Those folks who stored food in good times had it to sustain them in lean times. They survived, and passed their hoarding genes on to their offspring.

Ergo, amassing stuff is as human as apple pie.

©1989 SEATTLE
POST-INTELLIGENCER
NORTH AMERICA SYNDICATE

But on the other hand, for ninety-nine percent of the time we homo sapiens have existed on earth, we were hunter-gatherers. Our problem was that our food-seeking activities quickly depleted the areas we lived in of fruits, nuts, animals, and other edibles. So we often had to move on to allow those areas to rebound. Mobility was the name of the primitive game. And mobility didn't allow one to carry a whole lot of cargo. Hence a simpler, stuff-free life was a requirement for survival. A genetic propensity toward hoarding would have been downright deadly.

ORIGINAL AFFLUENCE

Life for hunter-gatherers was fraught with danger—from wild animals, accidents, disease, and an occasional enemy. Infant mortality was high, as were infirmities. Broken bones didn't heal too well. Modern medicine might have been a godsend.

But the Stone Age wasn't as miserable as most of us believe. Some anthropologists who have observed contemporary "Stone Age" cultures call them "the original affluent societies."[1] Studies of such groups as the !Kung Bushmen of the Kalahari Desert indicate that before modernization confined them in smaller regions and destroyed the biological habitats from which they found subsistence, these hunter-gatherers were able to provide for their basic needs on as little as three or four hours of work a day. So-called "Stone Age" life apparently included more leisure time than does our own.

UCLA anthropologist Allen Johnson and his family spent two years living with a tribe called the Machiguenga, hunter-gatherers who also practice some subsistence agriculture, and inhabit the upper regions of the Amazon rain forest in Peru. He says he came to Machiguenga country loaded down with a huge footlocker full of possessions. "One of the lessons we learned over a period of just a few months, actually, was to dispense with most of our possessions," Johnson recalls.[2] "This kind of minimalist existence became quite comfortable to us after awhile and we began to feel that all these other possessions were completely superfluous. I learned from the Machiguenga that we could be comfortable living a much simpler life."

Johnson found the Machiguenga not quite originally affluent enough to get by on a four-hour workday. "Anthropologists," he says "may have gone a little bit overboard in describing how easy it is to be a hunter-gatherer, but the Machiguenga are certainly able to meet all their needs with six to eight hours of work. And that leaves a lot of time. The Machiguenga struck me as people who always have enough time. They're never in a hurry."

He came to admire their gentle ways and kind interactions with each other, the pleasure they found in quiet observation of their surroundings, the fact that they never seemed to get bored. "There seems to be a kind of general satisfaction in the things that they do," Johnson says. "It's just a pleasure to be around the Machiguenga when they're working. They're calm, they're physically comfortable. They're sewing or weaving, or making a box or a bow and arrow. And there's a sense of them enjoying it as we might enjoy a hobby or a craft. No time pressure."

"One of the things they do in the evening," he observed, "is sit around telling stories. And as you go by a Machiguenga house in the evening, you'll see through the slats of the walls of the house. You'll see the fire glowing and hear people's voices softly telling stories. If a man went hunting, he'll tell the story with the sights and the sounds and the smells. They also tell folktales. I've translated a lot of them and they're absolutely beautiful, a real literature."

BACK IN THE U.S.A.

Like many travelers who return from time spent with so-called "underdeveloped" or "primitive" cultures, Johnson had trouble returning to the fast-paced, possession-laden life in the United States. Culture-shocked, he walked through a supermarket aisle entirely filled with cake mixes and wondered, "Where's the affluence? Is this really progress?"

Life in Los Angeles seemed surreal when Johnson first returned. His children complained regularly of boredom despite a plethora of toys and activities. People he met seemed constantly busy, but unsatisfied with their lives, working and consuming frantically as if to fill "some kind of hole or emptiness," an emotional state he never encountered among the Machiguenga.

Johnson doesn't romanticize Machiguenga existence. Their life expectancy was short, as they often fell victim to jungle diseases. But they hadn't a hint of affluenza.

So it's not "human nature." But it's easy to find evidence of early infection among societies that achieved agricultural surpluses sufficient to allow long-term settlements, class divisions, and the beginnings of city life. In such cultures, political and economic hierarchies flourished and, as they strove for greater riches, members of the upper echelon began to oppress the poor and subjugate their neighbors. Without naming it as such, prophetic traditions in all civilizations, East and West, challenged their lordly brethren who had been infected by affluenza. "Beware an act of avarice; it is a bad and incurable disease," warned an ancient Egyptian proverb.[3] Buddha taught that the way to happiness and enlightenment lies in reducing desire, which he thought to be the cause of suffering.

MORAL ANTIDOTES

The Hebrew prophets railed against those who amassed riches by oppressing the poor and the weak. Moderation was the key: "Give me neither poverty nor riches, but only enough," reads the book of Proverbs. One day each week, the Sabbath, was to be kept completely free of money-making and thereby remain holy. Of the Sabbath, the great Jewish scholar Rabbi Abraham Heschel writes, "He who wants to enter the holiness of the day must first lay down the profanity of chattering commerce . . . and fury of acquisitiveness."[4] The Book of Deuteronomy, written about 700 B.C., admonishes against wasting things, the natural corollary to a life of material desire. As Rabbi Daniel Schwarz puts it, "when you waste creation it's like spitting at God."[5]

The ancient Greeks, too, warned against affluenza. "Simplicity is an ancient, even a primordial ideal," says historian David Shi, author of *The Simple Life* and now president of Furman University. "The Greeks," Shi says, "spoke of the 'Middle Way,' that midpoint between luxury and deprivation."[6] Aristotle warned against those "who have managed to acquire more external goods than they can possibly use, and are lacking in the goods of the soul."

By contrast he suggested that happiness would come to "those who have cultivated their character and mind to the uppermost and kept acquisition of external goods within moderate limits." "Aristotle was the first to maintain the diminishing marginal utility of money," writes philosopher Jerome Segal. "His belief was that each additional increment of money is of progressively less benefit to its possessor, and beyond a certain point, having more is of no value, and may even be harmful."[7]

"Unlimited wealth," Aristotle wrote, "is great poverty." Two groups of Greek non-conformists, the Stoics and the Cynics, were even more critical of materialism. By the time of the birth of Christ, their ideas were widespread. The Roman philosopher Seneca, a Stoic, challenged his own culture: "A thatched roof once covered free men; under marble and gold dwells slavery."[8]

According to New Testament scholar Burton Mack, early Christian teachings bore a strong resemblance to those championed by Epictetus, Diogenes, and other followers of the Cynic tradition in Greece. Living simply, the Cynics mocked the conventional culture of their affluent peers. Their ideas were widely known throughout the Mediterranean region two millennia ago.

But perhaps the strongest rebuke to incipient affluenza came from Jesus himself. He continually warned of the dangers of wealth, declaring it the major impediment to entry into the Kingdom of Heaven. It would be easier for a camel to pass through a needle's eye than for a rich man to enter Heaven, he told his followers.

The rich man who wished to follow Jesus was told he would first have to sell his possessions and give the money to the poor. "He went away unhappy for he had great wealth."[9]

Don't store up treasures on earth, Christ commanded. Rather be like the birds and flowers who possess nothing. God takes care of them, and their beauty is not matched by Solomon in all his glory. The earliest of Jesus' disciples and believers lived in simple communities where they shared all things in common and preached that "the love of money is the root of all evil."

"I think one of the most riveting passages in the New Testament is where Christ warns about Mammon, which is the power of wealth, the power of money," says Dr. Richard Swenson, a physician who lectures widely in evangelical churches. "Christ says you cannot serve both God and Mammon. He didn't say it's hard, it's difficult, it's tricky. He said it's impossible."[10]

In fact, one of Jesus' final public acts was a stinging rebuke to the affluenza that had begun to permeate his society. By chasing the money-lenders from the temple and overturning their tables, he challenged physically (one might even say, violently) a profane commercialism that had crept into even the holiest of places.

Christian theologian (and environmental scientist) Calvin De Witt says our modern consumer philosophy turns scriptural teachings on their head: "Consume more, then you'll be happy. Remain discontented with everything so that you'll continue to strive for more and more. That's the message we hear. But the Biblical teaching is to be content with what you have, honor God, take care of creation, give your bread to the hungry, then joy comes as a by-product of service. If you take those teachings and just write their antithesis, you find yourself describing our current consumer society."[11]

A CLASH OF CULTURES

In the spring of 1877, the famous leader of a tribe of hunter-gatherers addressed a council of his people, gathered around him on the windswept plains of South Dakota. The Lakota Sioux chief Tatanka Yotanka (Sitting Bull), gave thanks for the change of seasons and the bounty that the earth freely provided. But he warned his people about "another race, small and feeble when our fathers first met them, but now great and overbearing." He described the pale-faced men and women who had come to mine and till the earth, carrying with them (and seeking to convert the Indians to) the words of a man who preached brotherhood, peace, and goodwill among all, a preference for the poor, and a life free from the encumbrances of worldly possessions.

Something, apparently, had gotten lost in the translation, because as Sitting Bull observed, "These people have made many rules which the rich may break but the poor may not. They take tithes from the poor and weak to support the rich who rule. They claim this mother of ours, the earth, for their own and fence their neighbors away; they deface her with their buildings and their refuse. Their nation is like a spring freshet that overruns its banks and destroys all who are in its path. We cannot dwell side by side."[12]

Of the White invaders, Sitting Bull said, one thing was certain: *The love of possession is a disease with them.* Today he might have called that disease "affluenza." Back then, he would have found that even among the whites, there were many who shared his fears of the virus in their midst.

CHAPTER 16

An ounce
of prevention

"The devaluation of the human world increases in direct relation to the increase in value of the world of things."

—KARL MARX,
Economic and Philosophical
Manuscripts of 1844

ear of affluenza, though never identified as such, has been part of the American tradition since some of the first colonists arrived here from Europe. It was a mixed bunch that risked life and livelihood to cross the Atlantic on small wooden ships. The first came seeking riches. The Spanish wanted gold, the French, furs. The Dutch sought new trade routes to the fabled Indies.

But among the early arrivals from England were refugees seeking to escape what they had come to view as a godless materialism rapidly taking root in Europe. "When the Puritans arrived in the New World, one of their major premises was their desire to try to create a Christian commonwealth that practiced simple living," explains historian David Shi.[1]

In their Massachusetts Bay Colony, the Puritans adopted what were known as sumptuary laws, forbidding conspicuous displays of wealth. They required colonists to wear simple clothing, for example. But because they were never applied fairly, the laws failed to stem a growing trade in luxury goods arriving in the New World from

Europe. Wealthier, politically powerful Puritans could effectively ignore the laws and wear whatever they chose, while their poorer brethren were punished for transgressions of the dress code. In effect, the sumptuary laws only exacerbated visible class differences.

In Pennsylvania the Quakers, under the leadership of John Woolman, were more successful in their efforts to keep affluenza at bay. "My dear friends," Woolman preached, "follow that exercise of simplicity, that plainess and frugality which true wisdom leads to."[2] "Among Quakers," writes philosopher Jerome Segal, "the restrictions on display and consumption became more widely applicable. Most important, the pursuit of luxurious consumption was linked to a broad range of injustices and social problems, including alcoholism, poverty, slavery and ill treatment of the Indians."[3]

YANKEE DOODLE DANDIES—NOT!

In some respects, the American Revolution itself was a revolt against affluenza. British colonial masters bled their American colonies in order to support a lifestyle of luxury approaching decadence. The English lords often spent half the day dressing, much of it on their ever-more-elaborate headpieces (this is the origin of the term "bigwigs"). Then they stuffed themselves on dinners that took hours to consume.

The American colonists, meanwhile, grew angry at the taxes imposed on them to keep British coffers full. But at the same time, colonial leaders were troubled by unbridled pursuit of wealth on the part of some of their own countrymen. "Frugality, my dear, must be our refuge," wrote John Adams to his wife Abigail, during the Revolution. "I hope the ladies are everyday diminishing their ornaments, and the gentlemen, too. Let us drink water and eat potatoes rather than submit to unrighteous domination."[4]

At the end of the eighteenth century, as the world changed politically with the triumph of the American and French revolutions, it was also changing economically. The industrial revolution's "dark, satanic mills" (William Blake) brought steam power and assembly-line techniques, making possible the production of textiles and other goods in a fraction of the time previously required. Benjamin Franklin argued that with such productive tools at humanity's disposal, it was possible to reduce the labor time needed to produce all the "necessaries" of life to three or four hours a day.[5]

But in fact, the opposite occurred. During the early industrial revolution, working hours were roughly doubled, rather than reduced. The medieval workday, scholars now estimate, averaged about nine hours; more in summer, fewer in winter.[6] Moreover, the pace of work was quite slow, with frequent breaks for rest. And in some parts of Europe, workers enjoyed nearly 150 religious holidays, when they didn't work at all. Pieter Breughel's sixteenth-century paintings of peasants dancing, feasting, or napping in their wheat fields in the afternoon were accurate portrayals of the life he witnessed.

THE SPIRIT OF SAINT MONDAY

But with the industrial revolution, factory workers—driven into desolate, Dickensian, industrial cities as the land they once farmed was enclosed for sheep-raising—were working fourteen, sixteen, even eighteen hours a day. In 1812, one factory owner in Leeds, England, was described as humane and progressive because he wouldn't hire children under ten years of age and limited children's working hours to sixteen a day.

But factory workers did not readily comply with the new industrial discipline. Stripped of their old religious holidays, they invented a new one: Saint Monday. Hung over from Sunday nights at the tavern, they slept in late, or failed to show up to work at all. Workers were paid on a piece-rate basis, and at first only worked as long as they needed to subsist. If an employer paid them more as an incentive to work more, he soon found that his strategy backfired. As Max Weber put it, "The opportunity of earning more was less attractive than that of working less."[7]

This was obviously a pre-affluenza situation.

Consequently, as Karl Marx repeatedly pointed out, employers sought to pay the lowest wages possible so that workers would have to keep working long hours simply to survive. But while such miserliness was rational behavior for individual employers, it undermined capitalist industry as a whole. Workers' lack of purchasing power led to overproduction crises that periodically destroyed entire industries.

"In these crises," Marx and Engels wrote in *The Communist Manifesto* (1848), "a great part not only of the existing products but also of the previously created productive forces are periodically destroyed. . . . Society suddenly finds itself put back into a state of momentary barbarism. . . . And how does the bourgeoisie get over these crises? On the one hand, by enforced destruction of a mass of productive forces; on the other, by the conquest of new markets, and by the more thorough exploitation of old ones."[8]

MARX ON AFFLUENZA

So just how is this "more thorough exploitation" accomplished? In effect, by exposing one's potential customers to affluenza, though, of course, Marx never used the term. But in a brilliant passage from *The Economic and Philosophical Manu-*

scripts of 1844, worth quoting from at length, he describes the process. "Excess and immoderation" become the economy's "true standard," Marx wrote, as

> the expansion of production and of needs becomes an ingenious and
> always calculating subservience to inhuman, depraved, unnatural and
> *imaginary* appetites . . . (Every product is a bait by means of which
> the individual tries to entice the essence of the other person, his
> money. Every real or potential need is a weakness which will draw
> the bird into the lime . . .) . . . The entrepreneur accedes to the most
> depraved fancies of his neighbor, plays the role of pander between
> him and his needs, awakens unhealthy appetites in him, and watches
> for every weakness in order, later, to claim the remuneration for this
> labor of love.[9]

That passage, written 157 years ago, accurately describes much of modern advertising, which, indeed, stimulates "imaginary appetites," consistently uses sex to sell products, and certainly, in cases such as the video game promotions described in the chapter "Dilated Pupils," "accedes to the most depraved fancies."

Ultimately, though, Marx believed that market expansion would always be inadequate, and that overproduction crises could only be prevented if the workers themselves gained ownership of the factories and used the machinery for the benefit of all. That didn't mean an ever-growing pie of material production simply shared more equitably. Marx's goal was never a materialistic one. Indeed, he stressed that to simply increase the purchasing power of workers "would be nothing more than a better remuneration of slaves and would not restore, either to the worker or to the work, their human significance and worth."[10]

WEALTH AS DISPOSABLE TIME

Neither would "an enforced equality of wages," made law by a socialist government, lead to happiness, which, Marx believed, was to be found instead in our relationships with other people and in the development of our capacities for creative expression. "The wealthy man," he wrote, "is one who needs a complex of human manifestions of life and whose own self-realization exists as an inner necessity." "Too many useful goods," he suggested, "create too many useless people."[11]

Of course, Marx understood that human beings must have enough wholesome food, decent shelter, and protective clothing. Mass-production, he believed, made it possible for everyone to achieve these ends. And to do so each person would have to perform a certain minimum amount of repetitive, noncreative labor. Marx called this time, which he and Engels estimated could be reduced (even in the mid-1800s) to as little as four hours a day, "the realm of necessity."

The work time necessary to satisfy real material needs could be reduced further by increases in productivity, "but it always remains a realm of necessity. Beyond it begins that development of human power, which is its own end, the true realm of freedom," when self-chosen activity prevails. Of this realm of freedom, Marx added, "the shortening of the working day is its basic prerequisite." "A nation is really rich if the working day is six hours rather than twelve," Marx wrote, quoting approvingly the anonymous author of a British article written in 1821: "Wealth is liberty—liberty to seek recreation, liberty to enjoy life, liberty to improve the mind: it is disposable time and nothing more."[12]

SIMPLY THOREAU

Meanwhile, across the Atlantic, an American movement offered a similar critique of industrialization and the acquisitiveness it engendered. The Transcendentalists, as they called themselves, idealized the simple life, close to nature, and started intentional communities (none destined to last very long) such as Brook Farm and Fruitlands, based on their principles.

Better remembered, if similarly short-lived, was Henry David Thoreau's 1845 sojourn to a one-room cabin he built on the shore of Walden Pond, near Boston. "Simplicity, simplicity, simplicity," wrote Thoreau in *Walden*. "Most of the luxuries and many of the so-called comforts of life, are not only not indispensible, but positive hindrances to the elevation of mankind."[13]

In *Life Without Principle,* Thoreau was even more damning of the acquisitive industrial personality, already in need of antibodies for affluenza. Like Marx, Thoreau believed that true wealth meant sufficient leisure for self-chosen creative activity, suggesting that half a day's labor should be enough to procure real material necessities. "If I should sell both my forenoons and my afternoons to society as most appear to do, I am sure that for me there would be nothing left worth living for," Thoreau wrote.

> Let us consider the way in which we spend our lives. The world is a
> place of business. What an infinite bustle. . . . There is no sabbath. It
> would be glorious to see mankind at leisure for once. It is nothing but
> work, work, work. I cannot easily buy a blank book to write thoughts in;
> they are commonly ruled for dollars and cents. . . . I think there is noth-
> ing, not even crime, more opposed to poetry, to philosophy, ay, to life
> itself than this incessant business.[14]

"If a man should walk in the woods for love of them half of each day, he is in danger of being regarded as a loafer, but if he spends his whole day as a speculator, shearing off those woods and making earth bald before her time, he is esteemed an industrious and enterprising citizen,"[15] Thoreau wrote, in words all the more relevant today, when such corporate speculators as Charles Hurwitz of Pacific Lumber Company shear off entire forests of old-growth redwoods to pay for junk bonds.

For Marx, Thoreau, and many other oft-quoted, but more often ignored, philosophers of the mid-nineteenth century, industrial development could only be justified because, potentially, it shortened the time spent in drudgery, thereby giving people leisure time for self-chosen activity.

Given a choice between more time and more money, these philosophers chose the former. For precisely a century following Thoreau's retreat to Walden, that choice, as our next chapter suggests, would engage Americans in a broad and energetic debate. Then, suddenly, it would be resolved—in favor of more money. But it would not be forgotten.

CHAPTER 17

The road not taken

We want bread, but roses, too
[and time to smell them].

—Female textile workers in Lawrence,
Massachusetts, 1912

After the horrors of the Civil War, a new, quieter conflict, ultimately as powerful in its impact, emerged in the United States. Two roads, as Robert Frost put it in his lovely poem "The Road Not Taken," presented themselves to Americans, and after a period of indecision that lasted nearly a century, we chose one of them, "and that has made all the difference."

Nineteenth-century Americans still had more respect for thrift than for spendthrifts, and the word "consumption" meant something different then. As Jeremy Rifkin explains, "If you go back to Samuel Johnson's dictionary of the English language, to consume meant to exhaust, to pillage, to lay waste, to destroy. In fact, even in our grandparents' generation, when somebody had tuberculosis, they called it 'consumption.' So up until this century, to be a consumer was not to be a good thing, it was considered a bad thing."[1]

Yet the factory system had made possible a tremendous efficiency in the time required to produce products. And herein lie the roots of the new conflict: what to do with all that time? One side suggested that we make more stuff; the other believed we should work less. Luxury or simplicity. Money or time.

THE RIGHT TO BE LAZY

Across the Atlantic, a similar argument was brewing. In 1883, while in a French prison, Paul Lafargue, a son-in-law of Karl Marx, wrote a provocative essay called "The Right to Be Lazy," challenging the make more/have more ethic. Lafargue mocked industrialists who "go among the happy nations who are loafing in the sun" and "lay down railroads, erect factories and import the curse of work."[2]

Lafargue deemed laziness "the mother of arts and noble virtues," and suggested that even then, factories were so productive that only three hours a day of labor should be required to meet real needs. Like Marx, he pointed out that Catholic Church law had given workers many feast days honoring the saints when work was forbidden. It was no surprise, he suggested, that industrialists favored Protestantism (with its work ethic), which "dethroned the saints in heaven in order to abolish their feast days on earth."

At the same time in England, William Morris, a poet, artist, essayist, and designer of the Morris chair, claimed that under the factory system, "the huge mass of men are compelled by folly and greed to make harmful and useless things." "An immensity of work" wrote Morris, was expended in making "everything in the shop windows which is embarrassing or superfluous." "I beg of you," Morris pleaded,

> to think of the enormous mass of men who are occupied with this miserable trumpery, from the engineers who have had to make the machines for making them, down to the hapless clerks who sit day-long year after year in the horrible dens wherein the wholesale exchange of them is transacted, and the shopmen, who not daring to call their souls their own, retail them . . . to the idle public which doesn't want them but buys them to be bored by them and sick to death of them.[3]

"The good life of the future," said Morris, would be totally unlike the life of the rich of his day. "Free men," he maintained, "must live simple lives and have simple pleasures." Morris defined a decent, wealthy life as requiring "a healthy body, an active mind, occupation fit for a healthy body and active mind, and a beautiful world to live in."

THE SIMPLE LIFE

Back in the United States, new institutions like the department store helped promote a life of conspicuous consumption. "Urban department stores came in during the 1880s," says historian Susan Strasser, "basically to create the sort of place where people would go and lose themselves and meanwhile spend their money."[4] By the 1890s, wealthy Americans proudly displayed the material signs of their success, wearing affluenza on their sleeves, you might say. But not everyone was impressed.

"In the late 19th century, there was a major revival of American interest in simple living," says historian David Shi. "Theodore Roosevelt was one of the foremost proponents of a simpler life for Americans during that period. Roosevelt was quite candid in saying that for all his support for American capitalism, he feared that if it were allowed to develop unleashed it would eventually create a corrupt civilization."[5] Shi provides other examples of this turn-of-the-century interest in simplicity in his wonderful book *The Simple Life*. Even America's best-selling magazine *The Ladies' Home Journal* promoted simplicity during that era.

THE SHORTER HOURS MOVEMENT

Organized labor, too, had not yet then accepted the definition of the good life as a goods life, in which the marker of progress was the making of stuff. Indeed, for more than half a century, the demand for shorter hours topped labor's agenda. In 1886, hundreds of thousands of workers filled American cities, demanding that an eight-hour workday be made America's legal standard. That didn't happen until 1938, when the Wagner Labor Relations Act made the eight-hour day and forty-hour week the law of the land. And by then, labor leaders were fighting for a six-hour workday. It was needed, they argued, as much for spiritual as economic reasons.

"The human values of leisure are even greater than its economic significance," wrote William Green, president of the American Federation of Labor, in 1926. Green claimed that modern work was "meaningless, repetitive, boring," and offered "no satisfaction of intellectual needs." Shorter working hours were necessary "for the higher development of spiritual and intellectual powers," Green claimed. His vice-president, Matthew Woll, charged that modern production ignored "the finer qualities of life. Unfortunately, our industrial life is dominated by the materialistic spirit of production [affluenza?], giving little attention to the development of the human body, the human mind or the spirit of life."[6]

Juliet Stuart Poyntz, education director of the International Ladies Garment Workers Union, declared that what workers wanted most of all was "time to be human." "Workers," she observed, "have declared that their lives are not to be bartered at any price." "No wage, no matter how high" was more important than the time that workers needed.[7]

TIME TO KNOW GOD

Behind them, as Professor Benjamin Hunnicutt of the University of Iowa points out in his book *Work Without End,* rallied prominent religious leaders, who worried that workers had no time for reflection and spiritual matters, no "time to know God." Jewish leaders challenged Saturday work as violating their Sabbath, and led the fight for a five-day work week. Catholic leaders backed Pope Leo XIII's call (in his encyclical *Rerum Novarum,* 1891) for a "living wage" or "family wage" that would guarantee the breadwinner in working families sufficient income for a life of "*frugal* comfort." But beyond that, they believed that more time was more important to workers than more money.

During the '20s, Monsignor John Ryan, editor of the *Catholic Charities Review,* pointed to St. Augustine's claim that natural law demanded a "maximum" standard of living as well as a minimum one. "The true and rational doctrine," Ryan wrote, "is that when men have produced sufficient necessaries and reasonable comforts, they should spend what time is left in the cultivation of their intellects and wills, in the pursuit of the higher life." They should, he said, "ask what is life for?"[8] Jewish scholar Felix Cohen pointed out that in the Biblical tradition work was a curse visited upon Adam for his sin in Eden, and suggested that with wasteful and unnecessary production abolished, it would soon be possible to reduce the workweek to ten hours![9]

THE GOSPEL OF CONSUMPTION

But industrial leaders in the 1920s had their own religion, the gospel of consumption. A reduction in working hours, they believed, might bring the whole capitalist system to its knees. Increased leisure, Harvard economist Thomas Nixon Carver warned, was bad for business:

> There is no reason for believing that more leisure would ever increase the desire for goods. It is quite possible that the leisure would be spent in the cultivation of the arts and graces of life; in visiting museums, libraries and art galleries, or hikes, games and inexpensive amusements . . . it would decrease the desire for material goods. If it should result in more gardening, more work around the home in making or repairing furniture, painting and repairing the house and other useful avocations, it would cut down the demand for the products of our wage paying industries.[10]

It would, you might say, reduce affluenza. He had a problem with that. We don't.

After the Model T began rolling from Henry Ford's assembly lines in 1913, a cornucopia of material products followed. Businesses sought ways to sell them—and the economic gospel of consumption—giving rise to an advertising industry that looked—and still looks—to psychology for help in pushing products.

"Sell them their dreams," a promoter told Philadelphia businessmen in 1923. "Sell them what they longed for and hoped for and almost despaired of having. Sell them hats by splashing sunlight across them. Sell them dreams—dreams of country clubs and proms and visions of what might happen if only. After all, people don't buy things to have things. They buy hope—hope of what your merchandise will do for them. Sell them this hope and you won't have to worry about selling them goods."[11]

People's wants, the captains of American industry declared, were insatiable, and business opportunities therefore boundless. During the '20s, their gospel of wealth had plenty of believers. The world's first mass-consumption society came in dancing the Charleston. Cash registers were ka-chinging, and the stock market soared—higher, higher, higher—like that of the '90s. There were those who thought it would never go down.

SHORTER HOURS DURING THE DEPRESSION

Then one Black Friday in October 1929, it all collapsed. "Wall Street Lays An Egg," declared the headline in *Variety*. Millionaires suddenly became paupers and leaped out windows. Breadlines formed. Millions were out of work and "Buddy" couldn't spare a dime. With so many people out of work, the idea of shortening work hours, "work sharing," was back in vogue. Even Herbert Hoover called shorter hours the quickest way to create more jobs.

Once again, labor leaders like William Green were demanding "the six-hour day and the five-day week in industry." Imagine their delight when word came from the Capitol in Washington on April 6, 1933 that the U.S. Senate had just passed a bill that would make thirty hours the official American workweek. Anything over that would be overtime. Thirty hours. That was nearly seven decades ago.

But the bill ultimately failed in the House by a few votes. President Roosevelt opposed it because he was convinced that federal job creation programs—the New Deal—offered a better way to both reduce unemployment and keep industry strong.

But some businesses had already adopted thirty-hour workweeks, with excellent results. Cereal tycoon A.K. Kellogg took the lead, in December of 1930. Kellogg was a paternalistic capitalist who ran his company with an iron hand. But he had a certain radical vision. In Kellogg's view, according to Benjamin Hunnicutt, leisure time, not economic growth without end, represented the "flower, the crowning achievement, of capitalism."[12] The vision came to Kellogg because he mourned his rigid childhood and his own addiction to long hours of labor. "I never learned to play," he once told his grandson, regretfully.

Kellogg offered his workers thirty-five hours' pay for a thirty-hour week, and he built parks, summer camps, nature centers, garden plots, sports fields, and other recreational facilities for them. The plan immediately created 400 new jobs in Battle Creek, Michigan, where Kellogg's plants were located. Productivity rose so rapidly that within two years Kellogg could pay his thirty-hour workers what he had previously paid them for forty hours. Polling of Kellogg's workers during the '30s showed overwhelming support for the thirty-hour week; only a few single males wished for more hours and higher pay.

OLD EIGHT HOURS HAS GOT US ALL

But after Kellogg died, the company waged a long campaign to return to the forty-hour week. The reason: benefits. As benefits increasingly became a larger part of the wage package, it made more sense to hire fewer workers and keep them on longer. But the thirty-hour week at Kellogg's wasn't fully abandoned until 1985, when the company threatened to leave Battle Creek if the remaining thirty-hour workers (about twenty percent of the company, and nearly all women) didn't agree to work longer. The women held a funeral (complete with a casket) for the thirty-hour week at Stan's Place, a local bar, and one, Ina Sides, wrote a eulogy:

> Farewell good friend, oh six hours/
> Tis sad but true/ Now you're gone and we're all so blue.
> Get out your vitamins, give the doctor a call/
> Cause old eight hours has got us all.[13]

While writing his book *Kellogg's Six Hour Day*, Ben Hunnicutt spent time with many former Kellogg workers in Battle Creek. Most remembered the thirty-hour week with deep fondness. They remembered using their leisure well—to garden, learn crafts, practice hobbies, exercise, and share in a vibrant community life. "You weren't all wore out when you got out of work," said one man. "You had the energy to do something else."

Chuck and Joy Blanchard, a married couple who both worked at the plant, remembered that Chuck took care of the kids and was a "room parent" at their school "long before anyone heard about women's liberation."[14] They also remembered that after the return to forty hours, volunteering in Battle Creek went down and crime went up. The Blanchards say they *had* little, but their lives, blessed with abundant leisure, were happier than those of young families today, who have so much more stuff but never seem to have time.

Never before or since in America had ordinary industrial workers traveled so far down that "other road"—the road of time instead of money. In that sense, the Kellogg's workers were, as Hunnicutt sees them, explorers in a new and wondrous land that all Americans might have come to had World War II not intervened, and—in demanding a vast national outpouring of labor—locked the gate. Today, we meet people who cannot quite believe that more than half a century ago, in a corner of the United States, full-time workers were spending only thirty hours a week on the job. But it happened. And it can happen again when we get a grip on affluenza.

CHAPTER 18

An emerging epidemic

Man today is fascinated by the possibility of buying, more, better, and especially, new things. He is consumption hungry.... To buy the latest gadget, the latest model of anything that is on the market, is the dream of every-body, in comparison to which the real pleasure in use is quite secondary. Modern man, if he dared to be articualte about his concept of heaven, would describe a vision which would look like the biggest department store in the world.... He would wander around open-mouthed in this heaven of gadgets and com-modities, provided only that there were ever more and new things to buy, and perhaps, that his neighbors were just a little less privileged than he.

—PSYCHOANALYST ERICH FROMM, 1955

During World War II, Americans accepted rationing and material deprivation. Wasteful consumption was out of the question. In every city, citizens gathered scrap metal to contribute to the war effort. Most grew some of their own food, in so-called "victory gardens." Driving was limited to save fuel. Despite the sacrifices, what many older Americans remember most from that time was the sense of community, of sharing for the common good, and uniting to defeat a common enemy.

But shortly after World War II ended, pent-up economic demand in the form of personal savings, coupled with low-interest government loans and mushrooming private credit, led to a consumer boom unparalleled in history. The G.I. Bill sparked massive construction of new housing at the edge of America's cities, beginning with the famous Levittown development on Long Island. The average size of a Levittown bungalow was only 750 square feet, but its popularity encouraged other developers to build sprawling suburbs with larger homes.

New families filled the new homes as the baby boom began. Each family needed lots of new appliances and—with transit service in the suburbs nonexistent—cars to get around. It's fascinating to watch the many corporate and government films produced during that period, both documenting and extolling the new mass consumption society.

THE GOODS LIFE

"The new automobiles stream from the factories," the narrator cheers, in one late-forties film. "Fresh buying power floods into all the stores of every community. Prosperity greater than history has ever known." In the same film, we see a montage of shots of people spending money, and hear more peppy narration: "The pleasure of buying, the spreading of money! And the enjoyment of all the things that paychecks can buy are making happy all the thousands of families!"[1] Utopia has arrived!

Another film proclaims that "we live in an age of growing abundance" and urges Americans to give thanks for "our liberty to buy whatever each of us may choose" (the words come with a heavenly chorus humming "America the Beautiful" and shots of the Statue of Liberty). A third reminds us that "the basic freedom of the American people is the freedom of individual choice" (of which products to purchase, of course).

One film appeals to women to take up where the soldiers of World War II left off and fight "the age-old battle for beauty." We've been told "you can't buy beauty in a jar," the narrator says, "but that old adage is bunk. We have the money to spend and we want all the lovely-smelling lotions, soaps, and glamour goo we can get with it." Joy in a jar. As women try on perfumes in an upscale department store, the narrator continues: "Our egos are best nourished by a well-placed investment in real luxury goods—what you might call discreetly conspicuous waste."[2] "Waste not, want not," Benjamin Franklin once admonished. But the new slogan might have been "waste more, want more." Almost overnight, the good life became the *goods* life.

PLANNED OBSOLESCENCE

"The immediate postwar period does represent a huge change in the kinds of attitudes that Americans have had about consumption," says historian Susan Strasser, author of *Satisfaction Guaranteed*.[3] "Discreetly conspicuous waste" got another boost from what marketers called "planned obsolescence." Products were either made to last only a short time so that they would have to be replaced frequently (adding to sales) or they were continually upgraded, more commonly in style than in quality. It was an idea that began long before World War II with Gillette disposable razors and soon took on a larger life.

Henry Ford, who helped start the '20s consumer boom by paying his workers a then-fantastic five dollars a day, was a bit of a conservative about style, once promising that consumers could have one of his famous Model Ts in any color as long as it was black. But just before the Great Depression, General Motors introduced the idea of the annual model change. It was an idea that took off after World War II. Families were encouraged to buy a new car every year. "They were saying the car you had last year won't do anymore and it won't do anymore because it doesn't look right," explains Susan Strasser. "There's now a new car and that's what we want to be driving."[4]

INSTANT MONEY

Of course, none but the richest Americans could afford to plunk down a couple thousand dollars on a new car every year, or on any of the other new consumer durables that families wanted. Never mind, there were ways to finance your spending spree. "The American consumer! Each year you consume fantastic amounts of food, clothing, housing, amusements, appliances, and services of all kinds. This mass consumption makes you the most powerful giant in the land,"[5] pipes the narrator in a cute, mid-'50s animated film from the National Consumer Finance Association (NCFA).

"I'm a giant," boasts Mr. American Consumer, as he piles up a massive mountain of stuff. And how does he afford it? Loans, says the film: "Consumer loans in the hands of millions of Americans add up to tremendous purchasing power. Purchasing power that creates consumer demand for all kinds of goods and services that mean a rising standard of living throughout the nation." You can probably already hear the drum roll in your mind.

A TV ad for Bank of America made about the same time shows a shaking animated man and asks, "Do you have money jitters? Ask the obliging Bank of America for a jar of soothing instant money. M-O-N-E-Y. In the form of a convenient personal loan." The animated man drinks from a coffee cup full of dollars, stops shaking and jumps for joy.[6]

It was a buy now, pay later world, only to become more so with the coming of credit cards in the sixties.

AMERICA THE MALLED

During the 1950s and 1960s, the rush to suburbia continued (it hasn't stopped yet). In 1946 a government program, the G.I. Bill, spurred it along. Ten years later, another government program did the same. President Eisenhower announced the beginning of a vast federal subsidy to create a nationwide freeway system. In part the system was sold as national defense—roads big enough to run our tanks on if the Russians invaded. The new freeways encouraged a mass movement to even wider rings of suburbs. All were built around the automobile, and massive shopping centers, whose windows, according to one early '60s promotional film, reflected "a happy-go-spending world."[7]

"Shopping malls," the film continues, "see young adults as in need of expansion [interesting choice of words]. People who buy in large quantities and truck it away in their cars. It's a big market!" "These young adults," the narrator gushes, "shopping with the same determination that brought them to suburbs in the first place, are the goingest part of a nation of wheels, living by the automobile." Going to the mall was, for these determined consumers, an adventure worthy of Mt. Everest, at least according to this film, which later describes the consumers' hardest challenge as finding their cars again in the giant mall parking lots.

By 1970, Americans were spending four times as much time shopping as were Europeans. The malls encouraged Sunday shopping, then as rare in the United States as it still is in Europe. To its everlasting credit, the Sears, Roebuck Company opposed opening its store on Sunday, on the grounds that it wanted "to give our employees their Sabbath." But by 1969 it caved to the competition, opening on Sundays "with great regret and some sense of guilt."[8]

THE BOX THAT ENLIGHTENED

The big economic boom wasn't the result of any one thing. A series of synchronous events made it possible: pent-up demand, government loans, expanded credit, suburbanization, longer shopping hours, and mallification. But perhaps no single cause was as responsible for the emerging postwar epidemic of affluenza than the ubiquitous box that found its way into most American homes by the 1950s.

Television showed everyone how the other half (the upper half) lived. Its programs were free, made possible only because of the sale of time to advertisers who hawked their wares during and between the features. Crude at first, the ads became increasingly sophisticated—both visually, because of improving technologies, and psychologically, as batteries of experts probed the human mind to find out how to sell most effectively.

The early TV ads relied a great deal on humor—"Any girl can find a good husband, but finding the right man to do your hair, now that's a problem." Like many print and radio ads before them, they played on anxieties about personal embarrassment, warning of horrors like "B.O. (body odor)." But mostly, they just showed us all the neat stuff that was out there just waiting to be bought.

On TV, convenience was the new ideal, disposability the means. "Use it once and throw it away." Out of sight, out of mind. TV dinners in disposable aluminum trays. "No deposit, no return" bottles. Dinner time, and the livin' is easy. People danced with products. The airwaves buzzed with jingles. John still can't stop singing that old one that must have been on the tube every night when he was a kid: "You'll wonder where the yellow went, when you brush your teeth with Pepsodent."

AFFLUENZA'S DISCONTENTS

Of course, not everyone wanted Americans to catch affluenza. "Buy only what you really need and cannot do without," President Harry Truman once said on TV. By the early '50s, educational films were warning school kids about overspending.

But they were, in a word, boring. No match for TV's wit and whiz. In one, a nerdy looking character called Mr. Money teaches students to save. One can imagine the collective classroom yawns it produced. In another, the voice of God says "You're guilty of pouring your money down a rathole. You forget that it takes a hundred pennies to make a dollar. The visuals are equally uncompelling: a hand puts a dollar in a hole in the dirt labeled—you guessed it—"Rathole."[9]

Meanwhile, far-sighted social critics from both left and right warned that America's new affluence was coming at a high price. Conservative economist Wilhelm Ropke feared that "we neglect to include in the calculation of these potential gains in the supply of material goods the possible losses of a non-material kind."[10] Centrist Vance Packard lambasted advertising (*The Hidden Persuaders*, 1957), keeping up with the Joneses (*The Status Seekers*, 1959) and planned obsolescence (*The Waste Makers*, 1960). And the liberal John Kenneth Galbraith suggested that a growing economy fulfilled needs it created itself, leading to no improvement in happiness. Our emphasis on "private opulence," he said, led to "public squalor"— declining transit systems, schools, parks, libraries, and air and water quality. Moreover, it left "vast millions of hungry and discontented people in the world. Without the promise of relief from that hunger and privation, disorder is inevitable."[11]

The affluent society had met its members' real material needs, Galbraith argued at the end of his famous book. Now it had other, more important things to do. "To furnish a barren room is one thing," he wrote. "To continue to crowd in furniture until the foundation buckles is quite another. To have failed to solve the problem of producing goods would have been to continue man in his oldest and most grievous misfortune. But to fail to see that we have solved it, and to fail to proceed thence to the next tasks, would be fully as tragic."[12]

YOUNG AMERICA STRIKES BACK

During the following decade, many young Americans sensed that the critics of consumerism were right. Raised in the suburbs, they rejected the suburban lifestyle with its "little boxes on the hillsides made of ticky-tacky" (as songwriter Malvina Reynolds called them), where everyone grew up to be "just the same." During Berkeley's tumultuous Free Speech Movement of 1964, its leader Mario Savio attacked a school system that wanted students to be "well-behaved children in a chrome-plated consumer's paradise."[13] A new "counterculture" arose, rebuking materialism. Thousands of young Americans left the cities for agricultural communes practicing simple living, the most successful of which still survive today.

Many of the young questioned American reliance on growth of the Gross National Product as a measure of the nation's health. In that they were supported by the popular Senator Robert F. Kennedy. During his 1968 campaign for President (which ended when he was assassinated) Bobby Kennedy stressed that

> We will find neither national purpose nor personal satisfaction in a mere continuation of economic progress, in an endless amassing of worldly goods. . . . The gross national product includes the destruction of the redwoods and the death of Lake Superior.[14]

By the first Earth Day, April 22, 1970, young Americans were questioning the impact of the consumer lifestyle on the planet itself. Leading environmentalists, like David Brower, founder of Friends of the Earth, were warning that the American Dream of endless growth was not sustainable.

Then, in 1974, a nationwide oil shortage caused many people to wonder if we might run out of resources. Energy companies responded as they still do today, by calling for more drilling. "Rather than foster conservation," writes historian Gary Cross, "President Gerald Ford supported business demands for more nuclear power plants, offshore oil drilling, gas leases and drilling on federal lands," as well as "the relaxation of clean air standards."[15]

CARTER'S LAST STAND

But Ford's successor Jimmy Carter disagreed, promoting conservation and alternative energy sources. Carter went so far as to question the American dream in his famous "national malaise" speech of 1979. "Too many of us now tend to worship self-indulgence and consumption," Carter declared. It was the last courageous stand any American President ever made against the spread of affluenza.

And it helped bring about Carter's defeat a year later. "Part of Jimmy Carter's failure," says historian David Shi, "was his lack of recognition of how deeply seated the high, wide, and handsome notion of economic growth and capital development had become in the modern American psyche."[16]

The Age of Affluenza had begun.

CHAPTER 19

The age of affluenza

Advertising separates our era from all earlier ones as little else does.

—CONSERVATIVE ECONOMIST
WILHELM ROPKE

Any space you take in visually, anything you hear, in the future will be branded.

—REGINA KELLY,
DIRECTOR OF STRATEGIC PLANNING,
SATCHI AND SATCHI ADVERTISING

I t's morning in America," announced the TV commercials for Ronald Reagan, whose message that Americans could have their cake and eat it too overwhelmed the cautious conservationist Jimmy Carter. And indeed, it was morning, the dawning, you might say, of the Age of Affluenza. Despite economic ups and downs, the last twenty years of the twentieth century would witness a commercial expansion unparalleled in history. Those Reagan commercials, small towns and smiling people in golden light, seem quaint now, more like the sunset of an old era than the morning of a new one. For one thing, there are no ads to be seen anywhere in the America pictured in those political commercials, no billboards, no product being sold except Reagan. That's not America anymore.

Reagan's decade may have been that of supply-side economics, but it was also the decade of demand creation. Yuppies were made, not born. "Greed is good," chirruped Wall Street's Ivan Boesky. The message of Reagan's first inaugural ball and

Nancy's $15,000 dress was clear: It's cool to consume and flaunt it. The tone of '80s advertising echoed the sentiment: "Treat Yourself, You *Deserve* a Break Today, You're Worth It." Look out for Number One.

Since 1980, few industries have grown as fast as advertising. Its importance is underscored by a little-known fact: Madison Avenue real estate is now the priciest on the planet. A mere ten square feet of space there—smaller than the size of a single bed—now rents for an astonishing $6500 a year!

ADFLUENZA

That advertising's prime purpose is to promote affluenza is hardly a secret, as even its prime proponents have frequently stated in different words. As Pierre Martineau, marketing director for the *Chicago Tribune,* put it back in 1957, "Advertising's most important social function is to integrate the individual into our present-day American high-speed consumption economy."[1] "The average individual doesn't make anything," wrote Martineau in his classic text *Motivation in Advertising.* "He buys everything, and our economy is geared to the faster and faster tempo of his buying, *based on wants which are created by advertising in large degree.*" This was no critic of advertising expressing himself, but one of its most prominent practicioners.

"Our American level of living is the highest of any people in the world," Martineau went on to say, "because our standard of living is the highest, meaning that our wants are the highest. In spite of those intellectuals who deplore the restlessness and the dissatisfaction in the wake of those new wants created by advertising and who actually therefore propose to restrict the process, it must be clear that the well-being of our entire system depends on how much motivation is supplied the consumer to make him continue wanting." Were Pierre Martineau still alive, he would doubtless be proud to see how much motivation is now supplied to keep consumers "wanting."

If, as the old saying goes, "a man's home is his castle," then Madison Avenue has battering rams galore. Two-thirds of the space in our newspapers is now devoted to advertising. Nearly half the mail we receive is selling something.

THE HIGH COST OF MOTIVATION

You could call it Couch Potato Blight. The average American will spend nearly two years of his or her lifetime watching TV commercials.[2] A child may see a million of them before he or she reaches the age of twenty. There is more time devoted to them now—the average half-hour of commercial TV now has eight minutes of commercials, up from six two decades ago. And there are more of them—faster editing (to beat the remote control clicker) and the increasing cost of commercial time has shortened the length of the average ad.

They are phenomenally expensive: a typical 30-second national TV commercial now costs nearly $300,000 to produce—that's $10,000 per second! By contrast, production costs for an entire hour of prime-time public television are about the same—$300,000, or $83 a second. Commercial network programming is somewhat more expensive, but can't hold a candle to the cost of the ads. Is it any wonder that some people say they're the best thing on TV?

Moreover, it costs companies hundreds of thousands of dollars every time their ads are broadcast during national prime-time programming. In fact, thirty-second slots during the Superbowl sold for as much as $2.4 million each. TV advertising, the prime carrier of the affluenza virus, is now a $200 billion a year industry and growing at a rate of 7.6 percent annually, more than twice the average rate of the economy as a whole.[3]

It's paying off. When NPR's Scott Simon asked teenagers at a Maryland Mall what they were buying, they ran off a list of brand names: Donna Karan, Calvin Klein, Tommy Hilfiger, American Eagle. A recent study showed that while the average American can identify fewer than ten types of plants, he or she recognizes hundreds of corporate logos.

WELCOME TO LOGOTOPIA

In the effort to create demand, marketers now seek to place commercial messages everywhere. Today, outdoor advertising is a $5-billion-a-year industry (and growing at a rate of ten percent a year), with more than a billion spent on billboards alone. "Outdoor advertising is red-hot right now," says Brad Johnson in *Advertising Age.* "There's a shortage of space available."[4]

Thirty-five years after Lady Bird Johnson's Beautify America Campaign, our landscape is filled with more billboards than ever. Ad critic Laurie Mazur calls them "litter on a stick." "From a marketers perspective, billboards are perfect," says Mazur. "You can't turn them off. You can't click them with remote control."[5]

Mazur points out that marketers themselves say the ad environment has become "cluttered," so smart sellers look for ever-new places to put ads. Schools, as discussed in the chapter "Dilated Pupils," are one target, reached in a myriad of ways, including corporate logos in math text books: "If Joe has thirty Oreo™ cookies and eats fifteen how many does he have left?" Of course there's a big picture of Oreos on the page. The publisher might want to add another question: How many cavities does Joe have?

Hollywood films now offer sliding scales for product placements, as Mazur points out: "$10,000 to have the product appear in the film, $30,000 to have a character hold the product. In *Other People's Money,* Danny De Vito holds a box of donuts, looks into the camera and says, 'If I can't depend on Dunkin' Donuts, who can I depend on?'"[6]

"Advertising is just permeating every corner of our society," says Michael Jacobson, co-author with Mazur of *Marketing Madness*. "When you're watching a sports event, you see ads in the stadium. You see athletes wearing logos. You see ads in public restrooms. Some police cars now have ads. There are ads in holes on golf courses. And there are thousands of people who are trying to think of one more place to put an ad where nobody has yet put the ad."[7]

Daniel Schifrin has found such a place. He started a Silicon Valley company called Autowraps. Drivers make their cars available as rolling billboards, sporting advertising logos. Schifrin pays their owners $400 a month, but tracks them by satellite to make sure they drive to the sorts of places where target audiences will see the ads. They are required to drive at least 1,000 miles a month.[8] Hucksters, start your engines.

THE MARKETER'S MOON

The extreme idea for advertising placement, says Michael Jacobson, "is the billboard that was proposed for outer space that would project logos about the size of the moon that would be visible to practically everyone on earth."[9]

When the moon fills the sky like a big pizza pie, it's—Domino's! Imagine a romantic walk at night in the light of the full—logo.

For now, the idea of logos in outer space is still a marketer's pipe dream, but, says Jacobson, "what is the limit? Maybe outer space, but down here on earth we're willing to accept just about everything."

DOT-COMMUNISM

By far the biggest expansion of commercialism in the Age of Affluenza is occurring on the Internet. Billboards are popping up like mushrooms on the information highway. What was hailed as an educator's Eden has become a seller's paradise instead, as e-commerce attracts billions of investment and advertising dollars.

In 1848, Karl Marx wrote, "A specter is haunting Europe—the specter of communism." Today, he could have written the "Dot-Communist Manifesto" instead. From the 1950s until the 1980s, Americans were worried about communism. Now we ought to be worried about dot-communism. There may not be any communists under our beds but there are lots of dot-communists in our computers. Dot-communism is ubiquitous, freely advertising itself even on public channels. Listen to *All Things Considered* on NPR. Count the number of thinly veiled commercials—euphemistically called "underwriting spots"—each hour that are for dot-coms.
That grating voice that keeps reciting over and over again such messages as, "On the Web at smartmoney.com." And then they ask you to send in pledges.

You may be old enough to remember the artwork in news magazines or government propaganda films: A red blob—communism—spreads out from Russia, covering Eastern Europe, then China, then Korea and Vietnam, threatening to engulf the world. Today, dot-communism threatens to engulf the World Wide Web. In 1993, only one percent of Web sites were commercial dot-coms. Today, the percentage is near eighty and still growing. Communist tanks never came close to our National Defense Interstate Highway System (that's what it was called), but dot-communists control the Information Highway.

Dot-communism threatens our privacy in ways the KGB could only have dreamed of, recording our tastes, consumer behavior, and hidden proclivities, collecting information about our families from our children without our permission. Remember how the communists were going to destroy the businesses in our towns? They didn't, but dot-communists might (led by DotComGuy, dot-communism's answer to Che Guevara). Consider your little local bookstore. Can it fend off an Amazon? Where is Joe McCarthy now that we really need him? Where is the John Birch Society now that we need it?

HYPERCOMMERCIALISM

Our hypercommercial era is one in which images are everywhere and "image," as tennis star Andre Agassi says in the sunglasses commercial, "is everything." The daily bombardment of advertising images leaves us forever dissatisfied with our own appearances and those of our real-life partners. "Advertising encourages us to meet nonmaterial needs through material ends," says Laurie Mazur. "It tells us to buy their product because we'll be loved, we'll be accepted, and also it tells us that we are not loveable and acceptable without buying their product."[10] To be loveable and acceptable is to have the image. Authenticity be damned.

We live in what Susan Faludi calls an "ornamental culture," which "encourages people to play almost no functional public roles, only decorative and consumer ones." "Constructed around celebrity and image, glamour and entertainment, marketing and consumerism," writes Faludi, ornamental culture "is a ceremonial gateway to nowhere. Its essence is not just the selling act but the selling of self, and in this quest every man is essentially on his own, a lone sales rep marketing his own image."[11]

Back in 1958, a prominent conservative economist and staunch defender of the free enterprise system warned that the twentieth century might well end up being known as "the Age of Advertising." Wilhelm Ropke feared that if commercialism were "allowed to predominate and to sway society in all its spheres," the results would be disastrous in many ways. As the cult of selling grows in importance, Ropke wrote, "every gesture of courtesy, kindness and neighborliness is degraded into a move behind which we suspect ulterior motives."[12] A culture of mutual distrust arises.

"The curse of commercialization is that it results in the standards of the market spreading into regions which should remain beyond supply and demand," Ropke added. "This vitiates the true purposes, dignity and savor of life and thereby makes it unbearably ugly, undignified and dull. Think of Mother's Day. The most tender and sacred human relationship is turned into a means of sales promotion by advertising experts and made to turn the wheels of business."

Only by limiting the scope of its reach, claimed Ropke, could the free market system be expected to continue to serve the greater good. Extreme commercialization, the very sine qua non of our era, would, if not kept in check, "destroy the free economy by the blind exaggeration of its principle."

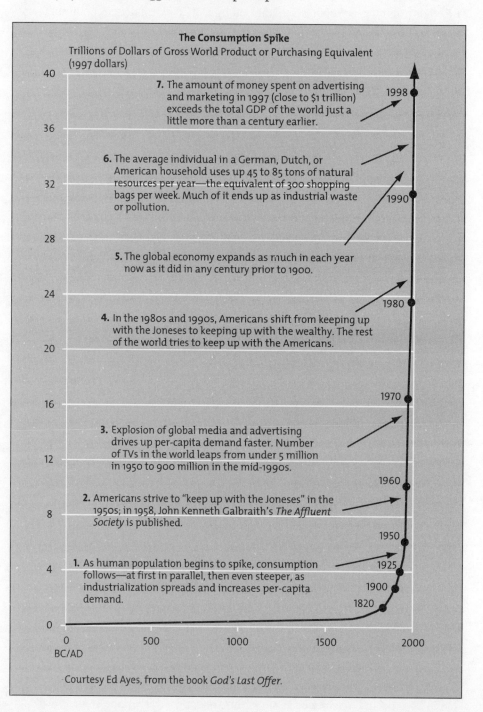

The Consumption Spike
Trillions of Dollars of Gross World Product or Purchasing Equivalent (1997 dollars)

7. The amount of money spent on advertising and marketing in 1997 (close to $1 trillion) exceeds the total GDP of the world just a little more than a century earlier.

6. The average individual in a German, Dutch, or American household uses up 45 to 85 tons of natural resources per year—the equivalent of 300 shopping bags per week. Much of it ends up as industrial waste or pollution.

5. The global economy expands as much in each year now as it did in any century prior to 1900.

4. In the 1980s and 1990s, Americans shift from keeping up with the Joneses to keeping up with the wealthy. The rest of the world tries to keep up with the Americans.

3. Explosion of global media and advertising drives up per-capita demand faster. Number of TVs in the world leaps from under 5 million in 1950 to 900 million in the mid-1990s.

2. Americans strive to "keep up with the Joneses" in the 1950s; in 1958, John Kenneth Galbraith's *The Affluent Society* is published.

1. As human population begins to spike, consumption follows—at first in parallel, then even steeper, as industrialization spreads and increases per-capita demand.

Courtesy Ed Ayes, from the book *God's Last Offer*.

CHAPTER 20

Is there a (real) doctor in the house?

> We have transformed information into a form of garbage.
>
> —NEIL POSTMAN

> In the public relations industry, the idea is to manage the outrage, not the hazard.
>
> —SHARON BEDER, GLOBAL SPIN

What happens when we ignore the symptoms of a disease? It usually gets worse. That's why affluenza is spreading around the planet. Although symptoms like the stress of excess, resource exhaustion, and social scars are right in our faces, we tend to look the other way—told over and over again that the market will provide. But will it?

Author and "adbuster" Kalle Lasn tells a tale about a large wedding party that takes place in a spacious suburban backyard. The party oozes affluence and "the good life": the live music is great, and everyone dances with abandon. The problem is that they're dancing on top of an old septic system, which causes the pipes to burst. "Raw sewage rises up through the grass," writes Lasn, "and begins to cover everyone's shoes. If anyone notices, they don't say anything. The champagne flows, the music continues, until finally a little boy says, 'It smells like shit!' And suddenly everyone realizes they're ankle deep in it."[1]

155

How many million Americans are now wheezing with affluenza, yet stubbornly in denial? "Those who have clued in apparently figure it's best to ignore the shit and just keep dancing," concludes Lasn. Meanwhile, the companies liable for the damages admit the pipes have cracked, but try to convince us there's nothing to worry about.

According to some trend watchers, at least forty million Americans are ready for recovery programs to beat affluenza. But where can we turn for the advice we'll need? There seem to be as many quacks and spin doctors out there as real doctors. With a strict policy of concealing their funding sources (as well as their planets of origin), the quack scientists do their best to make the world "safe from democracy." The first step is to encourage us to do nothing, just keep ignoring the symptoms. They tell us in voices that sound self-assured, "Go back to sleep, the facts are still uncertain, everything's fine. Technology will provide, just relax and enjoy yourself."

"TOXIC SLUDGE IS GOOD FOR YOU"

We all know how pervasive advertising is, because it's right in our faces. In fact, *we* pick up the tab for advertising, in the products we buy—at least $600 a year per capita. But as John Stauber, coauthor of *Toxic Sludge Is Good for You,* comments, "Few people really understand the other dimension of marketing—an undercover public relations industry that creates and perpetuates our commercial culture."[2] (In other words, our affluenza). What is PR, exactly? According to Stauber, it's covert culture shaping and opinion spinning. Not only do PR professionals alter our perceptions, they also finesse the political and cultural influence that ushers those perceptions into the mainstream. Unreported by the blindfolded eyes of the media, PR-managed initiatives are often signed into law and adopted as standard operating procedures while the public's civic attention is diverted by the most current scandal, crime, or catastrophe.

"The best PR is never noticed" is an unwritten slogan of an industry whose arsenal includes backroom politics, fake grassroots activism, organized censorship, and imitation news. The weapon of choice is a kind of stun gun that fires invisible bullets of disinformation. You can't remember how you formed a certain opinion or belief, but you find yourself willing to fight for it. For example, a popular corporate strategy staged by contracted PR firms is to form citizen advisory panels. This technique makes people feel included, rather than polluted. Citizens are carefully chosen to attend catered lunches around the corporate conference table, to discuss community issues.

Predictably, familiarity can breed content. One community advisory panel was content to approve a new waste incinerator and defend it vocally at a local hearing.

"You can't buy that kind of help at any price," comments Joel Makower, editor of *The Green Business Letter*.[3]

Similarly, on the advice of contracted PR experts, many corporations now fund and sponsor the very environmental groups that have dogged them for years. This "absorb the enemy" tactic accomplishes several things at once. It gives the company a buffed-up, green-washed image, and it distracts the environmental opponent/partner. Said one corporate partner, "We keep them so busy they don't have time to sue us."

"Another basic tactic is what I call book burning," says Stauber. "PR firms are hired to cast dark shadows on certain books. They often obtain book tour itineraries from inside sources and use a variety of tactics to sabotage the tours." For example, Jeremy Rifkin's tour for *Beyond Beef*, a critique of the meat industry, was derailed by fake phone calls, allegedly from the author's publicist, canceling each speaking appearance.

HOW MONEY TALKS

One of the most effective PR tactics is to fund "front groups" and give them very friendly, responsible-sounding names, like the American Council on Science and Health, whose experts defend petrochemical companies, the nutritional value of fast foods, and pesticides. The mission of front groups is to supply the "right" information on a product or industry, and debunk the "wrong" information. Writes Sharon Beder in *Global Spin*,

> The American Council on Science and Health is funded by Burger King, Coca-Cola, NutraSweet, Monsanto, Dow, and Exxon, among others. As in other front groups, the organization's scientists pose as independent experts to promote the corporate causes. The group's members portray themselves as moderates, often using words like 'reasonable,' 'sensible,' and 'sound.' They downplay the dangers of environmental problems while emphasizing the costs of solving them.[4]

Front groups are staunch defenders of the rights of Americans, such as the right to smoke (The National Smokers Alliance); the right to have employee accidents (Workplace Health and Safety Council, an employer organization that lobbies for the weakening of safety standards); the right to pay more for less health care (the Coalition for Health Insurance Choices); the right to choose large, fuel-inefficient cars (the Coalition for Vehicle Choice); and the right to dismantle ecosystems for profit (the Wise Use Movement). Front groups portray themselves as champions of free enterprise—strongholds of fairness and common sense—an image that helps

their PR products get circulated in influential circles. John Stauber, a director of
the organization PRWatch, first became involved in watchdogging the public relations industry when he was researching biotechnology through internal documents
and interviews with industry insiders. "We saw strong evidence of collusion
between Monsanto, a manufacturer of biotech products, and various government
agencies and professional organizations," he said. "The *Journal of the American
Medical Association* urged doctors to wave the flag for genetic engineering, and
pump up the new industry. Government agencies like the FDA and USDA did their
part by working with Monsanto to overcome farmer and consumer opposition to
the emerging products. Government agencies are supposed to be watchdogs, but
too often they are more like lap dogs."[6]

INVASION OF THE MIND-SNATCHERS

In effect, America's PR professionals create stage sets in which the rest of us play-
act our lives. Like Truman in the movie *The Truman Show*, we've never doubted
that the sets are real. Corporations alone contract fifteen to twenty billion dollars
in PR campaigns annually—campaigns that create consumer culture, buy political
agendas, and "spin" scientific opinion. As the average, underpaid journalist knows,

public relations—not journalism—is the profession to be in if you want to live in one of "those" neighborhoods. "Journalism students—even at the best colleges and universities—are more likely to graduate and work in PR and business communications than as journalists," says Stauber. "The schools combine PR and journalism classes as if they were one and the same." Fact is, the kids are going where the money is.

The PR industry cut its teeth in the 1920s on campaigns that promoted tobacco and leaded gasoline—products whose health effects badly needed to be swept under the carpet. Mark Dowie describes a classic perception coup executed by PR pioneer Edward Bernays in 1929: "On the surface it seemed like an ordinary publicity stunt for 'female emancipation.' A contingent of New York debutantes marched down Fifth Avenue in the 1929 Easter Parade, each openly lighting and smoking cigarettes, their so-called 'torches of liberty.' It was the first time in the memory of most Americans that any woman who wasn't a prostitute had been seen smoking in public."[7]

Bernays made sure publicity photos of the models appeared in worldwide press, and the tobacco industry quickly added sex appeal to its glorious if deadly parade through the twentieth century. Responding to the "1954 Emergency"—involving medical disclosures on the hazards of smoking—the tobacco industry hired PR firm Hill & Knowlton to launch a smoke-and-mirrors campaign to meet the enemy head-on. Among many other tactics, the firm combed 2,500 medical journals for any inconclusive or contrary findings about tobacco's health effects, and then showcased these gleanings-of-doubt in a booklet sent to over 200,000 doctors, members of Congress, and news professionals.[8] Tactics like these became standard procedures of the PR industry. "In a world of manufactured reality, the *perception* of a hazardous product or accident is what needs to be managed, not the hazard itself,"[9] explains author Sharon Beder.

GETTING THE LEAD IN

A similar tactic was used in the 1920s to promote leaded gasoline (ethyl). The mission was to boost both automobile performance and the profits of General Motors, DuPont, and Standard Oil. These allies soothed and massaged the American public's justified fear of leaded gasoline by performing health effects research in-house, with precedent-setting approval from the federal government. Word from the corporate labs was "no problem," even as factory workers making ethyl were dying by the dozen. A 1927 ad in *National Geographic* urged, "Ride with Ethyl in a high-compression motor and get the thrill of a lifetime." The overt message was "Don't let others pass you by," but the hidden tag line was ". . . even if it kills you."[10]

FLASHFLOODS OF INFORMATION

There's no shortage of information in America. Search for just about any keyword on the Internet and the cyber-hounds will retrieve gigabytes of "matches" of all shapes and flavors. It's true that a search for "art depicting the Madonna" may yield a colorful, profanity-spiked quote from a pop singer/actress by the same name—but hey, isn't that information too? Every day, on average, Americans dodge 3,000 commercial messages, each of them shouting louder or purring more seductively than the last. Soundbites, fun facts, and bad-news nuggets also compete for our attention, along with the million words a week some of us now process at work. Getting just the information we need is like trying to take a sip of water from a firehose.

Even more disturbing than the flood of information is its *quality*. We try to base intelligent civic, family, and marketplace decisions on vested-interest information. No wonder we can't shake our affluenza—the economy is programmed for sickness. Drug companies teach us how to overcome depression, and pesticide companies tell farmers how much pesticide to use. In the mania of media, good news is no news because it doesn't "work" on TV. The quality of our information is spiked throughout all sectors of our society, but we're forced to drink it anyway because it's the only information we can get.

"GREENING THE EARTH WITH GLOBAL WARMING"

If the true facts about global warming are thought of as the flow of a mighty river, the average American ends up with only a cupful. The complexity of global warming makes a third of the information unavailable even to scientists, who tell us they don't know enough yet about relationships among oceans, biomass, and atmospheric physics. They do know without any doubt that CO_2 levels have already increased by about thirty percent since the Industrial Revolution began, and that the decade from 1990 to 2000 was the warmest on record. They've known for a hundred years that a blanket of greenhouse gases like CO_2 can warm the planet the same way a car with rolled-up windows overheats in a parking lot.

However, PR firms and the PR/environmental offices of oil, mining, and automobile companies have a different story to tell—a story that sends a large portion of the information flow into a calculated whirlpool. Their mission is to craft "customized" information to create doubt, confuse the public, and protect the client's profits. Scientists are found whose skeptical views support the fossil-fuel industry. These "third-party experts" have an appearance of objectivity that sometimes fades when the scientists reveal, under oath, that their research funding comes from utilities and fossil-fuel consortiums. Even if the earth *is* warming, they maintain, it

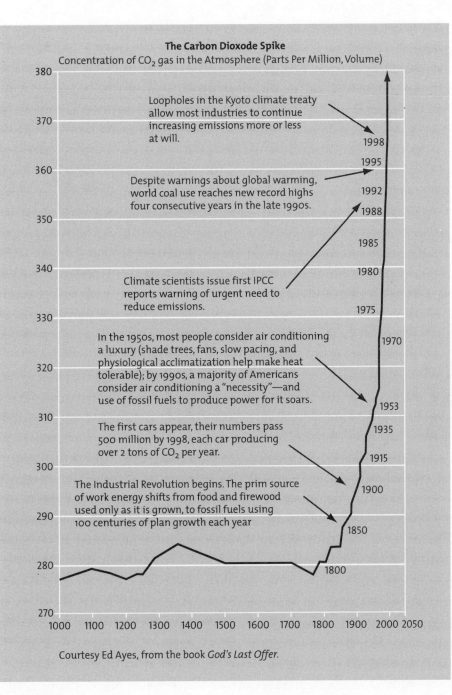

The Carbon Dioxode Spike

Concentration of CO_2 gas in the Atmosphere (Parts Per Million, Volume)

Loopholes in the Kyoto climate treaty allow most industries to continue increasing emissions more or less at will.

Despite warnings about global warming, world coal use reaches new record highs four consecutive years in the late 1990s.

Climate scientists issue first IPCC reports warning of urgent need to reduce emissions.

In the 1950s, most people consider air conditioning a luxury (shade trees, fans, slow pacing, and physiological acclimatization help make heat tolerable); by 1990s, a majority of Americans consider air conditioning a "necessity"—and use of fossil fuels to produce power for it soars.

The first cars appear, their numbers pass 500 million by 1998, each car producing over 2 tons of CO_2 per year.

The Industrial Revolution begins. The prim source of work energy shifts from food and firewood used only as it is grown, to fossil fuels using 100 centuries of plan growth each year

Courtesy Ed Ayes, from the book *God's Last Offer*.

could be a natural occurrence. In a recent Front Line/ Nova program, *What's Up With the Weather?* one fossil-fueled scientist summarized his stance on global warming: "Americans are moving to the Sun Belt by the millions," he said, "which proves we like warm climates." The question is, do we also like the spread of tropical diseases, drought, hurricanes, and economic disruption, and a rising sea level?

A video titled *Greening the Planet Earth* exposed many a congressional staff office to fantasy-science. Produced by the Greening Earth Society, the industry-funded program begins with dramatic narration: "The year 2085. The atmospheric level of carbon dioxide has doubled to 540 parts per million. What kind of world have we created?"

"A better world," answers a corporate-funded scientist. "A more productive world. Plants are the basis for all productivity on earth. . . . And they're going to be much more effective, much more efficient when the Earth is warmer"[11] (Never mind that 2,000 of the world's most eminent scientists signed a statement saying global warming will be a catastrophe, and that a 2000 UN report projected a temperature rise of up to ten degrees Fahrenheit by 2100). With pseudoscience like that of the Greening Earth Society in hand, fossil-fueled politicians are equipped to create happy-face scenarios about abundant cotton fields and prolific citrus trees. Who knows, maybe ferns three stories tall, and someday, the reappearance of dinosaurs—wouldn't that be cool?

GOOD NEWS IS NO NEWS

Journalists simultaneously supply and divert the information stream. Depending on a journalist's sources and biases, we may come away from a newspaper article knowing less than when we started (but thanks to the adjacent ads, we'll know where brassieres are on sale)! On perpetual deadline, and with a mandate for objectivity as well as controversy, journalists present both fabricated science-for-sale and its exaggerated, Chicken Little opposite. Effectively, they stage a "media clash of the titans." (Which expert will *you* root for, the kept professor or the chicken?)

Marching orders for the news media come from one of the half-dozen or so remaining media conglomerates—including AOL/Time Warner, Viacom, Disney, GE, and TCI—whose CEOs dictate what's newsworthy and what's not (when you're Rupert Murdoch, you buy newspaper companies like the rest of us buy newspapers). As recently as the 1980s, fifty corporations still had a slice of the media pie, but that elite clan has now shrunk to an incestuous handful that invest in each other's companies, are fattened by the same group of mega-advertisers, and get in-the-field reports from the same large wire services. Alarmingly, these companies are now pushing for the privatization—as opposed to licensing—of the airwaves. When these invisible yet very tangible wavelengths are controlled by a few multibillionaires, George Orwell's *1984* prophecies will be nearly complete: "The special function of certain Newspeak words . . . was not so much to express meanings as to destroy them."[12]

Because journalists are usually short on time, they are tempted to interview and quote experts conveniently supplied by PR firms through services like ProfNet. PR shadow-journalists also supply press releases, video news releases, and radio scripts by the thousands. One company, PR Newswire, pumps out 100,000 news releases every year for 15,000 private clients. RadioUSA supplies broadcast-quality scripts to 5,000 radio stations, and MediaLink distributes more than 5,000 "video news releases" to TV stations every year, ready to be aired as is, free of charge.[13]

According to the former managing editors of the *Washington Post*, the *New York Times*, and the *Wall Street Journal*, at least forty percent of the news in those papers is generated by "spin doctor" PR journalists.[14] Because newspaper, magazine, and Internet writers must also compress their stories into a given number of inches, they have little room for context and complexity. The same is true of TV news, sandwiched between the commercials and crime reporting that now make up a third of network news content. In 1968, the average interview soundbite was forty-two seconds; in 2000, the standard is eight seconds. Instead of political process, we get isolated events. Instead of context, we get vignettes about novelty and conflict. Information about change and reform takes too long to explain, so we are fed high-speed chases and newborn zoo animals instead. The goal is to keep us watching, not to keep us informed.

After journalists "dumb down" and abbreviate the remnants of the information stream, deep-pocketed advertisers divert more of the flow, often exerting enough pressure on editors to mop up a story altogether. Some advertisers issue policy statements to editors and news directors, requesting advance notice on stories that may put their products in an unfavorable light. Phone calls from CEOs of advertiser companies are like delete buttons on editors' computers: There goes a story from the front page of tomorrow's paper, or the six o'clock news.

By the time the truth about global warming reaches the American citizen, it's been siphoned and filtered down to a trickle of questionable pop science.

DELAYED, DISCOUNTED AND DILUTED FEEDBACK

Scientists like Donella Meadows argue that we need to be sensitive to scientific signals—"feedback"—or we risk crashing our civilization into a brick wall. She compares our world to a speeding automobile on a slippery road. "The driver goes too fast for the brakes to work in time."[15]

At the scale of an entire society in overdrive, she observes that "decision makers in the system do not get, or believe, or act upon information that limits have been exceeded." Part of our dilemma is from insufficient feedback: We don't even realize that caution is necessary. Another part of the problem is the speed we're travelling: Our "pedal to the metal" economy is based on beliefs that resource supplies are limitless and that the Earth can continually bounce back from abuse. These beliefs are in part scripted by public relations and advertising experts, just doing their jobs. What the heck, no harm done, right? Not exactly. Because of low-quality, incomplete information, we may be overlooking an obvious, and ominous, concept: The car will still achieve racecar speeds as always, even if the tank is almost empty.

PART THREE

Treatment

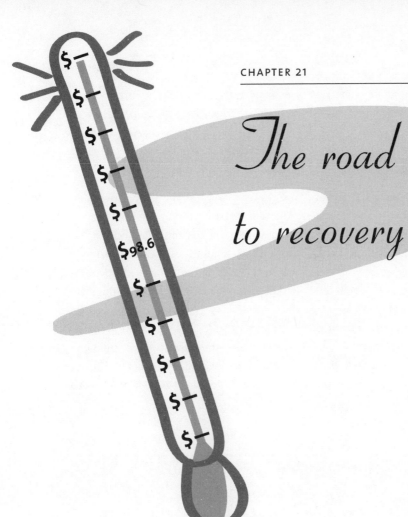

CHAPTER 21

The road to recovery

This situation imagined by *Affluenza* coproducer Vivia Boe has not occurred. Not yet.

*Y*ou're watching TV, in the middle of a program, when the screen goes black for a moment. The scene cuts to a breaking news story. A large crowd is gathered outside an expensive home with some equally pricey cars parked out front. A well-dressed family of four stands on the stairs, looking grim. One of the children is holding a white flag. The reporter, in hushed tones speaks into his microphone: "We're here live at the home of the Joneses—Jerry and Janet Jones—the family we've all been trying to keep up with for years. Well you can stop trying right now, because they have surrendered. Let's eavesdrop for a moment." The shot changes, revealing a tired-looking Janet Jones, her husband's hand resting on her shoulder. Her voice cracks as she speaks: "It's just not worth it.

We never see each other anymore. We're working like dogs. We're always worried about our kids, and we have so much debt we won't be able to pay it off for years. We give up. So please, stop trying to keep up with us." From the crowd our reporter yells, "So what will you do now?" "We're just going to try to live better on less," Janet replies. "So there you have it. The Joneses surrender," says the reporter. "And now for a commercial break."

The Joneses haven't really surrendered. Not yet. But millions of Americans are looking for ways to simplify their lives. And in the rest of this book, you'll learn about some of the ways they've tried, and how they are coming together to help create a more sustainable society, free from the clutches of affluenza. We suggest that you start by taking our "affluenza self-test," an admittedly unscientific, but we think useful, means of determining whether or not you've actually got affluenza, and if so, how serious your case is.

OK, now the moment of truth. In the privacy of your own home, without anyone looking over your shoulder, take the following diagnostic quiz, to see if you have affluenza, or are susceptible to it. If you have it, reader, you're not alone! There's help available in this part of the book, so read on. If you don't have it, read on anyway to stay healthy.

AFFLUENZA SELF-DIAGNOSIS TEST

YES NO

❏ ❏ 1. Do you get bored unless you have something to consume (goods, food, media)?

❏ ❏ 2. Do you try to impress your friends with what you own, or where you vacation?

❏ ❏ 3. Do you ever use shopping as "therapy"?

❏ ❏ 4. Do you sometimes go to the mall just to look around, with nothing specific to buy?

❏ ❏ 5. Do you buy home improvement products in a large chain store rather than the neighborhood hardware store?

❏ ❏ 6. Have you ever gone on a vacation primarily to shop?

YES NO

❏ ❏ 7. In general, do you think about things more than you think about people?

❏ ❏ 8. When you pay utility bills, do you ignore the amount of resource consumed?

❏ ❏ 9. Given the choice between a slight pay raise and a shorter workweek, would you choose the money?

❏ ❏ 10. Do you personally fill more than one large trash bag in a single week?

❏ ❏ 11. Have you ever lied to a family member about the amount you spent for a product?

❏ ❏ 12. Do you frequently argue with family members about money?

YES NO

❏ ❏ 13. Do you volunteer your time less than five hours a week to help other people?

❏ ❏ 14. Do you routinely compare the appearance of your lawn and/ or home with others in your neighborhood?

❏ ❏ 15. Does each person in your house or apartment occupy more than 500 square feet of personal space?

❏ ❏ 16. Do you routinely gamble or buy lottery tickets?

❏ ❏ 17. Do you check your investments at least once a day?

❏ ❏ 18. Are any of your credit cards "maxed out"?

❏ ❏ 19. Do worries about debt cause you physical symptoms like headaches or indigestion?

❏ ❏ 20. Do you spend more time shopping every week than you do with your family?

❏ ❏ 21. Do you frequently think about changing jobs?

❏ ❏ 22. Have you had cosmetic surgery to improve your appearance?

❏ ❏ 23. Do your conversations often gravitate toward things you want to buy?

❏ ❏ 24. Are you sometimes ashamed about how much money you spend on fast food?

❏ ❏ 25. Do you sometimes weave back and forth in traffic to get somewhere faster?

❏ ❏ 26. Have you ever experienced road rage?

❏ ❏ 27. Do you feel like you're always in a hurry?

YES NO

❏ ❏ 28. Do you often throw away recyclable materials rather than take the time to recycle them?

❏ ❏ 29. Do you spend less than an hour a day outside?

❏ ❏ 30. Are you *unable* to identify more than three wildflowers that are native to your area?

❏ ❏ 31. Do you replace sports equipment before it's worn out to have the latest styles?

❏ ❏ 32. Does each member of your family have his/her own TV?

❏ ❏ 33. Is the price of a product more important to you than how well it was made?

❏ ❏ 34. Has one of your credit cards ever been rejected by a salesperson because you were over the limit?

❏ ❏ 35. Do you receive more than five mail-order catalogs a week?

❏ ❏ 36. Are you one of those consumers who almost never takes a reusable bag to the grocery store?

❏ ❏ 37. Do you ignore the miles per gallon of gasoline your car gets?

❏ ❏ 38. Did you choose the most recent car you bought partly because it enhanced your self-image?

❏ ❏ 39. Do you have more than five active credit cards?

❏ ❏ 40. When you get a raise at work, do you immediately think about how you can spend it?

❏ ❏ 41. Do you drink more soft drink, by volume, than tap water?

❏ ❏ 42. Did you work more this year than last year?

YES	NO		YES	NO	
☐	☐	43. Do you have doubts that you'll be able to reach your financial goals?	☐	☐	47. Do you sometimes feel like your personal expenses are so demanding that you can't afford public expenses like schools, parks, and transit?
☐	☐	44. Do you feel "used-up" at the end of your workday?	☐	☐	48. Do you have more stuff than you can store in your house?
☐	☐	45. Do you usually make just the minimum payment on credit card bills?	☐	☐	49. Do you watch TV more than 2 hours a day?
☐	☐	46. When you shop, do you often feel a rush of euphoria followed by anxiety?	☐	☐	50. Do you eat meat nearly every day?

SCORING YOUR RESULTS (GULP!)

Each "yes" answer carries a weight of two points. If you're uncertain as to your answer, or it's too close to call, give yourself one point. If you score:

0 – 25   You have no serious signs of affluenza, but keep reading to stay healthy.

25 –50   You are already infected—keep reading to boost your immune system.

50 – 75   Your temperature is rising quickly. Take two aspirin and read the next chapters very carefully.

75 – 100 You've got affluenza big time! See the doctor, reread the whole book, and take appropriate actions immediately. You may be contagious. There's no time to lose!

PHOTO: FRANCINE STRICKWERDA

The Surrender of the Joneses

CHAPTER 22

Bed rest

Are you making a living or making a dying?

—JOE DOMINGUEZ

O.K. You've taken the affluenza self-test and you're admitting to your-self you've got a few of the symptoms, maybe more than a few. You sit back in your chair, wipe the sweat from your brow, cough a couple of times, sneeze mightily, and rummage around for a thermometer. You're wondering, "What do I do now?"

Remember what the doctor once told you when you had a bad case of the flu? "Go home and go to bed, take some aspirin and call me in the morning." (They don't want you to call them anymore in this age of HMOs, but that's a different issue.) Well, a case of affluenza calls for bed rest, too. We just define it a little differ-ently. But the point is the same: Stop what you're doing. Stop now. Cut back. Take stock. Give yourself a break.

FORCED TO REASSESS

Sometimes we have to hit bottom to do that. Fred Brown was once upwardly mobile, the personnel director of a large company. He was earning $100,000 a year. On the outside, it looked as if he had everything—a great job, a big home, and a beautiful family. But on the inside, Fred felt like a prisoner in golden handcuffs. He worked long hours and found little time for his wife and two daughters. Then his marriage broke up. His job was stressful: It was his responsibility to tell other employees they'd been laid off. Then he got a frightening phone call. His own job had been eliminated. "It's a different experience on the receiving end than on the giving end," he says, remembering that call.[1]

Though he was forced into involuntary simplicity, it wasn't the loss of income that hit Fred hardest. It was the loss of security, "letting go of what I thought I was supposed to do with myself." At first, Fred sought other opportunities in his field, but to find them, he'd have to move to another part of the country. He was suddenly forced to stop and take stock of his life, and the more he thought about it, the more he realized his work wasn't making him happy. "There came a point," he says, "when I realized I simply had to take the step off the cliff into the unknown."

In a stunning reversal of occupation and lifestyle, Fred went back to school and became a massage therapist. He now earns only about $20,000 a year and lives in a small apartment instead of the big house he once owned. But he is, he says, a much more contented man. And despite an eighty-percent drop in income, he manages to save a little money, and pay off debts he ran up when he was making five times as much! More importantly, he now has more free time and has renewed his relationship with his daughters. And he's doing work he finds intrinsically satisfying. "It turns out that for me living simply seems to be leading to more happiness. What a concept!" Fred says with a smile. "I'm thankful now that I was laid off, because I'm doing something that I love. It's what the Buddhists call 'right livelihood.' It feels to me like I've found my right livelihood."

ONE LIFE TO LIVE

Sometimes the shock that forces us to re-examine our lives is even more devastating than the loss of a job, as Evy McDonald found out. A feisty, cheerful woman, Evy was determined early on to make her mark. "My goal," she remembers, "was to become the youngest female hospital administrator in the country." By 1980, she was close to success. Promotions and pay raises were coming her way often, and so was a lavish life style. She bought a new house with each promotion, and a bigger car. "I talked about wanting to help people who were less fortunate than myself, but

I had seventy pairs of shoes and a hundred blouses. I had so much more than I needed."[2]

Then disaster struck. During an unusual bout of illness, Evy went to the doctor. Tests were done, and the doctor pronounced a grim verdict: Evy had a fatal disease—one from which there were no known survivors. She had, perhaps, only months to live. Stunned, she returned home, to find that the same day, her house had been broken into and practically everything she owned had been stolen. And she had no insurance. Suddenly, both sick and possessionless, Evy was confronted with questions about the meaning of her life.

"Who did I want to be when I died?" she asked herself. "And what I discovered was that I didn't want to have the most things. What I wanted my life to be about was understanding love, understanding service, and feeling whole and complete." Miraculously perhaps, Evy's disease went into remission and she recovered her strength and energy, though doctors have warned her the disease could always come back.

"And on my road to health," she says now, "I saw that I needed to integrate my life. I needed to become a whole person, and part of that was bringing my financial life, how I spent my money, what I did with it, into alignment with my values and life purpose." It was then that she met a couple whose ideas moved her so deeply she spent most of the next two decades working with them.

YOUR MONEY OR YOUR LIFE

Joe Dominguez was a former stockbroker, Vicki Robin a former actress. Believers in frugality and simple living, they taught others to get out of debt, save money, and work on saving the world. John got to know Joe Dominguez and had a chance to interview him less than a year before Dominguez died in 1997. By that time, Joe was a frail man, weak from fighting cancer for many years. But he had not lost any of the passion, moral courage, and biting sense of humor that had helped him influence the lives of thousands of people.

During one interview, Joe described the turnaround in his thinking that occurred while he was still a stock market analyst. "When I was on Wall Street," he said, "I saw that people who had more money were not necessarily happier and that they had just as many problems as the folks that lived in my ghetto neighborhood [in Harlem] where I grew up. So it began to dawn on me that money didn't buy happiness, a very simple finding."[3] Simple indeed, but mighty rare in the Age of Affluenza.

Dominguez tried frugality. He found he enjoyed life more and he found a way to save so much that he was able to retire at the age of thirty-one and live (very simply—when he died, he was living on $8,000 a year) on his interest. "A lot of people would ask me, 'How did you do it?'" Joe recalled. "How did you handle your finances so you're not an indentured slave like the rest of us?'"

So with his newfound time, he set out to teach other people how to cut their spending sharply. He soon met Vicki Robin, who became his partner for the rest of his life. Says Robin, "I found that I needed to learn how to fix things, and I became fascinated with living life directly and developing my skills and capacities and ingenuity, rather than just earning more money and throwing money at problems."[4]

Together, Dominguez and Robin resettled in Seattle, and went from conducting workshops in people's homes to producing an audiotape course that thousands of people ordered. "Then the publishing industry came to us to write a book," Joe remembered, "and the rest is history." The book, *Your Money or Your Life,* was published in 1992 and soon became a best seller that has now sold nearly a million copies. If the letters from readers that Joe and Vicki have received are to be believed, *Your Money or Your Life* has transformed countless lives.

Dominguez contrasted *Your Money or Your Life* with the plethora of financial self-help books on the market. "It's not about making a killing in the stock market. It's not about how to buy real estate with no money down or anything of that sort. It's just the opposite. It's about how to handle your existing paycheck in a much more intelligent way that creates savings instead of leading you deeper and deeper into debt. It's the stuff our grandparents knew, but we've forgotten or been taught to forget."

NINE STEPS TO FINANCIAL INTEGRITY

The book offers a nine-step "new frugality" program by which readers can get their financial feet back on the ground. When all steps are followed, many higher-income readers find that they can actually achieve "financial independence" in a decade or so, allowing them to devote their time to work they find more meaningful than their current jobs. But even lower-income readers have found they can cut their expenses sharply. "In fact, the steps will be most useful to low-income people," Dominguez told John, "because they're the ones who really need to know how to stretch a buck." Even following a few of the initial steps makes a big difference for many readers, who, on average, cut their spending by about twenty-five percent.

The initial steps include these four practices:

1. *Making peace with your past.* Calculate how much money you've earned in your life, and then what you have to show for it, your current net worth. You may be shocked at the total you've squandered, what we might call the toll of affluenza.

2. *Tracking your life energy* Calculate your real hourly income by adding hours spent in commuting and other work-related activities to your total workweek, and subtracting money spent on things needed for work (e.g. commuting, business clothing). Then keep track of every cent that comes into or goes out of your life. Your working time is an expenditure of your essential life energy. What are you getting for it and using it for?

3. *Tabulating all of your income and spending for one month.*

4. *Asking yourself whether you've received real fulfillment for the life energy you spent.* Joe and Vicki recommend plotting a "fulfillment curve," which rises as you spend for essential needs, then begins to fall as you spend on luxuries that aren't that important to you. The top of the curve is the point called "enough"— the point when you should stop spending and start saving.[5]

Doing these things means stopping your regular routine of activity to take stock. When you've got the flu, go to bed. When you're walking off the edge of a cliff, step back. When you've got affluenza, stop and think it over.

THE TIGHTWAD COUPLE

Since it was published in 1992, *Your Money or Your Life* has been translated into several other languages. The Dutch translation was done by Rob van Eeden and Hanneke van Veen, who are affectionately known in the Netherlands as "the tight-wad couple." Now, that is. "We spent a lot, bought everything we wanted," Hanneke remembers, "and after some years I started to feel empty. I did not want to live like that anymore. So I tried to convince Rob that another lifestyle, more simple, would be better."[6]

Rob, an environmental engineer whose computer scenarios showed that over-consumption was damaging Holland's ecology, agreed. They decided to see "how low they could go" in cutting back on consumption. But like Joe and Vicki, they found that small changes brought big savings without requiring enormous sacrifices in comfort and convenience. In time, they cut their spending by two-thirds while finding that the quality of their lives had actually improved. Now they talk about their transformation to appreciative audiences throughout the Netherlands. "We talk about the full closets of people, all the clutter in their lives and how they can reduce it," says Rob, "and everybody can relate to that."

THE NEW ROAD MAP FOUNDATION

Having written a best seller, Joe Dominguez and Vicki Robin could have put frugality on hold and cashed in on their success. But both had come to believe that our high-consumption lifestyle threatens the planet as well as ourselves. They were determined to continue the example they had set, and use their sudden new wealth to serve the common good. They decided that all profits from the book would go to a charity, the New Road Map Foundation, which supports projects that increase awareness of frugal lifestyles and the environment. Among simple-living devotees, their generosity is legendary.

Though she still lives on less than $10,000 a year, no one who knows Vicki Robin would ever consider her poor. Money can most certainly be a blessing, not a curse, she would argue. But most of all when it is used to make the world a better place.

DOWNSHIFTING

Of course, the "Your Money or Your Life" model isn't the only bed to rest in. Thousands of Americans have found other helpful ways to slow down, cut back, and reassess. They've taken personal steps to live better on less income. *U.S. News & World Report* correspondent Amy Saltzman calls them "downshifters." A 1995 poll found that eighty-six percent of them say they are "happier" as a result. Only nine percent report feeling worse.[7] People choosing to downshift can find tips for living more simply and less stressfully from dozens of journals and books, many of which are included in our bibliography. You can find others at your library or local bookstore. Web sites offer many more resources. Among the best are www.newdream.org (The Center for a New American Dream) and www.simpleliving.net (The Simple Living Network).

CHAPTER 23

Aspirin and chicken soup

"Study circles are beginning to develop,
newsletters, magazines, Internet resources
on the computer and so on, and that is now
beginning to create a culture of simplicity,
a culture of ecological living."

—DUANE ELGIN,
author, *Voluntary Simplicity*

Think, for a moment, back to your childhood. You were sick in bed with the flu and Mom came in with a little TLC. Words of comfort and maybe some medicine—aspirin for your fever, lozenges for your cough. And a bowl of hot chicken soup just to make you feel better. But the most important thing was having Mom there with her sympathy, so you wouldn't have to suffer alone.

The same goes for affluenza. To conquer it, most of us need to know we're not all by ourselves in the battle. We need support from others who are fighting the disease as well. Every addiction nowadays seems to have support groups for its victims, and conquering affluenza, the addictive virus, may require them even more, because there isn't any social pressure out there to stop consuming—just the opposite. But there is, you might say, an AA for affluenza—the Voluntary Simplicity Movement.

VOLUNTARY SIMPLICITY

"In our seventeen years of trend tracking," Gerald Celente of the Trends Research Institute said in 1996, "never have we seen an issue that's gaining such global acceptance as voluntary simplicity." He estimated that five percent of American baby boomers were practicing a "strong form of voluntary simplicity" and expected that number to reach fifteen percent by the year 2000. "They're finding a cure for affluenza," Celente declared. "They get rid of their stress and they say, 'You know I like living this way a lot better. How did I ever live like that before?'" [1]

It's now 2000, and voluntary simplicity has taken a bit of a hit from the new prosperity. Nonetheless, millions of Americans are still attracted to the idea of simpler, more environmentally friendly living. The voluntary simplicity "movement" if one wants to call it that, is alive, well, and still growing, if not quite as quickly as Celente predicted. It's a movement that's centered in discussion groups of many varieties, beginning with the kind Cecile Andrews first started nearly a decade ago.

STUDY CIRCLES CAN SAVE THE WORLD

Andrews, a 50-something Seattle teacher with a childlike sense of awe and wonder, and an ability to make people laugh that any stand-up comedian would envy, was promoting adult education classes as a community college administrator in 1989, when she read a book called *Voluntary Simplicity* by Duane Elgin. "I was really excited about it," she says, "but no one else was talking about it." She decided to offer a course on the subject. "But only four people signed up, so we had to cancel," she says with a laugh. "Then we tried it again three years later for a variety of reasons, and that time we got 175." [2]

Afterwards, participants told Cecile that her voluntary simplicity workshop had changed their lives. It wasn't the kind of thing a community college administrator hears every day, she says. "So I ended up resigning my fulltime position and devoting myself to giving these workshops."

She also remembered an idea she'd learned in Sweden. There, neighbors and friends organize discussion groups called "study circles" that meet in people's homes. Cecile began to organize her would-be voluntary simplicity students into such groups. Participants started with a short reading list, but most of the discussion focused on their personal experiences. People began to tell their own stories, "why they were there, that they have no time, they are working too much, they have no fun, they're not laughing anymore."

Some of the groups that Cecile began in 1992 still continue today. Participants give each other advice and build networks for tool-sharing and other activities that increase their sense of community. They find ways to help each other out that reduce their need for high incomes. They meet frequently in each other's homes and share tips, stories, and ideas for action. Everyone is expected to talk, and an egg timer, passed around the room, limits the time each can speak, preventing any-one from monopolizing the conversation.

The discussion often moves from the personal to the political. "People begin to talk about what institutional changes need to happen so they can find community and stop wasting money and resources," says Andrews. They talk about open space, parks for their kids, improved public transit, longer library hours, more effective local government. "Voluntary simplicity is not just a personal change thing. Study circles can save the world," Andrews adds with a wink.

SIMPLICITY AS SUBVERSION

Since 1992, Cecile Andrews has helped start hundreds of voluntary simplicity study circles. Seeds of Simplicity, a national organization she codirects, has start-ed many more. Her book, *Circle of Simplicity,* explains how anyone can start them. Most important, says Andrews, is that participants not see voluntary sim-plicity as a sacrifice.

"One person I know calls what we're doing the 'self-deprivation movement,' but it's not," she argues. "The way to fill up emptiness is not by denying ourselves some-thing. It's by putting positive things in place of the negative things, by finding out what we really need, and that's community, creativity, passion in our lives, connec-tion with nature. People help each other figure that out. They learn to meet their real needs instead of the false needs that advertisers create. They learn to live in ways that are high fulfillment, but low environmental impact."

In the good sense of the word, Andrews sees herself as a subversive (imagine Emma Goldman as Grandma Moses). "The thing about the voluntary simplicity movement is that it looks so benign," she suggests. "Like 'isn't that sweet, they're trying to cut back, to live more simply.' So people don't understand how radical it is. It's the Trojan Horse of social change. It's really getting people to live in a totally different way."

STUDY GROUPS IN CHURCHES

The voluntary simplicity discussion groups that began with Cecile Andrews can now be found in a variety of forms throughout the United States. One place where they're especially popular is in churches, many of whose leaders recognize that if we are indeed our brothers' keepers, Americans must "live simply so that others can simply live."

The United Methodist Church has produced a six-part video series called *Curing Affluenza,* featuring progressive evangelical theologian Tony Campolo, who was a spiritual advisor to President Clinton (he probably wished his ministrations had been more effective, but that's another issue). Churches use the videos to promote a continuing discussion of consumption issues.

Also popular are the discussion groups that begin with a book called *Simpler Living, Compassionate Life,* a collection of excellent essays edited and compiled by Michael Schut, a staff member of the Earth Ministry organization in Seattle. Churches use the book to conduct twelve-week courses in voluntary simplicity. Weekly topics include Time As Sacred, Your Money or Your Life, How Much Is Enough?, Everyday Food Choices, The Politics of Simplicity, Theology, History, and Widening the Community.

THE ROYS OF DOWNSHIFTING

Churches seem a natural arena to question ideologies built on greed, but Dick and Jeanne Roy's study groups take the battle against affluenza into unexpected places. Until he reached the age of fifty-three, Dick Roy was a leader in the most traditional fashion: president of his class at Oregon State University; officer in the Navy; and finally, a high-priced corporate attorney in one of America's most prestigious law firms, with a 32nd floor office overlooking all of Portland. But he was also married to Jeanne, a strong environmentalist and a believer in frugality.

So despite their six-figure income, the Roys lived simply and often had to weather teasing from their friends about their old clothes and used bicycles. They went backpacking on their vacations. Once they took their children to Disneyland—by bus, walking with backpacks on through the streets of Anaheim, California from the bus station to their motel.

Jeanne, in particular, found many ways to reduce consumption: using a clothesline instead of a dryer; sending junk mail back until it stopped coming; carefully saving paper; buying food in bulk and using her own packaging. Eventually, to the amazement of all her neighbors, she reduced the amount of landfill-bound trash the Roys produced to only one regular-sized garbage can a year! She says it wasn't a sacrifice. "If you ask people what kinds of activities bring them pleasure, it's usually contact with nature, things that are creative, and relationships with people, and the things we do to live simply bring us all of those satisfactions."[3]

Eventually, Jeanne took a leadership role in Portland's recycling program, conducting group workshops in people's homes to teach them how to save energy and water and use resources to maximum effectiveness.

Meanwhile, Dick raised a few eyebrows at work by putting in the fewest billable hours of anyone in the firm so that he could spend more time with his family. Such behavior almost brands you as a heretic in the legal profession, but Dick was a darned good lawyer and he got along well with his colleagues, so they overlooked his transgressions. Yet eventually he grew tired of corporate law. His children were grown and he wanted to do something that more directly expressed his values, especially his concern for the environment. In 1993, Dick Roy left his job, to live on his savings and devote his time to saving the earth.

WIDENING THE CIRCLES

He founded the Northwest Earth Institute in Portland, an organization that promotes simple living and environmental awareness by running discussion groups in existing institutions. Dick Roy's corporate connections helped him bring workshops—"Voluntary Simplicity," "Deep Ecology," "Choices for Sustainable Living," and "Discovering A Sense Of Place"—into many of Portland's largest corporations. Interested employees were encouraged to meet during lunch hours, in groups of a dozen or so, and conduct structured conversations that, Dick hoped, would lead to personal, social, and political action.

Only seven years later, the Northwest Earth Institute can look back at a surprising track record of success:

- more than 600 discussion courses conducted in private businesses (including such giants as Nike and Hewlett Packard), government agencies, schools, and nonprofits throughout the Pacific Northwest

- more than seventy church discussion groups in the Northwest

- establishment of outreach courses and sister Earth Institutes in thirty-seven states outside the Northwest

- involvement of more than 25,000 people in its courses

While the Earth Institutes now have a large and growing staff, Dick and Jeanne still work (fulltime) as volunteers. The Institutes conduct annual training programs for their organizers, always with a big dose of humor, music, and fun.

FINDING EACH OTHER

All of the study programs mentioned in this chapter start with aspirin and chicken soup: the premise that simplifying one's life (curing affluenza, if you will), is easier when we have the support and encouragement of others.

In the late seventies, Duane Elgin conducted a study of people who were choosing simpler, less consumptive lives for the Stanford Research Institute. He found they were "eating lower on the food chain," tending to vegetarian diets, wearing simple, utilitarian clothing, buying smaller, fuel-efficient cars, and cultivating their "inner" lives—living "consciously, deliberately, intentionally," mindful of the impacts of their activities.[4]

Elgin published his findings in the book *Voluntary Simplicity*. His timing was off by a bit. The book came out in 1981, just as Ronald Reagan was encouraging a return to excess and trend watchers were discovering the yuppies. Today Elgin, a gentle man with a gray beard and twinkling eyes, is an acknowledged leader in the new voluntary simplicity movement. Elgin believes that the embarrassment of riches that has marked the last few years of American history, and "the power of commercial mass media to distract us from real ecological crises and focus our attention on shampoo" are "creating a mindset for catastrophe right now."

But he sees hopeful signs in our times that weren't there during the '70s emphasis on simplicity. Elgin points to the rapidly expanding study circle movement and the countless ways that seekers of a cure for affluenza can now connect with one another: a plethora of new magazines, some real, some merely opportunistic; the Simple Living Network, a valuable internet resource; Web sites for dozens of simple living organizations; list serves and chat groups; radio programs; new books filled with practical tips and inspiration. Ten percent of the population, Elgin says, is making changes. "For a long time, they felt alone, but now they're beginning to find each other."

The change will take a generation, he feels, and he fears that's about all the time we have before we run into an ecological wall. "The leading edge of those people choosing a simple life," Elgin says, "have been relatively affluent. They've had a taste of the good life and have found it wanting, and now they're looking for a different kind of life." In that sense, the movement might be seen by some people as elitist. Yet, says Elgin, "it's only when such people begin moderating their consumption that there is going to be more available for people that now don't have enough."

Elgin likes to talk about Arnold Toynbee's "law of progressive simplification." He points out that the great British historian studied the rise and fall of twenty-two different civilizations and "summarized everything he knew about the growth of human civilizations in one law: *The measure of a civilization's growth is its ability to shift energy and attention from the material side to the spiritual and aesthetic and cultural and artistic side.*"

Thousands of Americans are coming together in small groups all across the country, trying to bring about that shift.

CHAPTER 24

Fresh air

*It's difficult to imagine being busy and
enchanted at the same time. Enchantment
invites us to pause and be arrested by
whatever is before us. Instead of doing
something, something is done to us....
We stumble across a roaring, resplendent
waterfall in the middle of a quiet forest,
and we become profoundly entranced.*

—THOMAS MOORE,
The Re-enchantment of Everyday Life

*A ditch somewhere—or a creek, meadow,
woodlot, or marsh .... These are places of
initiation, where the borders between ourselves and other creatures break down,
where the earth gets under our nails and
a sense of place gets under our skin.*

—ROBERT MICHAEL PYLE,
The Thunder Tree

I n the Age of Affluenza, American culture came indoors, in quest of
ever-greater convenience. Imagine Janet Jones talking to her neighbor
(before she surrendered, of course). *"We don't ever have to be hot
again,"* she confides as the air conditioning installer pulls into the driveway. *Right
behind him is a vanload of junipers, vincas, and a birdbath, to fill the space where
the vegetable garden used to be. As she pads slipper-footed across a carpet of Ken-
tucky bluegrass, Janet looks over her shoulder and adds, "Since we don't cook much
anymore, why have a garden?"*

In the '90s, the aphorism "Stop and smell the roses" sank to a more cynical
"Wake up and smell the coffee." We didn't have time for nature anymore. We
learned to just ignore the damn roses—let the landscaper take care of them.

NATURE GETS EVEN...

©1997 SEATTLE POST-INTELLIGENCER • NORTH AMERICA SYNDICATE

This chapter challenges a widespread, if unconscious, belief that if you make enough money, you don't need to know anything about nature, or have contact with it. Conversely, we suggest that the stronger your bond with nature, the less money you'll need, or want, to make. If kicking affluenza is your goal, proven natural remedies may be the way to go.

JUST SAY KNOW

Thirty-four percent of Americans polled in 2000 rank shopping as their favorite activity, while only seventeen percent prefer being in nature. The Las Vegas Strip is ranked as the number one "scenic drive" in the country. One fourth-grader, asked if he preferred to play indoors or outdoors, replied, "Indoors, 'cause that's where the electrical outlets are." Another child poked a stick at a dead beetle, commenting to her friend that the insect's batteries must have run out. On a field trip to trace the source of their drinking water, inner city New York middle-school kids were spooked by the cool, starry darkness and crescendo of silence in the Catskills.

"I thought potatoes grew on trees," one college student confided as Dave recently helped her plant a garden in her backyard. "I guess I need to know more about where my food comes from." Naturalists urge us to reintroduce ourselves to the real world by becoming familiar with our own backyards and county open spaces. This will help answer a question that malingers in the back of our minds: *Where exactly are we?*

Can you identify a few key species that live in your region, and the natural events that take place there?

BIOREGION QUIZ

1. Trace the water you drink from precipitation to tap.

2. Describe the soil around your home.

3. What were the primary subsistence techniques of the cultures that lived in your area before you?

4. Name five native edible plants in your bioregion and their seasons of availability.

5. Where does your garbage go?

6. Name five resident and any migratory birds in your area.

7. What animal species have become extinct in your area?

8. What spring wildflower is consistently among the first to bloom where you live?

9. What kinds of rocks and minerals are found in your bioregion?

10. What is the largest wilderness area in your bioregion?

(adapted from *Deep Ecology*, by Bill Devall and George Sessions)

A CIVILIZATION ON LIFE SUPPORT?

One after another, services that used to be provided free by nature have been packaged and put on the market. Take bottled water, home-delivered in five-gallon casks, or tanning salons, where creatures of the great indoors bask in simulated sunlight. Human contact with nature has become a *contract* with nature. Even oxygen is for sale. But many educators and thinkers refer to an "extinction of experience" that accompanies our pullback from nature. Like a washed-out sprig of parsley on a dinner plate, the community park is often biologically bland—and sometimes not secure from crime. The only way some know nature is by mentally crunching images of it on TV, like popcorn.

But television can't communicate a multidimensional, sensuous, interactive reality. It shows only the visual realm—and that through the tunnel of a lens. We're not actually *there* to smell nature, and touch it, and feel the breeze. Besides, television nature is often scripted nature—fake as a paper ficus. Spliced together from hundreds of nonsequential hours of tape, a typical nature program filmed in Africa zooms in on a majestic lion, relentlessly on the prowl for wildebeests, jackals, and gazelles. The reality is, lions are as lazy as your housecat, sometimes sleeping twenty hours a day. Even so, footage of two lions mating is predictably followed by "cubs, tumbling out after a two- or three-minute gestation, full of play. The timeless predatory cycle repeats…"[1]

In *The Age of Missing Information*, quoted above, Bill McKibben compares and contrasts the information contained in a day-long hike in upstate New York with the information content of a hundred cable TV stations, on the same day. He took a few months to watch every single taped program, and observed a vast, virtual wasteland that hawked a commercial mindset. Writes McKibben, "We believe that we live in the 'age of information,' that there has been an information 'revolution.'. . . Yet vital knowledge that humans have always possessed about who we are and where we live seems beyond our reach." In 100 hours of programming, he found very little to enrich his life.

On McKibben's day-long hike, however, all kinds of things were happening. Seven vultures leisurely circled directly above—so close he could count feathers. "It was nearly unbearable—almost erotic—this feeling of being watched," he writes. "At moments I felt small and vulnerable, like prey." Still, he knew the day's encounters with vultures, water striders, and thrushes would never be Spielberg material. "I had not been gored, chased, or even roared at. I had failed to tranquilize anything with a dart; no creature had inflated stupendous air sacs in a curious and ancient mating ritual."[2] Yet his real-world experiences made him feel actively, rather than passively, alive.

In the closing sentences of *The Age of Missing Information,* McKibben reminds us of the virtual canyon we've put between ourselves and the natural world:

> On *Now You're Cooking*, a lady is making pigs-in-a-blanket with a Super Snacker. "We have a pact in our house—the first one up plugs in the Super Snacker."
>
> And on the pond, the duck is just swimming back and forth, his chest pushing out a wedge of ripples that catch the early rays of the sun.

OVERCOMING ECOPHOBIA

As McKibben and many others point out, when we lose touch with the origins, habits, and needs of our earthly housemates, we lose our biological sense of balance. Writes psychologist Chellis Glendinning, "We become homeless, alienated from the only home we will ever have."[3]

In an evolutionary sense, we risk losing the living scaffold that supports our bio-logical sack-of-tricks. (For instance, without a healthy universe of decomposers, we'd all be knee-deep in dinosaurs). And we lose a way of knowing what's *right*. Ecologist Aldo Leopold believed "A thing is right when it tends to preserve the integrity, stability and beauty of the biotic community. It is wrong when it tends otherwise."[4] But let's face it: most of our daily activities and standard operating pro-cedures walk all over Leopold's law. We don't have a clue about the biotic commu-nity, or what it needs.

Educator David Sobel terms our separation from nature "ecophobia"—a symp-tom characterized by an inability to smell, plant, or even acknowledge the roses. "Ecophobia is a fear of oil spills, rainforest destruction, whale hunting, and Lyme Disease. In fact it's a fear of just being outside," Sobel explains. A fear of microbes, lightning, spiders, and dirt. Sobel's first aid for ecophobia emphasizes hands-on con-tact with nature. "Wet sneakers and muddy clothes are prerequisites for under-standing the water cycle," he says.[5] In the book *Beyond Ecophobia*, he describes the magic of overcoming "timesickness" and regaining a more natural pace.

> I went canoeing with my six-year-old son Eli and his friend Julian. The plan was to canoe a two-mile stretch of the Ashuelot River, an hour's paddle in adult time. Instead, we dawdled along for four or five hours. We netted golf balls off the bottom of the river from the upstream golf course. We watched fish and bugs in both the shallows and depths of the river. We stopped at the mouth of a tributary stream for a picnic and went for a long adventure through a maze of marshy streams. Fol-lowing beaver trails led to balance-walking on fallen trees to get across marshy spots without getting our feet wet. We looked at spring flowers, tried to catch a snake, got lost and found. How fine it was to move at a meanderous, child's pace![6]

NATURE: NOUN OR VERB?

One summer night, fifteen years ago, Dave's family was abruptly wrenched from sleep by an eerie, piercing sound that cut through the night like a Bowie knife. All four family members jerked upright in their beds, as lights went on in cabins throughout the little rural valley. At 4 A.M., Dave's kids stood shaky-legged on the couch, peering out into the darkness. They hoped to catch a glimpse of the moun-tain lions that had just "faced-off" in the front yard. This was a primordial experi-ence, connecting them with the fear and the wonder that humans have known throughout our evolution. They felt lucky to have the experience—though none of them slept for the rest of that night. Now, fast-forward twelve years or so to a rocky ledge overlooking Colorado's Sangre de Cristo mountain range. Dave's son, Colin, calls attention to the skeletal remains of an animal feast. As they study an antelope skeleton lying on the ledge, Colin imagines out loud, "A mountain lion dragged the antelope up here to eat it." He likes the idea of a real-world museum exhibit, and he likes the detective work, too.

But Dave was in a different place in his life cycle. Reaching down to the antelope skeleton, he cracked the skull away from the neck, to have a trophy from the hike. The sound of neck vertebrae cracking was one of the most abrupt, jarring sounds he'd ever heard—right up with the front yard face-off of years before. In fact, Dave was so alarmed he replaced the skull near its rightful place. Although Colin soon forgave the impulsive action, the two spent a few hours that afternoon debating the acquired trait of *having* nature versus the more unconditional *being* in nature.

Spoiled by the pace and panorama of TV nature, we're usually looking for the big event, the spectacle. But more often than adults, kids become absorbed in the small details of nature. "Where did you go?" asks the parent. "Out." "What did you do?" "Oh, nothing," answers the kid, but he's got a vivid image in his head that says otherwise: perhaps a nearly intact robin's eggshell, partially hidden under a bright red maple leaf.

NATURE'S MAGIC

Wilderness leader Robert Greenway has spent many years on the trail, and has allowed the child in himself to remain active. He tries to bring out that trait in others, too, with tangible results. Feedback from more than a thousand wilderness trip participants (both adult and child) indicates that nature is indeed working its magic:

90 percent described an increased sense of aliveness, well-being and energy;

77 percent described a major life change upon return (in personal relationships, employment, housing, or lifestyle);

60 percent of the men and 20 percent of the women stated that a major goal of the trip was to conquer fear, challenge themselves, and expand limits;

90 percent broke an addiction such as nicotine, chocolate, and pop;

57 percent of the women and 27 percent of the men stated that a major goal of the trip was to "come home" to nature;

76 percent of all respondents reported dramatic changes in quantity, vividness, and context of dreams after seventy-two hours in the wilderness. [7]

We know intuitively that nature is beneficial, even if we become estranged from it. Patients recover more quickly when they have beautiful, green views to look at. At the Way Station in Maryland, the suicide rate of emotionally and mentally challenged residents dropped dramatically when a sunny new brick and natural-wood building became their new home. Natural light and plants provided by windows and skylights seemed to calm and reassure them.

People like Greenway urge us to "come to our senses." By literally smelling, touching, and tasting nature, we begin to clear out some of the rubble in our heads. Says Greenway, "On a wilderness trip, it seems to take about four days for people to start dreaming nature dreams rather than 'busy' or 'urban' dreams. This recurring pattern suggests to me that our culture is only four days deep."[8] In contrast, John McPhee has called the history of life on earth "deep time." For example, without the ferns, algae, and protozoa of sixty-five million years ago (only yesterday as measured in deep time), we wouldn't be so preoccupied with petroleum.

COMING TO OUR SENSES

When we experience nature with our own noses, skin, lungs, and reptilian brains, we feel silly about the stress of obsessive projects and timelines. Self-importance begins to melt into something larger. We see that we're integral members of the Biosphere club, and it feels great! Rather than perceiving ourselves as simply human-paycheck-house-car, we finally understand who and where we are. We see that in reality, we're human-soil-grains-fruits-microbes-trees-oxygen-herbivores-fish-salt marshes, and on and on and on! We begin to question the logic and the ethic of parting nature out like a used-up car.

A few years ago, Lana Porter began to come to her senses. The garden she works is far more than just a lush, reclaimed vacant lot—it's a biological extension of her self, and a way of life. "I eat very well out of this garden, just about all year 'round," she says, "and the organic produce gives me energy to grow more produce and get *more* energy. It's a cycle of health that has cut my expenses in half. My grocery bills are lower, my health bills are lower, I don't need to pay for exercise, and my transportation costs are lower because I don't have to travel so much to amuse myself."[9]

Asked what she likes best about her personal Garden of Eden, she replies, "I like what it does for my head. Sometimes, when I'm watering a healthy crop, or planting seeds, or cultivating between rows, I'm not thinking anything at all—a radical switch from my previous life as an overworked computer programmer. People tell me I should take care of my crops more efficiently—with irrigation systems on timers, designer fertilizers and pesticides—so I could spend less time out here. But that way of growing disconnects the grower from the garden. The whole point is to spend *more* time with the plants, taking care of things, and less time trying to reshape myself to fit the changing whims of the world."

Like Lana, many Americans perceive the difference between natural complexity and oversimplified science. Between a juicy, tasty peach that confers health and a pulpy, worthless peach, grown in poor soil. Suddenly attuned to the frequency of natural law, they see with new eyes that many of our civilization's customs are counterproductive, because they're not grounded in biological reality. Just as leaving land fallow is a tenet of the Old Testament, optimizing solar income to prevent global warming should be one of the tenets of the Age of Ecology. But it seems that we won't protect backyard, bioregion, or planet unless we feel connected.

Nature is not "out there," it's everywhere. Finding out how well the timber was grown that went into your backyard fence is nature. Knowing if the ingredients in a cake mix are biologically compatible with human nutrition is nature. Walking to the store and stopping to ask your neighbor what kind of perennial flowers he's planting— that's nature, too.

HAPPY AS A RED-WINGED BLACKBIRD

For aquatic biologist and University of Wisconsin professor Cal De Witt, the Garden of Eden is a freshwater marsh that's just beyond his backyard. He knows the marsh so well that he can identify its birds by their calls alone. Standing knee-deep in it, in waders, De Witt traces the marsh's many cycles and life events. "When the stalk of the cattail here drops down to the marsh, it's converted again into soil, and in the structure of that soil grow all sorts of organisms which these geese feed on and the great herons that live here feed on," he exclaims. "It's things like this that really excite me, because they instill such a sense of awe and wonder. And I think that awe and wonder are really the things we're missing today." De Witt examines a dragonfly preening on a cattail stalk, then reflects, "This aquatic ecosystem is 11,000 years old. It's been doing all this for eleven millennia—without any human intervention."[10]

"As you stand for awhile, things begin to unfold if you are quiet enough to watch and listen. After a full day, you're still not fulfilled—there's so much to learn here. You're not tired either—you tend to be exhilarated from the experience." De Witt steps up on the bank of the marsh, water dripping from his waders. "Perhaps most curiously—in our consumptive society—you come home with your wallet just as full as when you left, and you've gotten all this pleasure, education, understanding, peace—for not a single penny."

CHAPTER 25

The right medicine

If you think your actions are too small to make a difference, you've never been in bed with a mosquito.

—ANONYMOUS

If we can harness the ingenuity that has made North America the richest, most successful society in history, our environment can start making a comeback in a single generation.

—ALAN DURNING

We need technologies that more efficiently digest a given resource, not technologies of larger jaws and a bigger digestive tract.

—HERMAN DALY

What if fifty *sinful* things could save the Earth? Wouldn't that be great? What if, for example, we Americans could deploy our favorite sin, greed, as a vaccine against itself, intentionally extending our spending spree at least a few more decades? Even environmentalists could put down their protest signs and join in the fun. Instead of "Doing all I can to save the Earth," they could consume all they wanted to save the Earth.

What if cigarettes increased lung capacity and prevented cancer; SUVs filtered the pollution out of urban air; and luxury beach vacations enhanced the health of habitats like coral reefs? The problem is, they don't.

Okay then, what if fifty *simple* things could save the Earth? We're talking about individual choices and actions taken by millions of Americans, without substantial changes in lifestyle. By each keeping a reusable grocery sack in the car, planting a tree, and screwing in some compact fluorescent light bulbs, maybe we can collectively reverse the decline of the planet's health. That, too, would be fantastic, but nothing on Earth is quite that simple. Our economy and the majority of its products are not *designed* to save the planet. They're designed to make money.

We can voluntarily cut back and do simple things by the boatload, but we'll still be paddling against a flashflood, no-conscience economy that's not designed to make sense. For example, we're willing to recycle a few sacks of aluminum cans, but we may have to drive twenty miles to do it. We'll pay a little more for nontoxic paints and cleaners, but we use them in houses glued together with toxic adhesives. We choose to buy natural fibers like cotton, unaware that conventionally grown cotton is drenched with pesticides (about a third of all pesticides used in the United States are applied to cotton crops).

As author and corporate futurist Paul Hawken points out, ninety percent of the waste we generate never even makes it into products or services, but remains at the point of extraction or manufacture, in slash and slag piles and on-site waste impoundments. Of the materials that do become products, eighty percent are thrown away after a single use. In a way, it's a Catch-22. To save the world, we need strong individual action, yet for effective individual action, we need to redesign the world. (Even a task that huge is achievable—we've totally redesigned the world in the last 100 years, haven't we?) Hawken believes we need to see a wider picture than we're used to seeing: "We've spent the last century working our tails off to make fewer people more productive using more resources. Yet we are doing this at a time when we have more people and *fewer* resources."[1] Hawken envisions an economy in which resources are many times more productive per molecule, electron, and photon; natural capital (lakes, trees, grassland) is valued as an indispensable living support system; and people bring their brains, their hearts, and their hands back into the workplace.

NOT ONLY SUFFICIENT, BUT ALSO EFFICIENT

Simple environmental fixes can be designed into our economy and political structure, so that they become as natural as breathing. By substituting efficient products like low-flow showerheads, compact fluorescent bulbs, and high-efficiency windows and refrigerators, we've already prevented millions of tons of pollution and environmental impacts in the last decade—and saved billions of dollars. Because they are "smarter" and designed for efficiency, newly available products like front-load washing machines can deliver better performance using fewer resources. A typical family now spends about $200 per year on energy, water, and detergent for doing laundry. A state-of-the-art model will cut that expense by about $75 a year.

Buying devices that score high on Energy Star and other rating systems not only lowers fuel bills but reduces the threat of global warming, reduces our reliance on unstable sources of energy like Middle Eastern oil, and reduces our guilt, too.

Howard Geller of the American Council for an Energy-Efficient Economy does not believe that simple, individual actions will save the planet by themselves, because many of the challenges we face are extremely complex. We need more earth-friendly economic incentives, more green-product certifications and efficiency ratings, and a revamping of codes and specifications—all designed specifically to make saving the Earth a cakewalk.

As an example, Geller cited regulations that mandate efficiency. "The nice thing is, regulations don't require consumer education or analysis." Refrigerator standards are one such regulation. "When your old refrigerator gives out, you need to replace it, ASAP. You usually don't have time to read *Consumer Reports*, you just make a beeline to the department store and get something with enough cabinet space to keep your teenagers alive."[2]

But much of the work to produce better refrigerators was already done behind the scenes, by lobbyists, legislators, engineers, and managers. As Geller explained, a series of progressive state laws were passed first, but each had different requirements. To reduce confusion and the need for many models of the same product, industry actually supported a standardized federal law that required higher efficiency. That law has produced models that use two-thirds less energy than a 1970s unit, but have more space, more features, and better performance. More for less, by design. Appliance standards in general that went into effect in 1990 have already saved more energy than is generated by thirty-one regional power plants. To keep our beer and forgotten leftovers cold, we don't have to cut back on anything, ponder anything, or become Greenpeace activists; we just need to harvest the fruits of environment-friendly laws. Now that's simplicity.

"If affluenza compels us to buy something," said Geller, "why don't we buy a state-of-the-art refrigerator or front-loading clothes washer—something that improves our quality of life and makes sense environmentally, too?"

Sometimes the life-cycle savings from high-efficiency devices like set-back thermostats and "low-E" windows are as good as returns on stock or bond investments, and you don't have to fret over the market. Monetary savings are only one of the "hidden benefits" of TLC for the Earth.

The changes that take place in our minds are perhaps the most important individual actions of all. We're discovering that it's not just how much or how little we consume as individuals that matters, but how well our purchases were *produced*. It's not just the quantity of our consumption—although that is important—but also the quality of our designs and choices.

In a super-efficient economy, we'll all save money, because we're not spending extra to clean up, recover our health, mine new materials, work in jobs we hate—requiring expensive vacations in compensation—and so on. Efficiency is especially beneficial for low-income consumers, who spend higher proportions of their income for utilities. When we learn to "ride the Earth in the direction it's going," by knowing how nature works and designing appropriately, everybody wins.

DRIVING AN SUV TO THE STEAKHOUSE

Meanwhile, we rejoin our regularly scheduled present-in-progress, where news stories about globally scaled environmental problems sometimes overwhelm us. They seem too big to be solved by informed consumer choices, let alone ignorant ones. But Michael Brower and Warren Leon, authors of *The Consumer's Guide to Effective Environmental Choices: Practical Advice from the Union of Concerned Scientists*, are here to help.[3] Their mission is to exorcise mental clutter and guilt by setting priorities in our consumer choices. Rather than stress over which forty things to do, the researchers suggest we address the worst problems first, to get the biggest bang for our collective buck. By their calculations, driving an SUV to the steakhouse is one of the worst consumer actions possible, because automobiles and meat are two primary pathways affluenza takes to infect the Earth.

Brower and Leon used a decade's worth of risk analysis from various agencies and experts to determine that air pollution, global warming, habitat alteration, and water pollution are the most critical consumption-related impacts. Big-pattern flaws in design and production often cause the worst impacts: the way our cities and suburbs are designed, the way we purify wastewater, the way agriculture is currently practiced, the way energy is generated, and the way industry designs and manufactures chemicals, computers, and cars. While consumer choices don't *directly* affect these production systems, informed choices do result in substantial hidden benefits that can speed the Earth's recovery. When we buy organic produce, for example, we are also buying farming techniques—such as crop rotation—that prevent erosion, insect damage, and other impacts. When we buy a fuel-efficient vehicle, we become rolling advertisements for a cool climate and clean air.

When we reduce our consumption of meat, we also dramatically reduce our impact on land, water, air, and atmosphere. Compared with a nutritionally equivalent intake of whole grains, "red meat is responsible for 20 times the land use (because of cattle grazing), seventeen times the common water pollution (because of animal wastes), five times the toxic water pollution and water use (from chemicals applied to feed grains and water for irrigation and livestock), and three times the greenhouse gas emissions (from greater energy use)," Brower and Leon contend.

Is the quantity of meat we consume a vestige from frontier days, or is it really more of a visual habit? Maybe we apportion servings by the way they should look on a plate. Dinner plate aesthetics—and meat consumption—have changed since 1970, but if we stop and think about it, wouldn't our plates look just as appetizing and far more colorful with larger proportions of fresh fruits, grains, and vegetables? That might mean reducing our meat intake from five pounds a week to one pound, and at the same time reducing our risk of heart disease and stroke.

PRIORITIES FOR AMERICAN CONSUMERS

Transportation

1. Choose a place to live that reduces the need to drive.

2. Think twice before purchasing a second or third car.

3. Choose a fuel-efficient, low-polluting car.

4. Set concrete goals for reducing your travel.

5. Whenever practical, walk, bicycle, or take public transportation.

Food

6. Eat less meat.

7. Buy certified organic produce.

Household operations

8. Choose your home carefully.

9. Reduce the environmental costs of heating and hot water.

10. Install efficient lighting and appliances.

11. Choose an electricity supplier offering renewable energy.

(adapted from *The Consumer's Guide to Effective Environmental Choices*)

Brower and Leon praise consumer efforts to reduce waste and promote efficiency, but they also urge us to go easy on ourselves. "The demonization of disposable cups, for example, has caused some individuals and groups to spend too much time worrying about them. One minister told us that his congregants wanted to purchase ceramic coffee mugs and install a dishwasher in their social hall, so they could avoid using plastic cups at meetings. When we discovered that their total cup use was only about forty a week, we urged them to spend their budgeted $450 on other measures, such as weather-stripping for their old drafty building."[4]

Some actions and activities are high-impact even though relatively few people do them, like power boating, and off-road joyriding in ATVs and snowmobiles. An hour of jet skiing, for example, can create as much smog as a car trip from Washington, D.C. to Orlando, Florida, because the engines in these vehicles don't have emission controls. (These small engines are prime candidates for redesign). The engines of gas-powered lawn mowers, in addition to ruining many an afternoon nap, also create red-advisory pollution right in our neighborhoods. In addition, homeowners apply ten times as much pesticide per acre as farmers, because reading labels is a bother, and isn't more better?

But some have opted to take the lawn into their own hands. "Xeriscaping" with water-conservative flowers and shrubs is popular in the arid west and elsewhere, and "lawn-busting" with edible landscapes may also become fashionable, as interest in organic produce continues to expand. Instead of spending hours a week to produce a bag of grass clippings, we'll go out and pick a bowl of cherry tomatoes.

An underlying cause of many environmental problems is "high-impact thinking" such as the compulsive need for spotlessness and tidiness. It seems that the more flawlessly green our lawns, the browner our streams, from all the nutrients and pesticides that run off. The cleaner our houses, the more toxic our environment, from runaway chemicals used to overpolish, oversterilize, and overdeodorize our homes.

Simple things to save the Earth? Sure, let's do as many as we can, because they reduce impacts, stimulate better design, and save money. In a sense, we're substituting information and awareness for overconsumption, a painless path to take, because not much change is required. But while we're at it, let's not forget a few other details that need to be taken care of by the week after next: redesigning the economy and many of its products, and recycling the American mindset.

SAVING THE EARTH BY DESIGN

When a toaster is designed well, it makes our day go better, because the toast comes out golden brown, and the appliance itself is so stylish! If the toaster is designed to be repairable, that's also a good thing, and if we could recycle it into another toaster, that too would be a good thing. We would have a smart product that created a minimum of impacts, by design. Many countries in Western Europe now mandate "extended producer responsibility" that includes taking back products at the end of their lives. In the future, your toaster might "swim upstream" to be recycled at the very factory where it was manufactured.

What kind of green design features do we want in other consumer products? The "hypercar" combines qualities such as efficiency, low levels of pollution, and low maintenance. Envisioned years ago by energy guru Amory Lovins, the next-generation vehicle is now being manufactured in prototype by Ford, GM, Honda, Toyota, and others. A Rocky Mountain Institute colleague of Lovins recently attended Detroit's annual Auto Show, where dinosaurs like the ten-mile-per-gallon Ford Excursion were on exhibit next to the high-tech seventy-mile-per-gallon Prodigy and the eighty-mpg GM Precept.

By reducing wind drag, mechanical friction, tire resistance, and weight, the designers of these high-IQ cars set the stage for a new kind of car engine—a flame-less, pollutionless fuel cell that will ultimately consume hydrogen as a fuel source and emit water vapor as exhaust.[5] By design, we may soon see the world's air pollution take a dramatic turn for the better—though of course, hypercars can't decongest the highways of a hyper society.

DESIGN Rx FOR AFFLUENZA

Non-toxic, non-polluting

Renewable energy and material sources

Socially Equitable and Affordable

Flexible, reversible

Durable, repairable

Diverse, unique

Efficient, precise

Easy to understand

Light "extraction footprint"

Low maintenance

Life sensitive, bio-compatible

Culture sensitive, people-friendly

The new-millennium wind generator, a child of aerospace and computer technologies, is another great example of how design can deliver a service much more elegantly than its old-millennium counterpart. Much cleaner and faster to build than coal-fired or nuclear power generators, state-of-the-art wind farms are already supplying enough electricity to power millions of homes. Between 1994 and 1998, the wind industry grew by forty percent. Says the American Wind Energy Association, if wind supplied ten percent of the world's energy, close to two million jobs could be created. One in four electricity customers in the United States now has the option of buying "green power" from renewable sources like wind. (One great example is Colorado's Wind Source program, in which Dave has invested.)

Howard Geller of the American Council for an Energy-Efficient Economy emphasized, "Efficiency is critical because the more wasteful we are, the more difficult it will be to make a transition to an economy powered by wind, biomass, and sun. With efficient products and processes, the transition can be relatively easy. Historically, the transitions from wood to coal and from coal to oil took place in a few decades."[6]

The potential for "smart stuff" to provide greater value with fewer impacts is nearly endless. Until now, industry has pursued other design goals such as cost per unit and ease of manufacture. "There's no reason why we shouldn't be able to manufacture footwear that lasts as long as the foot in this age of high technology," states Alan Durning of Northwest Environment Watch. "We can move from a hydrocarbon economy, based on nonrenewable petrochemicals, to a carbohydrate economy, based on plant materials," says David Morris of the Institute for Local Self-Reliance.[7]

Even everyday products like newspaper ink and toothpaste have been redesigned to meet needs precisely, without unwanted side effects. Tom Chappell of Tom's of Maine wondered, "Why were toothpastes filled with complex abrasives, dyes, artificial flavors, preservatives, binders, fluoride, and worst of all saccharin, long suspected as a cause of cancer? . . . Why were Americans spending more than a billion dollars a year to fill their mouths with chemicals?"[8] Chappell's innovative baking-soda toothpaste attracted millions of customers and prompted companies like Colgate and Procter and Gamble to market similar products.

CHANGING FOR GOOD

Why do people change behavior to become more environmentally friendly? Behaviorists report that the most effective stimulants for change emphasize a perception both of large benefits and of limited barriers. People need to know basic facts about global warming, water pollution, and so on, and understand how their actions can make a difference—without requiring Mission Impossible efforts.

Ecopsychologist Terrance O'Connor thinks environmental responsibility is really about enlightened self-interest. He asks, "If this is not my planet, whose is it? I am the cause, and I am the cure. When I act out of this realization, I act not out of guilt but out of self-love. I break through my denial and see that humankind is facing an absolutely unprecedented crisis. I act not out of obligation or idealism, but because I live in a straw house and I smell smoke."[9]

CHAPTER 26

Back
to work

Markets flatter our solitary egos but leave our
yearnings for community unsatisfied. They
advance individualistic, not social, goals, and
they encourage us to speak the language of
"I want" not the language of "we need."

—BENJAMIN BARBER,
A Place for Us

If you don't go to somebody's funeral, they
won't come to yours.

—YOGI BERRA

s there any better feeling than being back in the world after an extended illness? Good-bye daytime TV, Hello energy! The challenge is to
channel the energy productively.

Mohandas Gandhi said, "there's more to life than increasing its speed." We might
add that there's more to life than increasing its greed. And despite the million-dollar
ads to the contrary, there's more to life than "me." Buy the luxury car, the ads suggest (over and over!) and the pristine, deserted country roads roll out obediently,
like endless swaths of Persian carpet. On these mythical, mist-covered highways,
exotic women adorn the passenger seats, wearing short black dresses and pearl-
white smiles of delight. Speeding is mandatory, wet surfaces be damned! The ads
are all about "me," chasing an illusion of personal grandeur.

But political scientist Benjamin Barber is skeptical that those roads can take us where we want to go. In *A Place for Us,* Barber explains his gripe with an economy based solely on profit. "Markets are as likely to undermine as to sustain full employment, environmental safety, public health, social safety nets, education, cultural diversity, and real competition," he writes.[1] He believes these qualities need to be championed by *us,* the people—a slumbering yet historically potent third force in American society.

He urges us to rise up from our couches and collectively re-energize the third place, between big government and big business, where "citizens breathe freely and behave democratically without regarding themselves as passive complainers, grasping consumers, or isolated victims."[2] This third place, treasured throughout American history, is where civic life thrives. Barn raisings and Habitat for Humanity raisings; church philanthropic projects; holiday festivals and block parties; demonstrations and protests; volunteer activities like PTA and Red Cross; neighborhood watches, community gardens, and lively discussion groups—all these activities remind us that we belong to an extended family that needs and values our participation.

Barber's beef with big government is its inability, or refusal, to awaken and empower civic life. In the early 2000s, a mighty chorus of snores can be heard from coast to coast, which filmmaker Michael Moore praises facetiously in an open e-mail to the country's nonvoters. "Way to go!" he writes, "In 1996, you helped set the all-time American record for lowest turnout ever at a presidential election. And during the 2000 primaries, nearly eighty percent staged a sit-in on their living room couches."[3] (We did better in November 2000, but no doubt there are many silent Floridians who still wish they'd made time to vote).

In ancient Greece, the word "idiot" meant someone not involved in public life, but let's face it, since national politics became a corporate-funded media show in the '60s, we sometimes have to wonder if we're *all* idiots.

At the local level, where voices can be heard and politicians held accountable, we aren't doing much better. The living-room sit-ins continue during city council meetings, free concerts in the park, and public hearings—especially when their time slots compete with *ER* or *The Practice.* (Is that idiots, or "vidiots")?

Barber argues that there's much more to citizenship than voting and jury duty. The potentials are limitless for bringing civic energy back to the workplace, the health care industry, or the public review of new technologies—all sorely in need of new direction. He even proposes that public meeting spaces become mandated features in malls. How might malls be designed to make space for neighborhood health clinics, speaker's corners, child-care centers, and public art galleries?

EMERGING FROM LUXURY COCOONS

What do we want "people power" to accomplish? Social theorist Jean Elshtain believes that "The essential task of civil society, the families, neighborhood life, and community, and the web of religious, civic associations . . . is to foster competence and character in individuals, provide the foundations for social trust, and turn children into citizens."[4] But affluenza is often an obstacle to those lofty goals, because time-famine and chronic self-absorption limit our participation. We may wish we could look outside ourselves, but we're just too busy, too uncertain where to start, or too tired. What's more, we feel guilty about the time, money, and energy we've already invested to make things worse! But this painful awakening can be a first step on the road to recovery.

Of course, humans have always been a social species, guided by the shared wisdom of the tribe or clan. Gatherings around the fire weren't called "citizenship," but that's what they really were. They played an important role in formulating and expressing shared values and goals.

They still do, even if the fires are now artificial living room fireplaces. Portland residents Jeanne and Dick Roy, cofounders of the Northwest Earth Institute (see Chapter 23), organize discussion circles, often in peoples' homes, with the goal of "detaching participants from commercial messages and encouraging them to think for themselves."

The mission—self-discovery and personal motivation—is lofty, but the Institute's approach is low-key. "We don't claim to be teachers or preachers," says Roy, "we're simply a resource that enables people to express their highest values to others, *and then align their actions with those values.*"[5]

Why do people take the time to come to nine different sessions per course? Maybe because the classes offer easy access to citizenship and social expression they can't find in their communities or workplaces. Roy has found that groups of about ten encourage the sharing of opinions, stories, and convictions that stimulate personal change. "We see participants move from awareness and consciousness of an issue—let's say the impacts of the automobile—through motivation/inspiration, and intent to change, to action."

"One woman, Rosemarie Cordello, was a successful labor lawyer," he explains. "After taking our courses, she made basic changes in her life. She got rid of her car and her professional wardrobe and started a nonprofit organization in Portland, Sustainable Communities Northwest, to build 'green' housing for low income citizens. She says she's never been happier."

Roy also sees change happening right on his block. "We formed a neighborhood discussion group that continues to meet. The focus of our work is a physical feature, a ravine that's in back of twenty-five households in the neighborhood. We put together a neighborhood directory, organized a drop point where a local farmer delivers produce by subscription, and began meeting every Friday night for poker. We also have neighborhood work groups to clean up and restore the ravine, and we work on each other's home projects when help is needed."

It's an appealing notion—to have help when we need it. "I call our work 'gathering with a sense of purpose,'" says Roy. "I really believe that if we could get everyone in the country would go through our discussion courses, we could change the culture overnight."

Roy's beliefs are right on target with research about how, and why, behavior change happens. Commitment, trust, and intent are all key factors. In one classic study, conducted thirty years ago, a researcher posed as a sunbather, spreading a blanket near another sunbather. After a few minutes, he asked, "Excuse me, I'm here alone and have no matches—do you have a light?" The researcher then got up and walked down the beach, leaving his blanket and radio behind. When a second researcher ran by and "stole" the radio, the thief was pursued four times out of twenty. However, when the first researcher asked the person beside him to "watch his things," in nineteen out of twenty cases the thief was pursued.[6] We take action when we've made a commitment to others.

Similar research shows that written commitments are even more binding than verbal ones. Three different methods were used experimentally, urging households to recycle newspapers. One group of households received a pamphlet stressing the importance of recycling. The second group made verbal commitments, and the third group was persuaded to sign written commitments. Although verbal commitments yielded a higher recycling rate than pamphlet recipients, a follow-up survey a year later revealed that only those who had signed written commitments were still recycling.[7]

CHANGING THE WORLD, ONE NEIGHBORHOOD AT A TIME

About six years ago, Dave made a written commitment, in the form of a membership check, to a group of people interested in designing a neighborhood from scratch. The group took the formula for "cohousing," a design concept imported from Denmark, and applied it to a chunk of land in Colorado. They found a scenic, ten-acre property west of Denver, and, with help from an architect and a developer, they designed and contracted twenty-seven private homes, a workshop, a garden/orchard and a "common house." (The common house is used for group meals a few times a week, meetings, parties, and late-night soul sessions).

Cohousing emphasizes design for community: high density and lots of common space when possible. Many visioning sessions made even a slow-moving process exciting. In one brainstorming session, architect Matt Worswick (who's now a resident) led the group through a process of imagining what activities would be done, where. The group imagined the pedestrian walkways, the community garden, the kids' playgrounds, and various rooms in the common house. Since the architecture is southwestern, they pictured a mission bell in a bell tower. Five years later, that imaginary bell has a very real clang, and kids love to be asked to pull the rope that rings it. Salvaged from an old farm where one of the members grew up, the massive bell calls everyone in the community (called Harmony Village) for meals, meetings, and celebrations.

By clustering homes in blocks of two and four, Harmony residents preserved both land and energy, since heat is "borrowed" from the walls of neighboring homes. And by mandating that cars be parked in garages and parking spaces at the edge of the neighborhood, the group preserved the sanity of its members. There's a sense of calmness in the center of the neighborhood, kind of like a courtyard in a college campus. The design also helps the neighborhood's security, because there's usually activity in the common area, and there's also a good chance of having "eyes on the green" as people make dinner or do the dishes.

When Dave began to incrementally invest in the future of that neighborhood, he was also investing in his neighbors. Instead of wondering who lives six houses down, neighbors all knew each other very well before moving in, because they had met regularly with each other for two and a half years before a single foundation was dug. In the process of building the physical community, they also laid social foundations. They became citizens by necessity, because once the neighborhood was built, it had to be governed. Each resident serves on a team, and, once a month, a large gathering is held to take care of community business, work collectively on maintenance or building projects, or just have a big party or dance.

The neighborhood that emerged is a diverse band of individuals, ranging in age from one year old to eighty-three. Just about everybody has been profiled in the neighborhood newsletter, also an open forum for ideas, creative writing, and true confessions. Ginny Mackey is a retired minister who has made "restorative justice" a passion. This approach seeks genuine healing by creating a one-to-one dialog between criminal and victim.

Rich Grange is an entrepreneur whose telecommunications business provides local jobs for many of his neighbors. The company is committed to social activism, offering time off with pay for employees who volunteer. Edee Gail is a musician and community activist who helped "Save the Mesa"—a landmark we see from our property. Recently, she was singing a song in an assisted-living center. An elderly woman walked away from the group and, according to a nurse who was there, died singing the song.

Virginia Moran is an expert on environmentally and socially responsible investing. Her expertise developed as she researched corporate involvement during the Vietnam war. "It was to their benefit to keep the War going," she says, recalling her initial research. "I decided to teach myself so I could help people align their investments with their values. Then I happened to be in San Francisco and attended some of the early meetings of the Social Investment Forum. After Desmond Tutu came to the United States asking investors to withdraw financial support for South African apartheid, we began canvassing specific sectors, asking them to participate in that cause. Churches were especially effective in getting the word out. Five years later, the [South African] economy started to falter, partly as a result of our efforts."[8]

Virginia has personal investments in diversified hardwood tree plantations in Costa Rica, and in small loans to micro-enterprises, which she calls "bootstraps banking." You can see her excitement as she explains how well some of the funds she works with are performing. "Four socially responsible mutual funds beat the S & P 500s ninety-five percent total return in 1996 through '99," she says. One of the reasons is that a lot of waste, liability, and pollution are screened out. You don't see companies that have EPA citations or labor trouble. And, with most of these companies, you don't have to support products that are frivolous and short-lived, like Pet Rocks. Returns like those we are now seeing—a lot of them in high-tech companies—will continue to cause more people to put their money where their political and ethical beliefs are."

These are just a few of the residents of Harmony Village, and most of the others are also involved with activities that stretch the conventional meaning of the word "value." The way they spend their time makes money less critical. Save enough for retirement? Sure. But do they need a new car, to "keep up with the Joneses?" Not really, because the Joneses drive a well-maintained Saab old enough to wear plates that label the car "antique."

Harmony's mission statement is *"To create a cooperative neighborhood of diverse individuals sharing human resources within an ecologically responsible community setting.*" To make good on that mouthful of intentions, the group recycles, composts, cultivates a community garden, and works on local issues like battling the last leg of a metro beltway (it worked!). Like the rest of the country, Harmony residents are victims of an economy that doesn't always "get it." Recently, they caught employees of the recycling company red-handed—mixing carefully sorted materials together with trash bound for the landfill.

The group also experiments with more innovative activities, like community-supported agriculture. Since their own garden is still evolving, many in the neighborhood subscribe to produce from a local farmer whose wife comes every Tuesday with eight or ten bushel baskets of produce. This enables J.P., the farmer, to know at the beginning of the growing season how much to plant. ("So who's got a great coleslaw recipe?")

Another concept being actively discussed is an effective, businesslike car-sharing cooperative. As Worldwatch Institute writer Gary Gardner phrases it, "Cars spend most of their lives (an average of 95%) parked, taking up space, not taking people where they want to go—*not* doing what they were built to do."[9] In an era with high percentages of at-home workers and retired people, and a desperate re-emergence of public transportation, some Harmony residents wonder why we can't get around in fewer cars, which would use less land for parking spaces and roads and gobble smaller bites of income for car insurance.

The neighborhood already has an informal network of car lending, and a very supportive approach to transportation. "When you need to pick your car up from the shop, just walk around the neighborhood and see who's around," says Laura Herrera, a renter in the community. One Sunday morning at 4:20 A.M., Dave got a frantic call from a neighbor who was trying to board a plane to go on vacation, but whose ID had expired. "Do you think you could go into my house, get my work ID, and be out here at the airport in less than forty-seven minutes, when the plane leaves?" he asked, hopefully. Since there was no traffic, Dave made it in thirty-six minutes.

Though the residents don't call their neighborhood Utopia, they're learning trial-by-fire citizenship—an exciting and challenging, if sometimes frustrating, proposition. Cohousing is only one of many ways to create vital, people-friendly neighborhoods, and it doesn't have to take place in newly constructed buildings. (The Nomad community in Boulder, Colorado, for example, shares public space with an existing theater, while the On-Going Community in Portland, Oregon, rehabilitated old neighborhood houses that members were able to purchase cheaply). Whenever developers, city leaders, and active citizens successfully create a place that optimizes social opportunities and minimizes wasted effort (including resources, time, and money), they are taking a swipe at affluenza.

RESPONSIBLE WEALTH

As we've seen throughout this section of the book, many Americans' economic values may be changing—perhaps just in time. Another indication comes from a seemingly unlikely place—the ranks of the rich and famous. The phrase "a roomful of millionaires" may bring to mind high-powered, aggressive deals struck behind closed doors, but if it's a meeting of an organization known as Responsible Wealth, the millionaires may actually be plotting to give money *away*.

More than four hundred of its members have already redistributed millions in profits they could have reaped from a recent law cutting capital gains taxes. They also opposed recent efforts to abolish the Estate Tax, a tax that only affects people like them. Says one of the group's founders, Mike Lapham, "It's not in society's long-term interest to have people at the top living in gated communities while people at the bottom are behind bars or living in poverty." Among the members of Responsible Wealth are the singer Cher and the actress Christine Lahti.

Another member, software millionaire Michele McGeoy, says, "If I'm earning money watching my stocks grow and someone else is working hard as a teacher, why should I pay a lower tax rate? That may be good for me economically, but it doesn't build a healthy society."[10]

What's up with these people? Why don't they get over it, rake in the money, and get back to the mergers and takeovers? Apparently because they've reached a point of having "enough." Now, greater satisfaction comes from acting for the common good. In a sense, they *are* reinvesting the money—not just for profit, but for people.

CHAPTER 27

Vaccinations and vitamins

> People who for years have been fighting the pollution of the physical environment suddenly realize that we have a perhaps even bigger problem that has to be solved first, and that is cleaning up the toxic areas of our mental environment.
>
> —KALLE LASN,
> *Adbusters*

An ounce of prevention is worth a pound of cure, or so the old saying goes. Many of us take that suggestion seriously each fall when we line up dutifully for flu shots. When we feel a virus coming on, we pop some Vitamin C tablets into our mouths, hoping Linus Pauling knew what he was talking about. Of course, there are no real shots or pills that can prevent or soften the impact of affluenza (with one exception: for the small percentage of Americans who are truly addicted, compulsive shoppers, psychiatrists sometimes prescribe anticompulsion drugs and antidepressants, with promising results). But in a metaphorical sense, some powerful antiviruses are floating around that can help vaccinate us against affluenza, and so are some equally effective vitamins that can help keep us from harm's way.

ADBUSTERS

Vancouver, British Columbia, might be called the headquarters of anti-affluenza vaccine research. It's the home of Kalle Lasn, author of *Culture Jam,* who may one day be viewed in relation to overconsumption the way Jonas Salk is to smallpox. Lasn is the director of The Media Foundation, publisher of a popular quarterly called *Adbusters* magazine. The publication is a mix of scholarly critiques of consumerism and clever "uncommercials," anti-ads that often mock real ads. For example, a parody of Calvin Klein's "Obsession" ads shows men staring into their underwear, while another mocking Absolut Vodka, shows a partially melted plastic vodka bottle, with the caption "Absolute Impotence," and a warning in small print that "drink increases the desire but lessens the performance."

Another ad mocks no real product but shows a handsome young businessman who says he's one of many who are turning to "Mammon," because "I want a religion that doesn't complicate my life with unreasonable ethical demands." It's an obvious play on Christ's declaration that "you cannot serve both God and Mammon." "We're not the biggest player in the spiritual arena, but we're the fastest growing," the Mammon anti-ad declares. It's a subtle but powerful reminder of the decline of true spirituality in the Age of Affluenza.

Perhaps the most successful of *Adbusters'* parodies are its anti-smoking ads. In one, two Marlboro Man–type cowboys ride side by side in the sunset. "I miss my lung, Bob," reads the caption. A series of anti-ads mocks Joe Camel, a cartoon character devised to sell cigarettes to kids according to anti-smoking critics. Joe Camel becomes "Joe Chemo," a camel dying of cancer, lying in a hospital bed hooked to an array of life-support equipment, or already dead from cancer and lying in his coffin.

TURNING ADVERTISING AGAINST ITSELF

The anti-ads work like vaccines because they use the virus itself to build up resistance. "We discovered early on in the publication of *Adbusters* that if we come up with an ad that looks like a Chevron ad or a Calvin Klein ad and fool people for a couple of seconds before they realize it's saying exactly the opposite, then we have created a kind of moment of truth that forces them to think about what they've seen," says Lasn.[1]

Born during World War II in Estonia, Lasn spent the early years of his life in a refugee camp. He remembers those early years as tough in a material sense, "but it was a time when our family was very together, when the community in which we

THE SURGEON GENERAL WARNS THAT
SMOKING IS A FREQUENT CAUSE OF
WASTED POTENTIAL AND FATAL REGRET.

© 1996 BY ADBUSTERS

lived was very together, and I recall it with fondness." Lasn moved around a lot, from Germany to Australia to Japan, where he worked for ten years in marketing until he had a sudden change of heart. He emigrated to Vancouver and became a documentary filmmaker. In 1989 Lasn produced his first television "uncommercial," a parody of British Columbia Tourist Commission ads that showcased the province's stunning natural beauty. Lasn's spoof showed what was happening to that beauty as logging companies clearcut B.C.'s ancient forests. Not surprisingly, television stations refused to air the uncommercial even though Lasn was willing to pay for the airtime.

Lasn started *Adbusters* magazine as an alternative way to get his anti-commercial message out. But his real goal is still to get uncommercials on commercial television, which he calls "the command center of our consumer culture." Lasn and his coworkers, most of whom are less than half his age, have now produced dozens of TV uncommercials. One trumpets "the end of the age of the automobile," as a metal dinosaur constructed from model cars topples to the ground. Others promote "TV Turnoff Week," challenge the "beauty" industry for promoting anorexia and bulimia, and depict a bull running through a china shop while criticizing the gross national product as a measure of economic health.

Many of the uncommercials are produced by people who actually work in the advertising industry. "They have qualms about the ethics of their business," says Lasn, "so clandestinely they come and help us to come up with our messages, which are trying to use television to change the world for the better."

NO ROOM IN THE BOX

But Lasn admits he's still had virtually no success in getting those messages on television. He says, "All the major networks in North America have rejected just about all of our television uncommercials." He describes a discussion with an executive at CNN. It came when Lasn wanted to buy time for one of his anti–beauty industry ads during a CNN fashion show.

"Listen, personally I like your campaign," the executive told Lasn. "I think it says something very important about our society. We should be airing spots like this, but on an official level I can tell you right now, we will never air that spot because we would have Revlon and Maybelline and Calvin Klein coming down our throats the very next day, and that's where our bread and butter is."

Lasn continues to challenge the rejections in court, but the courts nearly always rule that his ads are political commercials and the only political commercials networks must accept are those for candidates in election campaigns. So much for free speech and first amendment protections. "We need a free marketplace of ideas instead of a closed shop where only consumption messages are allowed," Lasn says with a touch of anger. "This is really a battle for the right to communicate. I think it's one of the really great human rights battles of our information age."

BUY NOTHING DAY

CNN did agree (alone among the networks) to air one of Lasn's uncommercials, a spot showing a pig protruding from a map of North America. After a short narration: "The average North American consumes five times more than a Mexican, ten times more than a Chinese person and thirty times more than a person from India. We are the most voracious consumers in the world," the pig burps loudly. "Give it a rest," the narrator continues. The spot promotes an annual event called "Buy Nothing Day," held on the Friday after Thanksgiving, which, in the United States, kicks off the Christmas shopping season.

Begun in Vancouver in 1992, Buy Nothing Day is now celebrated in at least twenty other countries. Participants agree not to purchase anything that day, cut up their credit cards, and demonstrate to encourage others to follow suit. In Vancouver, just before Buy Nothing Day, teams of young adbusters race through the streets ahead of the police, slapping hard-to-remove Buy Nothing Day posters on store windows.

"Buy Nothing Day has exploded," says Lasn. "It's becoming a truly international celebration of frugality and living lightly on the planet, and of voluntary simplicity." Lasn believes the spirit of Buy Nothing Day must catch on as an effective vaccine against affluenza, because the North American lifestyle is simply unsustainable. "Over-consumption is the mother of all of our environmental problems," he says, before settling back to work on another uncommercial.

CREDIT CARD CONDOMS

When the producers of *Affluenza* included several of Lasn's uncommercials in the program, viewers got to see them on PBS. Many found them to be one of the highlights of that program. But when John and his coproducers tried to create an uncommercial of their own—a fake public service announcement (PSA)—to include in the follow-up program, *Escape from Affluenza,* they were required to remove it. Otherwise, PBS wouldn't show the program in prime time.

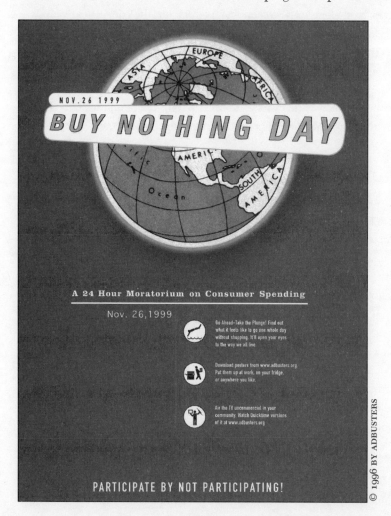

The fake PSA—"a public service announcement from your heirs"— promoted a protection device against affluenza called a credit-card prophylactic. It's a little envelope to store your credit card in with a warning on the outside. "Before you buy, ask yourself: Do I really need it? Can I borrow it from someone else? Are the materials in it reusable or recyclable? How much time will I need to work to afford it?" An older woman tells a young friend to "practice safe shopping" using the prophylactic. "And remember," she says with a smile, spoofing American Express, "don't leave home without it."

PBS refused to allow the PSA in *Escape from Affluenza* because programmers would have to alert local stations to the reference to credit-card prophylactics. The programmers were convinced that fifty or more local PBS affiliates in conservative rural areas wouldn't air the program because in their markets, condoms are taboo. PBS knows its audience. But call it what you want, we think the credit-card condom is a great idea that can help people think twice before spending.

MASTERS OF MONEY

To be truly effective against affluenza, vaccination and vitamin programs will have to start with children. Models of effective preventative programs already exist—none, perhaps, as promising as the one used in San Diego, California. In San Diego area schools, the Money Masters Program runs from preschool through high school.

Staff members from the Consumer Credit Counseling Service speak in the schools, showing students how to save money and spend wisely. One asks students to guess how much he paid for his sharp-looking outfit. Their guesses are about five times the actual price. His secret: buying used clothes in thrift stores and consignment shops. The kids are duly impressed. "This just goes to show you that you don't have to spend a lot of money to look professional," CCCS staffer Gerardo Favela tells them.[2]

Irene Wells, CCCS director in San Diego, explained that her volunteer board of trustees had grown alarmed over the dramatic rise in bankruptcies in San Diego. "And they said, when does it stop?" Gabriella Lopez, who designed the Money Masters Program for the schools said she had been surprised to see that the number of high school students using their own credit cards was rising every semester, and that many of them had gotten into debt problems.

Now, San Diego students don't graduate until they've learned to manage money wisely. Tanya Orozco, a single mother in San Diego, is pleased that her teenage daughter Anita went through the program. It gave Anita a better understanding of her mother's efforts to save on a tight budget. A few years earlier Tanya had needed help from CCCS to handle her own debts. Now she and Anita keep careful track of all their expenses.

CCCS staffers even take the program into preschools, offering bilingual presentations that show four and five year olds how to save their money in a piggy bank and think carefully about spending it. Parents tell CCCS staffers that their tiny children are now telling them that they have to save money. "I have parents coming in saying that every time they buy something now their children are asking them 'do we really need this?'" Gerardo Favela explains with a laugh. Those are kids with a good dose of affluenza vaccine in their veins.

MEDIA LITERACY

In many other schools around the country, teachers help their students protect themselves from affluenza-carrying commercials by teaching them to analyze how media messages manipulate them. The concept is called "media literacy" and in the Age of Affluenza it may be as important as learning to read. Students dissect television ads, to discover the psychological techniques the ads use to convince them to buy. They analyze what needs each advertisement suggests the product might fill, then ask if there are better, less-costly ways to meet the same needs. Increasingly, enlightened school districts require media literacy courses.

Often, the most successful combine ad analysis with video production workshops so that students learn directly the techniques that make television effective. Malory Graham, who teaches video production and media literacy in Seattle, has received support from the county's solid waste division to teach video techniques to high school students and then have them produce their own PSAs promoting recycling and sustainable consumption. Despite the fact that Seattle has one of the best recycling rates in the U.S., increased consumption means that landfills are still growing—recycling can't keep pace with the accelerating rate of waste.

Graham's media literacy and production classes combine the opportunity for hands-on production, which is very exciting for the students, with a greater understanding of the impact of their consumption. "I think it's harder for advertisers to manipulate students who've gone through a program like this," says Graham.[3]

Around the U.S., many students who have been exposed to media literacy are also learning about the deplorable wages and working conditions in factories that make some of the products and brands teenagers have been taught to desire. They demonstrate against child labor and sweatshops in other countries where their products are made, and refuse to be walking billboards for global corporations.

"Today's teens and preteens are going to be tomorrow's revolutionaries," says trend-watcher Gerald Celente. "They're going to very antimaterialistic."[4] But only if they get vaccinated.

CHAPTER 28

Political prescriptions

Our country is set up structurally to oppose voluntary simplicity.

—MICHAEL JACOBSON,
author, Marketing Madness

We are today paying the debt for the material growth that characterized the postwar "Golden Age": disfigured landscapes, polluted air and water, erosion of the ozone layer, the greenhouse effect. Since the Third World also needs significant growth of its material production, only a reorientation of the overdeveloped countries towards a model of development centered on the immaterial growth of free time is capable of guaranteeing our common future.

—ALAIN LIPIETZ,
French Green Party economist

In the previous chapters we've been exploring voluntary personal, community, and workplace strategies for beating the affluenza bug. All are necessary, and will help keep the disease in check for millions of people. But sometimes an epidemic reaches such proportions that political action is called for, usually in the form of a quarantine. We believe that point has been reached in the case of affluenza.

Despite twenty years of bad-mouthing that has left the American public deeply cynical about whether government can ever do anything right, we believe it can play an important role in helping create a society that is affluenza-unfriendly, or, to put it in more positive terms, simplicity-friendly. We line up squarely on the side of those who say our social ills won't be cured by personal action alone.

Just as the symptoms of affluenza are many and interconnected, so must be public efforts to quarantine it. There is no silver bullet that by itself will do the trick. It will take a comprehensive strategy, at all levels of government from local to federal, built, we believe, around several key areas of action:

- reducing working hours
- restructuring the tax and earnings systems
- corporate reform, including responsibility for entire product cycles
- investment in a sustainable infrastructure
- redirection of government subsidies
- a new concept of child protection;
- campaign finance reform

and finally,

- new ideas about economic growth.

BACK TO THE ROAD NOT TAKEN

First of all, if we want to put a lid on the further spread of affluenza, we should restore a social project that topped organized labor's agenda for half a century, then suddenly fell from grace. In Chapter 16 we argued that since the Second World War, Americans have been offered what economist Juliet Schor calls "a remarkable choice." As our productivity more than doubled, we *could* have chosen to work half as much—or even less—and still produce the same material lifestyle we found "affluent" in the '50s. We could have split the difference, letting our material aspirations rise somewhat but also taking an important portion of our productivity gains in the form of more free time. Instead, we put all our apples into making and consuming more.

Established as law in 1938, the forty-hour workweek is still our standard. By law, we could set a different standard, and we should. It need not be a one-size-fits-all standard, like a thirty-hour week of six-hour days as proposed in the 1930s (and more recently in a 1993 Congressional bill written by Democratic representative Lucien Blackwell of Pennsylvania) or a thirty-two-hour week composed of four eight-hour days, though for many working Americans either of those choices would be ideal.

More important, perhaps, is to get annual working hours—now averaging about 2,000 per year and exceeding those even of the workaholic Japanese—under control. Two thousand hours equals 250 eight-hour days. Add to that 104 weekend days and nine national holidays and you've got 363 days—leaving only two days for vacation, which is about where America seems to have come.

Were the average workday to be six hours, we'd be putting in only about 1500 hours a year, about the norm in western Europe. That's an additional 500 hours— twelve and a half weeks!—of free time. So here's a suggestion: Set a standard working year of 1500 hours for fulltime, keeping the forty-hour a week maximum. Then allow workers to find flexible ways to fill the 1500 hours.

FLEXIBLE WORK REDUCTION

Some excellent international ideas for shortening working hours can be found in Anders Hayden's little-known but important book, *Sharing the Work, Sparing the Planet*.

Any of these scenarios could be voluntarily agreed upon between worker and employer, but shorter hours legislation would include stiff employer penalties for work required beyond the 1500-hour maximum per year.

Polls have shown that half of all American workers would accept a commensurate cut in pay in return for shorter working hours.[1] But the cut needn't be based on a one-to-one ratio. Workers are more productive per hour when they work fewer hours. Absenteeism is reduced and health improves. Therefore, as W. K. Kellogg recognized in the 1930s, their thirty-hour weeks should be worth at least thirty-five hours' pay and perhaps more. In fact, Ron Healey, a business consultant in Indianapolis, has convinced several local industries to adopt what he calls the "30-40 now" plan. They offer prospective employees a normal forty-hour salary for a thirty-hour week. Increased employee productivity has made the experiment successful for most.

LESS OVERTIME, MORE VACATION

But to combat affluenza, we ought not fear trading income for free time. Beyond the reduction to 1500 hours per year, legislation could ensure the right of workers to choose further reductions in working hours—instead of increased pay—when productivity rises, or further reductions in working hours at reduced pay, when productivity is stagnant.

In the short run, we need immediate legislation to outlaw the practice of mandatory overtime, which employers now frequently use to require their workers to put in fifty-hour work weeks or more, often over long periods of time. Several recent industrial strikes have centered on eliminating this employer prerogative, which has meant that hundreds of thousands of workers hardly ever see their families.

And if a 1500-hour work year seems too ambitious as an immediate goal, an increase in vacation time (three weeks after one year's employment and four weeks after three years) as a recent article in the travel magazine *Escape* proposed, seems almost a no-brainer. *Escape* editor Joe Robinson is now leading a campaign called "Work to Live" to get Congress to pass federal legislation requiring vacations comparable to those taken for granted in Europe.[2] Asked about the longer vacations idea, a staff person for then-candidate George W. Bush, said, "That sounds great. We need that here." But of the candidates themselves, only Ralph Nader actually endorsed the idea. As things stand now, even the Japanese are guaranteed twenty-five annual vacation days by law. And how many are we guaranteed? Zero.

WORK SHARING WHEN RECESSION COMES

Plans for spreading work around by shortening hours should begin now for another reason: the current economic boom is not going to last forever (it may not even last until this book is published). Even now—November 2000—the Nasdaq is dropping and dot-coms are disappearing daily (the fall of Dot-Communism?), with a new upsurge in layoffs. When a real recession does come will we simply say "sayonara, tough luck" to those whose jobs are lost? There is a better way. Say a company needs to reduce production by twenty percent and believes it must lay off one-fifth of its workforce. What if, instead, it cut everybody's workweek by one day?

Sure, all workers would have to learn to live with less—not a bad idea anyway— but no one would be tossed to the wolves. And we predict that everyone would soon *love* the time off. On the other hand, if we don't make such plans and millions suddenly face unemployment, then all other negative social indicators—crime, family breakdown, suicide, depression, and so forth—can be expected to skyrocket again. Remember, you read it here.

RETIRING STEP BY STEP

There are other ways of exchanging money for time. Many academics receive "sabbaticals," anything from a quarter to a year off every several years, usually accepting a reduced salary during the period. Why not a system of sabbaticals every seven to ten years for all workers who desire them and are willing to take moderate salary reductions when they are on sabbatical? We all need to recharge our batteries every so often.

Or how about a system of graduated retirement? For many of us, self-esteem takes a hit and boredom a bounce when we suddenly go from forty-hour weeks to zero upon retiring. Instead, we could design a pension and social security system that would allow us to retire gradually. Let's say that at fifty we cut 300 hours from our work year—nearly eight weeks. Then at fifty-five we cut 300 more. At sixty, 300 more. And at sixty-five, 300 more. Now, we're down to 800 (given no change in the present annual pattern). We might then have the option to stop paid labor entirely, or to keep working 800 hours for as long as we are capable.

What this would do would allow us to begin learning to appreciate leisure, volunteer more, and broaden our minds long before final retirement. It would allow more young workers to find positions and allow older workers to stay on longer to mentor them. It would allow older workers to both stay involved with their careers and also find time for more balance in their lives.

A variation on this idea that also has merit is to allow workers to take some of their "early retirement" at different stages of their careers, perhaps when they need more parenting time, for example. The ultimate idea, promoted in some European countries, is that a certain number of hours would constitute a total *paid work life,* with considerable flexibility around when the hours are worked.

TAXES

In one sense, the 2000 election was about taxes. Gore wanted to tax Americans less, and Bush wanted to tax them even less than Gore did. What was missing was a discussion about the kinds of taxes and what they might do. There was one exception: As an even stronger cheerleader for affluenza than was Gore, Bush advocated ending the Estate Tax, a tax currently paid by only the richest one or two percent of Americans.

But a change in the tax system, similar to one already underway in parts of Europe, could help considerably to contain affluenza. The first step toward a change could come through an idea called the progressive consumption tax. Proposed by economist Robert Frank in his book *Luxury Fever,* the tax would replace the personal income tax. Instead, people would be taxed on what they consume, at a rate rising from twenty percent (on annual spending under $40,000) to seventy percent (on annual spending over $500,000). Basically the idea is to tax those with the most serious cases of "luxury fever" (which seems to be Frank's synonym for affluenza) at the highest rates, thus encouraging saving instead of spending.

At the same time, we must make it possible for lower-income Americans to meet their basic needs without working several jobs. The old Catholic idea of a family or living wage could be accomplished by a negative income tax or tax credits that guarantee all citizens a simple but sufficient standard of living above the poverty line.

Equally promising are so-called "green taxes." Their proponents would replace taxes on "goods" such as income—and payroll taxes, which discourage increased employment—with taxes on "bads" such as pollution or waste of nonrenewable resources. The point would be to make the market reflect the true costs of our purchases. We'd pay much more to drive a gas-guzzler, for example, and a little more for this book (to cover the true costs of paper), but no more for a music lesson or theater ticket.

Additional *carbon taxes* would discourage the burning of fossil fuels. *Pollution taxes* would discourage contamination of water and air. The costs of cleaning up pollution would be added as a tax on goods whose production causes it. Such a tax could make organic foods as cheap as pesticide-laced produce. *Depletion taxes* would increase the price of nonrenewable resources and lower the comparative price of goods made to last.

While such a green tax system would be complicated, it could go a long way toward discouraging environmentally or socially harmful consumption, while encouraging benign alternatives. As things currently stand, we more often subsidize what we should be taxing—extractive industries like mining ($2.6 billion in subsidies a year), and air and auto travel, for example. We could, and should, turn that around, subsidizing clean technologies and activities (see Chapter 25) like wind and solar power or organic family farms (for example) instead of oil and agribusiness.

CORPORATE RESPONSIBILITY

Another way to reduce the impact of consumption is to require that corporations take full responsibility for the entire life cycle of their products, an idea now gaining widespread acceptance in Europe. The concept is simple, and it is well-explained in the book *Natural Capitalism* by Paul Hawken, and Amory and Hunter Lovins. In effect, companies would no longer sell us products but lease them. Then, when the products reach the end of their useful lives, the same companies would take them back to re-use and recycle them, saving precious resources.

This cradle-to-the-grave idea is winning considerable corporate support already, with leadership from Ray Anderson, CEO of Interface Corporation, an industrial carpet company, and from businesses that have joined the "Natural Step" movement, agreeing to full life-cycle responsibility for their products. If companies take such full responsibility, they will have to include the attendant costs in the prices of their goods.

GOING DUTCH

Such responsibility will be made law by 2006 in the European Union, for automobile companies at least. But with so many companies and so many products traveling all over the world, a Dutch law may provide a more effective solution. In the Netherlands, car buyers pay an additional "disassembly tax" when they buy their vehicle. When the car reaches the end of its useful life, they take it to an auto disassembly plant, where it is carefully stripped of anything that can still be used. Then only the metal shell is crushed and recycled (in the United States everything—wires, plastic, and so forth—just gets crushed, and a large percentage is simply lost as waste). The Dutch plants, which are cheap and low-tech, employ many workers and take any cars. The disassembly tax is part of the Dutch National Environmental Policy Plan (or "Green Plan") and will soon be extended to include many other consumer goods.[3]

STOPPING CHILD ABUSE

Consumer advocate Ralph Nader has called the recent upsurge in marketing targeting children a form of "corporate child abuse." It's as if marketers have set out knowingly to infect our children with affluenza by spreading the virus everywhere kids congregate. It's time to protect our kids. At a minimum, we can keep commercialism out of our schools, starting with Channel One. The fight against Channel One unites Left and Right—Nader and Phyllis Schlafly both testified in Congress against it—and offers a place to begin building bridges in a country increasingly torn apart by ideology.

Secondly, we can begin to restrict television advertising aimed at children. Already, places like Sweden and the Province of Quebec don't allow it. If you're a parent like each of us, you probably long for relief from TV advertising's manipulation of your kids. Moreover, a stiff tax on all advertising would send a strong message to corporate America that curbing the spread of affluenza is serious business.

CAMPAIGN FINANCE REFORM

There are, of course, dozens of other good anti-affluenza legislative ideas out there and no space to mention them here, but none will come to fruition as long as those who profit most from affluenza pull the strings in our political system. The sheer cost of elections—a single New Jersey Senate race in 2000 resulted in $100 million in spending—leaves candidates beholden to those who pay, and those who pay are "those that has and wants to keep."

So the first anti-affluenza legislation has to be campaign finance reform, taking the PACs out of politics and offering competing candidates equal media time to present their ideas, but no time for clever, yet meaningless thirty-second commercials. Former Texas agriculture commissioner Jim Hightower has it right. "The water won't clear up," he says, "until you get the hogs out of the creek."[4]

BUT WON'T OUR ECONOMY COLLAPSE?

What if Americans started buying smaller, more fuel-efficient cars, driving them less and keeping them longer? What if we took fewer long-distance vacations? What if we simplified our lives, spent less money, bought less stuff, worked less, and enjoyed more leisure time? What if government began to reward thrift and punish waste, legislated shorter work hours, and taxed advertisers? What if we made consumers and corporations pay the real costs of their products? What would happen to our economy? Would it collapse, as some economists suggest?

Truthfully, we don't know exactly, since no major industrial nation has yet embarked on such a journey. But there's plenty of reason to suspect that the road will be passable, if bumpy, at first, and smoother later. If we continue on the current freeway, however, we'll find out it ends like Oakland's Interstate 880 during the 1989 earthquake—impassable and in ruins.

Surely we can't deny that if every American took up voluntary simplicity tomorrow, massive economic disruption would result. But that won't happen. A shift away

from affluenza, if we're lucky enough to witness one, will come gradually, over a generation perhaps. Economic growth, as measured by Gross Domestic Product, will slow down and might even become negative. But as economist Juliet Schor points out, there are many European countries (including Holland, Denmark, Sweden, and Norway) whose economies have grown far more slowly than ours, yet whose quality of life—measured by many of the indicators we say we want, including free time, citizen participation, lower crime, greater job security, income-equality, health, and overall life contentment—is higher than our own. Such economies show no sign of collapse. And their emphasis on balancing growth with sustainability is widely accepted across the political spectrum. As former Dutch Prime Minister Ruud Lubbers, a conservative, put it:

> It is true that the Dutch are not aiming to maximize gross national product per capita. Rather, we are seeking to attain a high quality of life, a just, participatory and sustainable society. While the Dutch economy is very efficient per working hour, the number of working hours per citizen are rather limited. We like it that way. Needless to say, there is more room for all those important aspects of our lives that are not part of our jobs, for which we are not paid and for which there is never enough time.[5]

TIME FOR ATTITUDE ADJUSTMENT

If anti-affluenza legislation leads to slower rates of economic growth or a "steady state" economy that does not grow at all, so be it (as we argue in the next chapter, growth of GDP is a poor measure of social health anyway). Beating the affluenza bug will also lead to less stress, more leisure time, better health, and longer lives. It will offer more time for family, friends, and community. And it will lead to less traffic, less road rage, less noise, less pollution, and a kinder, gentler, more meaningful way of life.

In a '60s TV commercial, an actor claims that Kool cigarettes are "as cool and clean as a breath of fresh air." We watch that commercial today and can't keep a straight face, but when it first aired, nobody laughed. Since that time, we've come to understand that cigarettes are unhealthy, silent killers. We've banned TV ads for them. We tax them severely, limit smoking areas, and seek to make tobacco companies pay the full costs of the damage cigarettes cause. We once thought them sexy, but today most of us think they're gross.

Where smoking is concerned, our attitudes have certainly changed. Now, with growing evidence that affluenza is also hazardous, it's surely time for another attitude adjustment.

CHAPTER 29

Annual check-ups

The gross national product includes air pollution and advertising for cigarettes, and ambulances to clear our highways of carnage. It counts special locks for our doors, and jails for the people who break them. . . . It does not allow for the health of our families, the quality of their education, or the joy of their play.

—ROBERT KENNEDY, 1968

A patient in remission from cancer requires routine check-ups to evaluate how things are going. It's the same with affluenza. Once we're on the road to recovery, annual check-ups help prevent costly, energy-sapping relapses. Lingering germs like debt, susceptibility to advertising, and possession obsession can cause recurrences not only in individuals, but communities and national economies as well. Check-ups help track these germs down where they hide, and wipe 'em out!

We argue here that quantitative indicators such as return on investment, tax revenues, and GDP can't tell us everything we need to know about our health. We present alternative indicators that give a more holistic picture: personal consumption audits, community indicators, and the Genuine Progress Indicator (GPI).

Too often, life's complexities get boiled down to a single, nagging question: "Do we have enough money?" Vicki Robin, coauthor of *Your Money or Your Life,* believes this question is far too narrow. Pointing out that money is really what we trade our life energy for, she asks,

> Do we receive fulfillment, satisfaction, and value in proportion to life energy spent?

> Is this expenditure of life energy in alignment with our values and life purpose?

You wouldn't expect weight alone to measure whether a person is sick or well. Nor would blood pressure, by itself, tell you if a person is healthy. Similarly, a grand total of expenditures (like GDP) blindly measures quantity but not quality. It can't distinguish thriving from surviving.

MAKING PERSONAL HISTORY

A very simple measurement of well-being, or gladness to be alive, is whether you're anxious to get out of bed in the morning. But the cold, hard truth is, you may jump energetically out of bed one morning only to be laid off by mid-afternoon (so much for gladness to be alive). Or worse, you could suddenly find out you have an illness even more critical than affluenza, and only have a year to live. Are you really doing what's most important, such as making connections with people, ideas, and nature? What have you always wanted to do that you haven't done yet, because you've been too busy making and spending money? How can you do more of what you're most proud of accomplishing?

These are the kinds of questions that enable us to take stock, and take control of our lives. Honest answers strip away illusions and worn-out patterns. They help get to the heart of what really matters. As Irvin Yalom observed, "Not to take possession of your life plan is to let your existence be an accident."[1]

A good first step in repossessing your life is to identify what you value most. Record the most significant events of your life in a notebook, including personal relationships, births and deaths, achievements, adventures, enlightenments, and disappointments. Recall the first house of your adult life, the first time you fell in love. Note the relative importance of material possessions. Have they satisfied as fully as the connections, emotions, and actions of your life?

Now, jot down a list of principles that are most important to you—things like fairness, trust, unconditional love, taking care of nature, financial security, fearlessness, maintenance of health. These are the principles to base your life decisions on, because they are your greatest, highest values. Apply these principles in your relationships, your career, and your plans for the future, and ask yourself if the constant pursuit of wealth and stuff isn't more effort than it's worth.

When you perform your annual check-up, get out your notebook and review the memoir-in-progress. Do any events of the past year deserve inclusion in life's "greatest hits?" With another year behind you, are there events that now seem less important? Which people from the past year of your life do you most admire? Have you followed your personal code of ethics, with maybe a few, forgivable exceptions?

WHAT REALLY MATTERS

Now comes the knock-out punch—good night, affluenza! By cross-referencing your personal history and values with your annual expenditures, you can determine if you're living life on your terms. Every year when you file your taxes, also file your self-audit—but don't give yourself a deadline. (After all, the idea here is to give yourself a *life*line.) Are your consumption expenditures consistent with what really matters? Have you spent too much on housing, entertainment, or electronic gadgets? Did your expenditures cause you to work overtime, in turn reducing family time? Are you happy with the charitable contributions you made? Are you getting anything back from the money you spent?

COMMUNITY CHECK-UP: INDICATORS OF SUSTAINABILITY

A recent issue of the *Denver Post* reported various surveys in which the mile-high city ranked high, nationally, in terms of "livability." But the same issue reported that Denver's growing traffic problem also ranked near the top. Sure, you take some bad with the good, but how much bad do you take?

That's essentially the question community activists asked themselves a decade ago in Seattle, when they pulled together a cross-section of business leaders, elected officials, doctors, environmentalists, and others to create a checklist of sustainability indicators for the metropolitan area. (By "sustainability," they mean "long-term health and vitality—cultural, economic, environmental, and social.") Keeping track of forty indicators is no small feat, but project coordinator Lee Hatcher is convinced the indicators provide more comprehensive feedback on the health of people, places, and the economy of Seattle than conventional gauges like property values and housing starts. Already, hundreds of Seattle citizens have put in thousands of hours of volunteer time to create and maintain the indicators.

Hatcher points out how linkages among indicators help foster holistic thinking in a community. "Take the indicator for the number of wild salmon returning to spawn," he says. "That one is linked to the economy—tourism, recreation, and fishing—as well as the environment—logging and runoff from streets that pollute streams. If

FORTY SUSTAINABILITY INDICATORS, SEATTLE

- Wild Salmon
- Wetlands
- Biodiversity
- Soil Erosion
- Air Quality
- Pedestrian-friendly Streets
- Open Space in Urban Villages
- Impervious Surfaces
- Population
- Residential Water Consumption
- Solid Waste Generated and Recycled
- Pollution Prevention and Renewable Resource Use
- Farm Acreage
- Vehicle Miles Traveled and Fuel Consumption

- Renewable and Non-renewable Energy Use
- Employment Concentration
- Real Unemployment
- Distribution of Personal Income
- Health Care Expenditures
- Work Required for Basic Needs
- Housing Affordability Ratio
- Children Living in Poverty
- Emergency Room Use
- Community Capital
- Adult Literacy
- High School Graduation
- Ethnic Diversity of Teachers

- Arts Instruction
- Volunteer Involvement in Schools
- Juvenile Crime
- Youth Involvement in Community Service
- Equity in Justice
- Low Birthrate Infants
- Asthma Hospitaliza-tion Rate for Children
- Voter Participation
- Library and Commu-nity Center Usage
- Public Participation in the Arts
- Gardening Activity
- Neighborliness
- Perceived Quality of Life

we begin to see larger populations of salmon, it probably means we're taking better care of the habitat we share with them."[2]

If a community has excellent *arts education* for children, the *juvenile crime rate* may fall, *high school graduations* may increase, and overall *employment* may also improve. However, if the number of *children in poverty* increases, both crime and sickness may increase, resulting in long-term scars in the community.

For Linda Storm, a Seattle resident for eighteen years, the indicators provide important feedback about specific qualities she values. "What sustainable Seattle means to me is being able to find places close to home where I can walk and see my neighbors (*Pedestrian-Friendly Streets, Open Space in Urban Villages, Neighborliness*), breathe fresh, clean air (*Air Quality*) and see native plants (*Biodiversity, Wetlands*)." Yet many of these qualities are declining in proportion to the increase in negative indicators such as *Impervious Surfaces* (fifty-nine percent of Seattle's land area has now been paved over).[3]

The news isn't always what we want to hear, but having relevant feedback about community health can at least stimulate intensive care. Says Lee Hatcher, "Indicators are like the gauges and dials of an aircraft's instrument panel. By designing them carefully and watching them closely, we know the status of our flight and can make good decisions about where to go. Without indicators, we're just flying by the seat of our pants."

NATIONAL CHECK-UP: THE GENUINE PROGRESS INDICATOR (GPI)

Newscasters, investment brokers, and lenders are among those who rely on the Gross Domestic Product (GDP) as an indicator of national prosperity. But does GDP really tell us if our economy is healthy? Economists with an organization called Redefining Progress (RP) don't think so. In a report titled "Why Bigger Isn't Better" they write,

> Imagine receiving an annual holiday letter from distant friends, reporting their best year, because more money was spent than ever before. It began during the rainy season when the roof sprang leaks and their yard in the East Bay hills started to slide. The many layers of roofing had to be stripped to the rafters before the roof could be reconstructed, and engineers were required to keep the yard from eroding away. Shortly after, Jane broke her leg in a car accident. A hospital stay, surgery, physical therapy, replacing the car, and hiring help at home took a bite out of their savings. Then they were robbed, and replaced a computer, two TVs, a VCR, and a video camera. They also bought a home security system, to keep these new purchases safe.[4]

These people spent more money than ever and contributed slightly to a rise in GDP, but were they happier? Not likely, in that year from hell. And what about a nation in which GDP continues to grow? Are its citizens happier? Clearly, that depends on *how the money is being spent.*

A central mission of Redefining Progress is to spotlight the "bads" that are hiding out in the Gross Domestic Product, a yardstick that has for the last half-century been a drug of choice for conventional economists. As long as the GDP goes higher, everything's cool. Politicians point to a swelling GDP as proof that their economic policies are working, and investors reassure themselves that with the overall expan-

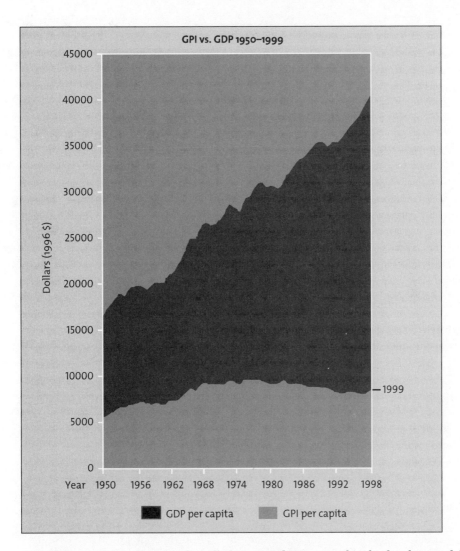

sion of the economy, their stocks will also expand. Yet even the chief architect of the GDP (then GNP), Simon Kuznets, believed that "The welfare of a nation can scarcely be inferred from a measurement like GNP."[5]

Here's why: although the overall numbers continue to rise, many key variables have grown worse. As we have already mentioned, the gap between the rich and everyone else is expanding. In addition, the nation is borrowing more and more from abroad, a symptom of anemic savings and mountains of household debt. The economic and environmental costs of our addiction to fossil fuels continue to mount.

When a city cuts down shade trees to widen a street and homeowners have to buy air conditioning, the GDP goes up. It also goes up when parents divorce, when new prisons are built, and when doctors prescribe antidepressants. Pollution is a big hitter, too, as Redefining Progress' Joanne Kliejunas explains. "The GDP counts pollution at least four times—when it's produced, when it's cleaned up, when there are health care costs, and when there are legal fees to settle lawsuits."[6] In fact, careful analysis reveals much of the economy as tracked by GDP is based on crime, waste, and environmental destruction!

In contrast to GDP—which lumps all monetary transactions together—GPI *evaluates* the expenses, adding in "invisible" assets such as housework, parenting, and volunteer work, but subtracting the following "bads" from the national economy:

GPI EXPENSES

Cost of Crime	Cost of Air Pollution
Cost of Family Breakdown	Cost of Noise Pollution
Loss of Leisure Time	Loss of Wetlands
Cost of Underemployment	Loss of Farmland
Cost of Consumer Durables	Depletion of Nonrenewable Resources
Cost of Commuting	Cost of Long-term Environmental Damage
Cost of Household Pollution Abatement	
Cost of Automobile Accidents	Cost of Ozone Depletion
Cost of Water Pollution	Loss of Old-Growth Forests

As a tool for an annual check-up of the nation, Kliejunas and a growing legion of top-level economists propose that the Genuine Progress Indicator be reported right alongside the annual GDP, to show the *quality* of the economy.

And additional measures are needed to track our use of natural resources—what we have versus what we use. Measures like RP's Ecological Footprint help us to see how our consumptive lifestyles are annually eating up resources faster than Nature can regenerate them. Like the spendthrift who goes on a shopping spree with a savings account, we won't have the steady supply of interest coming to us from Nature in future years if we keep this up.

Says Redefining Progress economist Mathis Wackernagel, "The ecological footprint is gaining a gaining a foothold in the market analysis. Some banks have hired us to analyze the security of government bonds. They want to know, 'Do countries have ecological deficits? Are they overspending their natural wealth?'"

The Genuine Progress Indicator and the Ecological Footprint are really common sense with an analytical, pragmatic edge. National vitality, like personal health and community health, is not really about Powerpoint graphs and mindless business-as-usual, but about real things like the health of people, places, natural capital, and future generations. At all levels of our society, it's time to schedule a holistic annual check-up.

CHAPTER 30

Healthy again

*... one word to you and your children: stay
together, learn the flowers, go light.*

—GARY SNYDER,
Turtle Island

veryone knows the feeling of waking up after a long illness and suddenly, miraculously, feeling full of life again! Being anxious to dive back
into things that have been neglected, and try new things, too. Not feeling isolated, powerless, or estranged anymore. That's what happens when we beat
affluenza. Imagine a dial on your wristwatch, with only two readings—"Life" and
"Death." (Wouldn't that simplify things?) When you shift priorities to pursue what
really matters, the needle on that dial buoyantly wobbles back toward Life.

In the course of writing this book, we've talked with many people whose ideas
became part of our own thought processes. One early reader of the manuscript saw
similarities between victims of affluenza and prisoners of war. "Except we're prisoners of an economy that destroys our environment, our communities, and our peace
of mind," he said. "Imagine what it must feel like when the war is over, and we're

liberated. Or when affluenza is purged from our lives. We'll feel such a sense of freedom, and such a sense of lightness."

After reading about historically low savings rates in the United States, another reviewer imagined fifty million people retiring all at once with virtually no savings, and rapidly gearing down their lifestyles. "There's gonna be one huge garage sale," he said, shaking his head. "I can see the signs now: 'Ford Excursion, near-new, $300,' 'Big Screen TV (56 inch), free. Hot tub, free."

A third reader commented that each of our homes seems to have an elephant in the living room that we try desperately to ignore. "We can't figure out how to chase it out, so we learn to just live with it," he said.

But maybe we don't have to. There are thousands of actions we can take to beat the Bug—and oust the elephant. Though largely out of sight of mainstream media, much is already being done, in classic grassroots style. There are changes in the workplace, from dress codes to employee ownership. There's a resurgence of faith and spirituality, and a growing commitment to better health, including high-quality food, alternative medicine, and personal care products "green" enough to eat (skin cream made of oatmeal, shampoo made from rice and ginger). A recent poll conducted by professional homebuilders found that energy efficiency has in the past year become one of the top considerations for homebuyers. Connections are being made between what we consume and what's happening to the environment. Clearly, our economy is in transition.

We hope this book equips readers with remedies for affluenza that have already worked for thousands of people. A common thread in the recovery process is being able to admit we have a problem—which is equally true at the scale of the individual, the community, the bioregion or the nation.

COMING BACK TO LIFE

Spiritual leader Joanna Macy urges our civilization to take a deep breath, admit we have a major problem, and collectively go cold turkey. She's working to create a new world ethic based on the way nature—and human nature—actually work (lifestyles based on reality—what a concept). In the past, as she discusses in the book *Coming Back to Life*, we've looked at the world as a collection of parts and pieces, but now we're ready for a Great Turning, a new way of understanding.[1]

The idea that life is interdependent and self-organizing has always been perceived on a spiritual level, and now that perception is manifesting itself in biology and physics. Faith, says Macy, is becoming fact, as scientists compile evidence that the world's living systems "are not heaps of disjunct parts, but are dynamically organized and intricately balanced—interdependent in every movement, every function, every exchange of energy and information."

Macy points out that the Earth's systems use feedback just as a thermostat does, to stay healthy. But she believes human feedback is being squelched by an economy with a one-track mind. "It's natural for us to be distressed over the state of the world," she believes. "We are integral components of it, like cells in a larger body. When that body is traumatized, we feel it. . . . However, our culture conditions us to view pain as dysfunction. A successful person, as we conclude from commercials and electoral campaigns, brims with optimism. . . . 'Be sociable,' 'Keep smiling,' 'If you can't say something nice, don't say anything at all.'"

But until we acknowledge that our environment and many aspects of our culture are sick, how can we take focused action to heal them? "The problem lies not with our pain for the world, but in our repression of it," she concludes. "Our efforts to dodge or dull it block effective response." Similarly, our voluntary separation from political and social participation diminishes the collective power of citizens. When we operate strictly as "me" rather than "we," we've essentially been divided and conquered.

We live our lives in the shadow of delirious assumptions such as "We own the Earth," and "Faster is better." (To this latter belief, Mohandas Gandhi responded, "Speed is irrelevant if you're traveling in the wrong direction.") A vintage Doritos commercial typifies our flu-contaminated worldview: "Crunch all you want, we'll make more." But Macy and many others present new ways of seeing the world that strengthen our immune systems against this conveyor-belt mindset. They see beyond the glitter and glitz to a more grounded, abundant reality. Instead of window-shopping (or e-shopping) to *buy* life, they urge us to more passionately *live it*.

DREAMING A NEW DREAM

Betsy Taylor, director of the Center for a New American Dream, consciously operates in the "we" mode. She has the courage to see the damage we're doing and work actively to counter it. "Our house is on fire," she says with conviction, "and there are children inside."[2] (Like many of her colleagues, she believes the smoke alarm went off when the Industrial Revolution began.) "Global warming now threatens the very fabric of life," she says. "Yet man remains in denial."

"Individuals acting alone can't solve the problem," says Taylor, though she acknowledges the critical role that each of us plays. She envisions a positive future—a new dream—shaped by a combination of technological innovation, policy reform, and a significant shift in consciousness. "In twenty-five years, we will have new government policies that provide incentives for us to use materials and energy differently," she predicts. "New policies for transportation, waste management, recycling, and taxes will help individuals and institutions consume wisely. . . . Prices of goods will reflect the true environmental costs of natural resource use and waste. Government will use its purchasing power to create markets for environmentally friendly products."

In effect, Taylor sees strong evidence that our sleepwalking culture is right on the verge of waking up! "Go into any bookstore and you'll see hundreds of books about values, balance, meditation, and simplicity," she says, adding, "Our Web site is another example. This year we'll have eight to ten million hits on it, as people learn more about sustainable living." The overall goals of the Center are not just to *reduce* consumption, but also to *redirect* it with smarter choices about how to purchase sustainable products. In other words, if we're smart, we'll increasingly substitute better design and more complete information for consumption. For example, we'll support sustainable farming in which natural pest control—a biologically rich bank of information—substitutes for pesticide applications. We'll support better design of walkable communities, reducing the need to spend hours lost in wasteful gridlock.

"People assume that a so-called sustainable economy means we have to make sacrifices and give up 'the good life,'" says Taylor. "But look what we're already giving up in our current dream: we're losing cultural traditions, indigenous wisdom, species, languages, relationships, trust, community, and health—all things that are precious beyond money." In Taylor's new dream, the word *simplicity* means far more than cutting back on consumption. It means cutting back on unwanted thoughts, waste, and stress—scrapping the artificial and superficial in favor of the authentic. It's not just simplicity of stuff, but also simplicity of purpose, and clarity of mind. It's about being contented and connected, rather than confused.

The emerging dream she describes is not meager and sparse, but precise, elegant, and full of quality. When we wake up from our current, troubled sleep, we won't be wearing burlap bags—we'll be meeting needs *well*, without having to lug extraneous, expensive baggage. We'll still have the same or better value, but it will be redistributed to more productive ends. Taylor cites the emerging generation of cleaner, leaner vehicles; "green power" like space-age wind turbines; clothing made without petroleum fibers; organic food, grown locally; and buildings that don't make us sick—(especially when we open the utility bills). "Look what's happening in the corporate culture, as companies promote green product lines, like Philips' more efficient computer chips, which may eliminate the need for a half-dozen huge power plants. Or look at a city like Santa Monica, California, which has solar-heated public buildings and organic salad bars in public schools."

"Much of what is being marketed is not tied to quality of life, but status and image. We can change that, with the help of better role models." She points to basketball star Hakeem Olajuwon, who worked with Spalding to offer a $35 athletic shoe under Olajuwon's name (compared to many shoes that cost more than $100). "When growing numbers of people act on their convictions, and those convictions are based on positive values, we'll be dreaming a new dream," says Betsy Taylor.

MOVING AT THE SPEED OF QUALITY

The people we interviewed agree that our current repertoire of assumptions is out of date. One of the most time-worn slogans is "the show must go on." But those who have successfully kicked affluenza ask, "Why?" If the buyer must always beware, and if our economy seems to resemble a pyramid scheme in which risks are pushed onto the poor and the environment, why don't we change the script? they ask. Why don't we announce a new mission, much bigger than going to the moon, or even stopping the Nazis? Why don't we move (quickly!) toward a new Renaissance, in which quality, ecology, equity, diversity, flexibility, and democracy blend together in a sustainable economy? It's clear that by redistributing the unprecedented wealth of this generation, we can make historic improvements in our own lives as well as those of our great great grandchildren. Why settle for junk when we can have quality?

In a way, quality is to affluenza what garlic is to vampires. Durability, appropriate materials, and good design eliminate the need for mountains of stuff, without reducing overall value. It's a different kind of math, which asks not how *much*, but rather how *well*.

Throughout this book, we've talked about hidden costs in an economy that tolerates waste, loss of natural capital, and social impacts. On the other hand, there are many hidden *benefits* in an economy designed for sustainability. For example, eating organic produce has the hidden benefits of preventing soil erosion from farmland and protecting algal blooms in lakes from wasted, runaway nutrients. Healthy food generally comes from healthy farms. Similarly, buying recycled paper has the hidden benefit of helping to create a viable recycling industry, complete with products made solely from recycled material. We're talking about very productive yet relatively effortless changes in the way we live our lives. Though it sometimes seems overwhelming to think about changing something as huge as a "worldview," Macy's Great Turning and Taylor's New Dream are really just part of our everyday lives, as Paul Hawken sees it:

> Join a diverse group of people in a room—different genders, races, ages, occupations, and levels of education—and ask them to describe a world they want to live in 50 years from now. Do we want to drive two hours to work? No. Do we want to be healthy? Yes. Do we want to live in places that are safe? Do we want our children to grow up in a world where they are hopeful? Do we want to be able to worship without fear of persecution? Do we want to live in a world where nature is rebounding and not receding? No one disagrees; our vision is the same. What we need to do is identify, together, the design criteria for how we get there.[3]

With inspired design, we can have architecture that lasts a thousand years (instead of eight, like many Wal-Mart buildings). With maturing knowledge about ecology, we can have waste treatment that mimics nature, like John Todd's "Living Machines," which use diverse, efficient biosystems to purify water, aesthetically. We can have energy that comes directly from income (the sun) rather than savings (fossil fuels). We can support local banks that in turn support local needs. We can have less stressful lifestyles and more time with family and friends, as advocated by members of the "slow food" movement, for whom fast food is synonymous with anxiety. Chances are we can have what we want, if we recycle our worn-out paradigm into a new one, in which our decisions and our policies are driven more by our hopes than by our fears. We know what a dysfunctional future would feel like: an endless string of bad-news days that deplete our energy and strip away our sense of balance. If we continue on the same path, our economy will ultimately crash like the Titanic, and the waters will be icy.

"It can't happen," we tell each other, "our economy is now unsinkable." But it can—and will—happen, unless we get busy. We need to convert convictions into public policy, and ideas about sustainability into reality.

THE LAST PICTURE SHOW

As individuals, we don't need to be millionaires to eat well, sleep soundly, or get to know our neighbors. Without any doubt, we *do* need to consume less, because we're running out of affordable resources as well as tolerable places to dump our wastes. But the core issue of this book goes beyond consuming less to *wanting* less, and *needing* less. From Lifestyles of the Rich and Famous we can progress to the more rewarding Lifestyles of the Content and Healthy.

Think about all the money we spend to fight various diseases, many of which (like allergies, cancer, diabetes, and stroke) are caused or aggravated by affluent lifestyles. Then remember that affluenza is one disease that we can cure by spending *less* money, not more.

The bottom line is this: When your time comes and your whole life flashes before you, will it hold your interest? How much of the story will be about moments of clarity and grace, kindness and caring? Will the main character— you—appear as large and noble as life itself, or as tiny and absurd as a cartoon figure, darting frantically among mountains of stuff? It's up to you, and indeed, it's up to all of us!

CHAPTER ENDNOTES

INTRODUCTION

1. Al Gore, *Earth in the Balance,* p. 221.
2. Personal interview, April 1996.
3. Personal interview, October 1996.

CHAPTER 1

1. *Statistical Abstract of the United States,* 1999.
2. *Harper's* Index, July 1999.
3. *All-Consuming Passion* (1998 pamphlet produced by the New Road Map Foundation and Northwest Environment Watch), p. 6.
4. KCTS Television interviews, October 1995.
5. *All-Consuming Passion,* p. 7.
6. Personal interview, April 1996.
7. *All-Consuming Passion,* p. 6.
8. Bob Walker, "Mall Mania," *The Sacramento Bee,* October 19, 1998.
9. Ibid.
10. Paula Felps, "DotComGuy," *The Seattle Times,* February 20, 2000.

CHAPTER 2

1. Personal interview, May 1996.
2. Robert Frank, *Luxury Fever,* p. 46.
3. *Statistical Abstract of the United States,* 1999.
4. Personal interview, May 1996.
5. Leslie Earnest, "Household Debt Grows Precarious As Rates Increase," *Los Angeles Times,* May 13, 2000.
6. Elizabeth Warren, "Bankruptcy Borne of Misfortune, Not Excess," *The New York Times,* September 3, 2000.
7. *Los Angeles Times,* op cit.
8. *New York Times,* op cit.
9. Michael Mantel, "What Bush v. Gore Means for Empty Piggy Banks," *Business Week,* September 11, 2000.

10. *USA Weekend* magazine, May 12–14, 2000.

11. *All-Consuming Passion*, p. 11.

CHAPTER 3

1. David Meyer, *The American Paradox,* p.136.

2. Personal interview, April 1996.

3. Personal interview, September 1996.

4. Personal interview, September 1996.

5. Keith Bradshear, "GM Has High Hopes for Road Warriors," *New York Times,* August 6, 2000.

6. See the wealth of information on changing expectations in Richard McKenzie's *The Paradox of Progress.*

7. Paul Andrews, "Compaq's new iPac may be the PC for your pocket," *Seattle Times,* November 5, 2000.

8. *All-Consuming Passion*, p. 4.

9. Personal interview, October 1987.

10. Personal interview, May 1997.

11. James Lardner, "The Urge to Splurge," *U.S. News and World Report,* May 24, 1998.

CHAPTER 4

1. Michael Kidd, White Paper on Self-Storage, Self-Storage Association, March 2000.

2. Personal interview, January 2000.

3. John Fetto, "Time for the Traffic," *American Demographics,* January 2000, www.americandemographics.com.

4. Steven Ashley, Ed., *Mechanical Engineering* online, 1997.

5. Stephanie Simon, "Scientists Inspect Humdrum American Lives," *Los Angeles Times,* October 28, 1999.

6. Ellen Goodman, as quoted in *All Consuming Passion*, 1998.

7. Erich Fromm, *To Have or To Be?*, p. 5.

8. Goodman, op cit.

9. Personal Interview with Rathje, September 2000.

CHAPTER 5

1. Personal interview, September 1996.

2. Personal interview, September 1996.

3. From the film *Running Out of Time,* 1994.
4. Ibid.
5. Staffan Linder, *The Harried Leisure Class,* p. 4.
6. Staffan Linder, op cit., p. 40.
7. Rodney Clapp, "Why the Devil Takes Plastic," *The Lutheran,* March 1999.
8. Linder, op cit. p. 71.
9. Personal interview, October 1992.
10. Personal interview, September 1993.
11. Personal interview, October 1992.
12. Personal interview, May 1993.
13. See for instance, Martin Moore-Ede, *The Twenty-Four Hour Society.*
14. From the film *Running Out of Time,* 1994.
15. Personal interview, October 1993.
16. Personal interview, October 1993.

CHAPTER 6

1. From the documentary *Running Out of Time,* 1994.
2. William Bennett, *The Index of Leading Cultural Indicators,* p. 68.
3. Personal interview, May 1996.
4. Personal interview, May 1996.
5. Personal interview, May 1996.
6. Personal interview, May 1996.
7. Arlie Russell Hochschild, *The Time Bind,* back cover.
8. Personal interview, May 1996.
9. Personal interview, October 1996.

CHAPTER 7

1. Personal interview, April 1996.
2. See for example James McNeal, *Kids As Customers.*
3. Harwood poll, Yearning for Balance, 1995.
4. Personal interview, October 1999.
5. Geoffrey Cowley and Sharon Begley, "Fat for Life," *Newsweek,* July 3, 2000, pp. 40–47.
6. As seen in the TV program *Affluenza,* 1997.
7. Personal interview, October 1999.
8. Personal interview, April 1996.
9. Personal interview, May 1996.
10. Personal interview, April 1996.

11. Interview with Alex Molnar, April 1996.

12. Interview with psychologist David Elkind, October 1993.

13. David Korten, *The Post-Corporate World,* p. 33.

14. Personal interview, May 1996.

CHAPTER 8

1. Ray Oldenburg, *The Great Good Place,* p. xv

2. Personal interview, March 1997.

3. Robert Putnam, *Bowling Alone: the Collapse and Revival of American Community*, p. 49.

4. Eileen Daspin, "Volunteering On the Run," *Wall Street Journal,* November 15, 1999, p. W1.

5. "Our Separate Ways," *People,* September 25, 1995, p. 125.

6. Jeremy Rifkin, *The Age of Access*, p. 59.

7. Personal interview with Stacy Mitchell, Institute for Local Self-Reliance, February 2000.

8. Personal interview with Jeff Milchen, Boulder Independent Business Alliance, February 2000.

9. Personal interview, February 2000.

10. Personal interview, October 1998.

11. Edward J. Blakely and Mary Gail Snyder, *Fortress America: Gated Communities in the United States.*

12. Dyan Machan, interview with Daniel Yankelovich, *Forbes,* November 16, 1998, p. 194.

13. Personal interview with William O'Hare, Annie Casey Foundation, March 2000.

14. Ibid, p. 114.

15. Personal interview with March Miringoff, May 2000.

CHAPTER 9

1. Personal interview, October 1999.

2. Personal interview, April 1999.

3. Personal interview, September 1996.

4. Lee Atwater, "Lee Atwater's Last Campaign," *Life* magazine, February 1991.

5. Michael Lerner, *The Politics of Meaning*, pp. 5–8.

6. David Myers, *The American Paradox*, pp. 6–7.

7. Tim Kasser and Richard Ryan, "A Dark Side of the American Dream," *Journal of Personality and Social Psychology,* Vol. 65, No.2, 1993.

8. Tom Hayden, *Reunion*, p. 82.

9. Personal interview, May 1998.

10. William Willimon and Thomas Naylor, *The Abandoned Generation*, pp. 7–8.

11. Wilhelm Ropke, *A Humane Economy*, p. 102.

12. Ibid, p. 113.

13. Ibid, p. 114.

14. Ernest van den Haag, "Of Happiness and of Despair We Have No Measure," in *Man Alone*, p. 184

15. Ibid, p. 197.

CHAPTER 10

1. From the film, *Affluenza*, 1997.

2. Personal interview, November, 1996.

3. Sylvia Nasar, "Even Among the Well-Off, the Richest get Richer," *New York Times*, May 24, 1992.

4. Felicity Berringer, "Giving by the Rich Declines," *New York Times*, May 24, 1992.

5. "The Widening Income Gap," *Center on Budget and Policy Priorities*, Sept. 4, 1999.

6. "Millions Still Going Hungry in U.S., Report Finds," *Reuters*, Sept. 9, 2000.

7. "Is Greed Good?" *Business Week*, April 19, 1999.

8. David Broder, "To Those who Toil Invisibly Amid Billionaires," *Seattle Times*, April 16, 2000.

9. Barbara Ehrenreich, "Maid to Order," *Harper's*, April, 2000.

10. Ibid.

11. Personal interview, October 1996.

12. Ibid.

13. Barry Yeoman, "Steel Town," *Mother Jones*, May/June 2000. See also Drew Leder, "It's Criminal the Way We've Put 2 Million in Cages," *The San Francisco Examiner*, Feb. 10, 2000.

14. Personal interview, October 1996.

CHAPTER 11

1. Paul Hawken, Amory Lovins and Hunter Lovins, *Natural Capitalism: Creating the Next Revolution*, pp. 51–52.

2. Sandra Postel, *Dividing the Waters*, Vol. 132.

3. Energy Information Administration, *Annual Energy Review 1997*, DOE/EIA-0384(97), Washington, D.C., July 1998, Tables 5.1 and 1.5.

4. John C Ryan and Alan Thein Durning, *Stuff: The Secret Lives of Everyday Things*, p. 43.

5. Donella Meadows, "How's a Green Group to Survive Without Junk Mail?" *Global Citizen*, June 2000.

6. Ryan and Durning, op. cit., p. 55.

7. Gary Gardner and Payal Sampat, "Forging a Sustainable Materials Economy," in Worldwatch Institute, *State of the World 1999*, p. 47.

8. Ryan and Durning, op. cit., p. 8.

9. Personal interview with Alan Durning, July 1995.

10. Personal Conversation with Mathis Mackernagel, August 2000.

11. Anthony Ricciardi, "Mass Extinction in American Waters," Society for Conservation Biology, September 30, 1999

12. Ibid.

CHAPTER 12

1. Theo Colburn, Diane Dumanoski, and John Peterson Myers, *Our Stolen Future: Are We Threatening Our Fertility, Intelligence, and Survival? A Scientific Detective Story*, p.137.

2. Personal interview, March 2000.

3. *Living Downstream: An Ecologist Looks at Cancer and the Environment*, p. 99.

4. Ibid, p. 6–7.

5. "Phasing Out Persistent Organic Pollutanta," *State of the World 2000*, p. 85.

6. Dan Fagin, Marianne Lavelle, Center for Public Integrity, *Toxic Deception: How the Chemical Industry Manipulates Science, Bends the Law, and Endangers Your Health*, p. 43.

7. Chris Bowman, "Medicines, Chemicals Taint Water: Contaminants Pass Through Sewage Plants," *Sacramento Bee*, March 28, 2000, online.

8. Douglas Frantz, "E.P.A. Asked to Crack Down on Discharges of Cruise Ships," *American* online, March 20, 2000.

9. Colburn, op. cit., p. 24.

10. Colburn, op. cit., p. 236.

11. Webster Donovan, "The Stink About Pork," *George*, April 1999, p. 94.

CHAPTER 13

1. National Institute on Drug Abuse, Bethesda, Maryland.

2. Scott Cohen, "Shopaholics Anonymous," *Elle*, May 1996, p. 120.

3. "News and Trends," *Psychology Today,* January/February 1995, p. 8.

4. David G. Myers, "Wealth, Well-Being, and the New American Dream," Center for a New American Dream website, July 4, 2000.

5. Personal interview, August 1997.

6. "Money Changes Everything," *American Behavioral Scientist,* July/August 1992, p. 809.

7. Ibid.

8. Alex Prud'Homme, "Taking the Gospel to the Rich," *New York Times,* February 14, 1999, p. BU 13.

CHAPTER 14

1. Personal interview, June 2000.

2. Donella H. Meadows, Dennis Meadows, and Jorgen Randers, *Beyond the Limits.*

3. Taichi Sakaiya, *The Knowledge-Value Revolution, or, A History of the Future,* p. 43.

4. Edward Hoffman, *The Right to Be Human: A Biography of Abraham Maslow,* pp. 122, 128.

5. Andrew Weil, *Eating Well for Optimum Health,* p. 21.

6. Fromm, Eric, *To Have or to Be?,* p. 155.

7. Jane Brody, "Cybersex Gives Birth to a Psychological Disorder," *New York Times,* May 16, 2000, p. D7.

8. Jerry Mander, *Four Arguments for the Elimination of Television,*

9. Eric Schlosser, "Fast Food Nation: The True Costs of America's Diet," *Rolling Stone,* September, 3, 1998, p. 3.

10. Personal interview with D.J. Forman, December 2000.

11. Rocky Mountain News editorials, June 20, 2000, p. 31.

CHAPTER 15

1. Marshall Sahlins, "The Original Affluent Society" in Goodwn, Ackerman, and Kiron (Eds.) *The Consumer Society,* pp. 18–20.

2. Personal interview, May, 1993.

3. Cited in James Child Jr., *Greed,* p. 1.

4. Jerome Segal, *Graceful Simplicity,* p. 167.

5. Personal interview, April 1996.

6. Segal, op. cit. p. 6.

7. Ibid, p.189.

8. Personal interview, October 1996.

9. Personal interview, April 1996.

10. T.C. McLuhan, *Touch the Earth,* p.90.

CHAPTER 16

1. Personal interview, April 1996.

2. Jerome Segal, *Graceful Simplicity,* p. 13.

3. Ibid, p. 13.

4. Ibid, p. 14.

5. from the documentary film *Running Out of Time,* 1994.

6. Juliet Schor, *The Overworked American,* p. 44.

7. Rodney Clapp, *The Consuming Passion,* p. 173.

8. Marx and Engels, *The Communist Manifesto,* in Lewis Feuer, *Marx and Engels: Basic Writings on Politics and Philosophy,* pp. 1–41.

9. Marx, *The Economic and Philosophical Manuscripts of 1844,* in Erich Fromm, *Marx's Concept of Man,* p. 55.

10. Erich Fromm, *Marx's Concept of Man,* p. 107.

11. Ibid, p. 37.

12. Karl Marx, *Capital III,* p. 954.

13. Perry Miller, *The American Transcendentalists,* p. 313.

14. Ibid, p. 309–310.

15. Ibid, p. 310.

CHAPTER 17

1. Personal interview, April 1996.

2. Paul Lafargue, *The Right to Be Lazy,* p. 40.

3. William Morris, in A.C. Morton, *The Political Writings of William Morris,* p. 112.

4. Personal interview, April 1996.

5. Ibid.

6. Benjamin Hunnicutt, *Work Without End,* p. 82.

7. Ibid, p. 75.

8. Ibid, pp. 88–97.

9. Ibid, p. 99.

10. Ibid, p. 53.

11. James Twitchell, "Two Cheers for Materialism, *Utne Reader,* November/December, 2000.

12. Personal interview, October 1993.

13. Ibid.

14. Ibid.

CHAPTER 18

1. From the documentary *Affluenza*, 1997.

2. Ibid.

3. Personal interview, April 1996.

4. Ibid.

5. From the documentary *Affluenza*, 1997.

6. Ibid.

7. Ibid.

8. Gary Cross, *An All-Consuming Century*, p. 169.

9. From the documentary *Escape From Affluenza*, 1998.

10. Wilhelm Ropke, *A Humane Economy*, p. 109.

11. John Kenneth Galbraith, *The Affluent Society*, p. 258.

12. Ibid, p. 266.

13. Tom Hayden, *Reunion*, p. 264.

14. Mario Savio, "Stop the Machine," address to the Free Speech Movement, Berkeley, 1964.

15. Gary Cross, op cit., p. 161

16. Personal interview, April 1996.

CHAPTER 19

1. Pierre Martineau, *Motivation in Advertising*, p. 190.

2. New Road Trip Foundation, *All-Consuming Passion*, p. 6.

3. Kim Chapman, "Americans to Spend More on Media than Food in 2003," *Denver Rocky Mountain News*, December 17, 1999.

4. Michael Jacobson and Laurie Mazur, *Marketing Madness*, p. 131.

5. Personal interview, April 1996.

6. Personal interview with Laurie Mazur, April 1996.

7. Ibid.

8. Pat Kearney, "Driving for Dollars," *The Stranger*, May 4, 2000.

9. Personal interview, April 1996.

10. Personal interview, April 1996.

11. Susan Faludi, *Stiffed*, p. 35.

12. Wilhelm Ropke, *A Humane Economy*, p. 128–129.

CHAPTER 20

1. Kalle Lasn, *Culture Jam,* p. 27.
2. Personal interview, April 2000.
3. Joel Makower, *The Green Business Letter,* March 1994, pp. 1, 6–7.
4. Sharon Beder, *Global Spin: The Corporate Assault on Environmentalism,* pp. 28–29.
5. Greening Earth Society Web page.
6. Personal interview, April 2000.
7. Mark Dowie, introduction to John C. Stauber and Sheldon Rampton, *Toxic Sludge Is Good for You: Lies, Damn Lies and the Public Relations Industry,* p. 1.
8. John C. Stauber and Sheldon Rampton, *Toxic Sludge is Good for You: Lies, Damn Lies and the Public Relations Industry,* p. 28.
9. Beder, op. cit., p. 32.
10. Jamie Lincoln Kitman, "The Secret History of Lead," *The Nation,* March 20, 2000, p. 6.
11. Joyce Nelson, "Great Global Greenwash: Barston-Marsteller, Pax Trilateral and the Brundtland Gang vs. the Environment," *CovertAction, 44,* pp. 26–33, 57–8.
12. George Orwell, *1984,* p. 312.
13. Stauber, op. cit., p. 28.
14. Beder, op.cit., pp. 112–113.
15. Donella Meadows, Dennis Meadows, and Jorgen Randers, *Beyond the Limits.*

CHAPTER 22

1. Personal interview, October 1997.
2. Personal interview, November 1996.
3. Ibid.
4. Ibid.
5. See also the book *Getting a Life,* by Jacqueline Blix and David Heitmiller.
6. Personal interview, June 1996.
7. Harwood poll, "Yearning for Balance," 1995.

CHAPTER 23

1. Personal interview, October 1996.
2. Personal interview, November 1996.

3. Personal interview, September 1996.

4. Personal interview, July 1996.

CHAPTER 24

1. Bill McKibben, *The Age of Missing Information*, p. 70.

2. Ibid, p. 71.

3. Chellis Glendinning, "Recovery from Western Civilization," in *Deep Ecology for the 21st Century*, ed. George Sessions, p. 37.

4. Aldo Leopold, *A Sand County Almanac*, p. 24.

5. Personal interview.

6. David Sobel, *Beyond Ecophobia: Reclaiming the Heart in Nature Education*, p. 34.

7. Robert Greenway, "The Wilderness Effect and Ecopsychology," in *Ecopsychology*, ed. Theodore Roszak, Mary E. Gomes, and Allen D. Kanner, p. 128–9.

8. Ibid.

9. Personal interview, March 2000.

10. Personal interview, April 1996.

CHAPTER 25

1. Personal interview, March 1997.

2. Personal interview, June 2000.

3. Personal interview, July 2000.

4. Michael Brower and Warren Leon, *The Consumer's Guide to Effective Environmental Choices*, p. 134.

5. Michael Brylawski, "Car Watch: Move Over, Dinosaurs," *RMI Solutions Newsletter*, Rocky Mountain Institute, Spring 2000, page 12.

6. Personal interview, June, 2000.

7. Personal interview, September, 2000.

8. Tom Chappell, *The Soul of a Business: Managing for Profit and the Common Good*.

9. Terrance O'Connor, "Therapy for a Dying Earth," in *Ecopsychology*, ed. Theodore Roszak, Mary E. Gomes, and Allen D. Kanner, p. 153.

CHAPTER 26

1. Benjamin R. Barber, *A Place for Us*, p. 73.

2. Ibid, p. 10.

3. "A Letter from Michael Moore to the Non-Voters of America," Internet August 1, 2000.

4. "Off the Playground of Civil Society," Harry C. Boyte paper, Duke University, October 1998, p. 5.

5. Personal interview, August 2000.

6. Doug McKenzie-Mohr and William Smith, *Fostering Sustainable Behavior*, p. 49.

7. Ibid, p. 53.

8. Personal interview, October 2000.

9. Gary Gardner, "Why Share?" *World Watch*, July–August 1999, p. 10.

10. Leah Brumer, "Capital Idea," *Hope*, Fall 1999, pp. 43–45.

CHAPTER 27

1. Personal interview, November 1996.

2. Personal interview, October 1997.

3. Personal interview, April 2000.

4. Personal interview, October 1996.

CHAPTER 28

1. New Road Map Foundation, *All-Consuming Passion*, p. 16.

2. *Utne Reader*, September–October 2000.

3. From the TV documentary *Green Plans*, 1995.

4. Speech at Santa Barbara, California, May 13, 2000.

5. Anders Hayden, *Sharing the Work, Sparing the Planet*, p. 36.

CHAPTER 29

1. Irvine D. Yalom, *Existential Psychotherapy*, p. 12.

2. Personal interview, October 1998.

3. Personal interview, October 1998.

4. *Redefining Progress*, "Why Bigger Isn't Better: The Genuine Progress Indicator 1999 Update."

5. Personal interview, October 1998.

6. Personal interview, October 1998.

CHAPTER 30

1. Joanna Macy and Molly Young Brown, *Coming Back to Life: Practices to Reconnect Our Lives, Our World*, p. 27.

2. Personal interview, October 2000.

3. Paul Hawken, "Natural Capitalism," interview by Allan Hunt Badiner, *Yoga Journal*, September/October 1994, pp. 68, 70.

BIBLIOGRAPHY AND SOURCES

Abdullah, Sharif. *Creating a World that Works for All*. San Francisco: Berrett-Koehler, 1999.

Ableman, Michael. *From the Good Earth*. New York: Abrams, 1993.

———. *On Good Land*. San Francisco: Chronicle Books, 1998.

Acuff, Dan. *What Kids Buy and Why*. New York: The Free Press, 1997.

Andrews, Cecile. *The Circle of Simplicity*. New York: Harper/Collins, 1997.

Aronowitz, Stanley, and William DiFazio. *The Jobless Future*. Minneapolis: University of Minnesota, 1994.

AtKisson, Alan. *Believing Cassandra*. White River Jct., Vt.: Chelsea Green, 1999.

Barber, Benjamin R. *A Place for Us*. New York: Hill and Wang, 1998.

Bartlett, Donald, and James Steele. *America:Who Really Pays the Taxes?* New York: Touchstone, 1994.

———. *America: What Went Wrong?* Kansas City: Andrews and McNeal, 1992.

Beder, Sharon. *Global Spin: The Corporate Assault on Environmentalism*. White River Junction, Vt: Chelsea Green Publishing Company, 1997.

Bellah, Robert, et al. *The Good Society*. New York: Knopf, 1991.

———. *Habits of the Heart*. Berkeley, CA: University of California Press, 1985.

Blakely, Edward J., and Mary Gail Snyder. *Fortress America: Gated Communities in the United States*. Washington, D.C.: Brookings Institution Press, 1997.

Blix, Jacqueline, and David Heitmiller. *Getting a Life*. New York: Viking, 1997.

Bodnar, Janet. *Dr. Tightwad's Money-Smart Kids*. Washington, D.C.: Kiplinger, 1997.

———. *Mom, Can I Have That?* Washington, D.C.: Kiplinger, 1996.

Boyte, Harry, and Nancy Kari. *Building America*. Philadelphia: Temple, 1996.

Brandt, Barbara. *Whole Life Economics*. Philadelphia: New Society, 1995.

Brockaway, Sandy, ed. *Macrocosm USA*. Cambria, Calif.: Macrocosm USA, Inc., 1992.

Brower, Michael, and Warren Leon. *The Consumer's Guide to Effective Environmental Choices*. New York: Three Rivers Press, 1999.

Callenbach, Ernest. *Living Cheaply With Style*. Berkeley, CA: Ronin Publishing, 1993.

Celente, Gerald. *Trends 2000*. New York: Warner, 1997.

Chappell, Tom. *The Soul of a Business*. New York: Bantam, 1993.

Childs, James. *Greed*. Minneapolis: Fortress, 2000.

Clapp, Rodney, ed. *The Consuming Passion*. Downer's Grove, Ill.: Intervarsity, 1998.

Cobb, Clifford W. "Roads Aren't Free: Estimated the Full Social Cost of Driving and the Effects of Accurate Pricing," *Working Paper Number 3*. San Francisco: Redefining Progress, July 1998.

———, Gary Sue Goodman, and Joanne Kliejunas . *Blazing Sun Overhead and Clouds on the Horizon: The Genuine Progress Report for 1999*. San Francisco: Redefining Progress, December 2000.

Cohen, Joel. *How Many People Can the Earth Support?* New York: Norton, 1995.

Colburn, Theo, Diane Dumanoski, and John Peterson Myers. *Our Stolen Future: Are We Threatening Our Fertility, Intelligence, and Survival? A Scientific Detective Story*. New York: Dutton, 1996.

Courtright, Alan. *The 6/12 Plan*. Self-published, 1989.

Cross, Gary. *An All-Consuming Century*. New York: Columbia, 2000.

Daly, Herman. *Steady-State Economics*. Washington, D.C.: Island Press, 1991.

——— with John Cobb. *For the Common Good*. Boston: Beacon, 1994.

De Bell, Garrett, ed. *The Environmental Handbook*. New York: Ballantine, 1970.

DeGrote-Sorenson, Barbara and David. *Six Weeks to a Simpler Lifestyle*. Minneapolis: Augsburg, 1994.

Devall, Bill. *Living Richly in an Age of Limits*. Salt Lake City: Gibbs Smith, 1993.

DeWitt, Calvin. *Earth-wise*. Grand Rapids, Mich.: CRC Publications, 1994.

Dickson, Paul. *Timelines*. Reading, Mass.: Addison-Wesley, 1991.

Dlugozima, Hope, James Scott, and David Sharp. *Six Months Off*. New York: Henry Holt, 1996.

Dominguez, Joe, and Vicki Robin. *Your Money or Your Life: Transforming Your Relationship with Money and Achieving Financial Independence*. New York: Viking, 1992.

Doyle, Kenneth. *The Social Meanings of Money and Property*. Thousand Oaks, Calif.: Sage, 1999.

Durning, Alan. *How Much Is Enough?* New York: Norton, 1992.

——— and John C. Ryan. *Stuff: The Secret Lives of Everyday Things*. Seattle: Northwest Environment Watch, 1997.

Ehrenhalt, Alan. *The Lost City*. New York: Basic Books, 1995.

Elkind, David. *The Hurried Child*. Reading, Massachusetts: Addison-Wesley, 1988.

Ellul, Jacques. *The Technological Society*. New York: Vintage, 1964.

Elwood, J. Murray. *Not For Sale*. Notre Dame, Ind.: Sorin, 2000.

Etzioni, Amitai. *The Spirit of Community*. New York: Crown, 1993.

Faludi, Susan. *Stiffed*. New York: Morrow, 1999.

Fassel, Diane. *Working Ourselves to Death*. San Francisco: Harper San Francisco, 1990.

Folbre, Nancy. *The New Field Guide to the U.S. Economy*. New York: New Press, 1995.

Forbes, Peter, ed. *Our Land, Ourselves*. San Francisco: Trust for Public Land, 1999.

Foster, Richard. *Freedom of Simplicity*. San Francisco: Harper & Row, 1981.

Fox, Matthew. *The Reinvention of Work*. San Francisco: Harper San Francisco, 1994.

Frank, Robert. *Luxury Fever*. New York: The Free Press, 1999.

Frank, Thomas. *One Market Under God*, New York: Doubleday, 2000.

Fromm, Erich. *Marx's Concept of Man*. New York: Frederick Ungar, 1971.

———. *The Anatomy of Human Destructiveness*. Greenwich, Conn.: Fawcett, 1973.

———. *The Heart of Man*. New York: Harper & Row, 1964.

———. *The Sane Society*. New York: Rinehart, 1955.

———. *To Have or To Be?* New York: Bantam, 1982.

Fukuyama, Francis. *Trust*. New York: The Free Press, 1995.

Galbraith, John Kenneth. *The Affluent Society*. Boston: Houghton Mifflin, 1998.

Galeano, Eduardo. *Upside Down*. New York: Metropolitan, 2000.

Giddens, Anthony. *Beyond Left and Right*. Stanford: Stanford University, 1994.

Goldberg, M. Hirsh. *The Complete Book of Greed*. New York: William Morrow, 1994.

Goodwin, Neva, Frank Ackerman, and David Kiron, eds. *The Consumer Society*. Washington, D.C.: Island Press, 1997.

Gore, Al. *Earth in the Balance*. Boston: Houghton Mifflin, 1992.

Hammond, Jeff, et al. *Tax Waste, Not Work: How Changing What We Tax Can Lead to a Stronger Economy and a Cleaner Environment*. San Francisco: Redefining Progress, April 1997.

Hawken, Paul. *The Ecology of Commerce*. New York: Harper Business, 1993.

——— with Amory and Hunter Lovins. *Natural Capitalism*. Boston: Little Brown, 1999.

Hayden, Anders. *Sharing the Work, Sparing the Planet*. London: Zed Books, 1999.

Hayden, Tom. *Reunion*. New York: Random House, 1988.

Heloise. *Hints for a Healthy Planet*. New York: Perigee, 1990.

Hertsgaard, Mark. *Earth Odyssey*. New York: Broadway Books, 1998.

Hochschild, Arlie Russell. *The Time Bind*. New York: Metropolitan, 1997.

Hoffman, Edward. *The Right to Be Human: A Biography of Abraham Maslow*. Wellingborough, U.K.: Crucible Press, 1989.

Holy Bible. New International Version. Colorado Springs, International Bible Society, 1984.

Hunnicutt, Benjamin. *Work Without End*. Philadelphia: Temple, 1988.

———. *Kellogg's Six-Hour Day*. Philadelphia: Temple, 1996.

Ikuta, Yasutoshi. *Cruise O Matic*. San Francisco: Chronicle Books, 1988.

Illich, Ivan. *Shadow Work*. Boston: Marion Boyars, 1981.

———. *Tools for Conviviality*. New York Harper & Row, 1973.

———. *Energy and Equity*. New York: Perennial, 1974.

Jacobson, Michael, and Laurie Ann Mazur. *Marketing Madness*. Boulder, Colo.: Westview, 1995.

Josephson, Eric and Mary, eds. *Man Alone*. New York: Dell, 1970.

Kelley, Linda. *Two Incomes and Still Broke*. New York: Times Books, 1996.

Klein, Naomi. *No Logo*. New York: Harper Collins, 2000.

Korten, David. *When Corporations Rule the World*. San Francisco: Kumarian/Berrett-Koehler, 1995.

———. *The Post-Corporate World*. San Francisco: Berrett-Koehler/ Kumarian, 1999.

Lafargue, Paul. *The Right to be Lazy*. Chicago: Charles Kerr, 1989.

Lasch, Christopher. *The Revolt of the Elites*. New York: Norton, 1995.

———. *The Culture of Narcissism*. New York, Norton, 1978.

———. *The Minimal Self*, New York, Norton, 1984.

———. *The True and Only Heaven*, New York, Norton, 1991.

Lasn, Kalle. *Culture Jam*. New York: Eagle Brook, 1999.

Leider, Richard and David Shapiro. *Repacking Your Bags*. San Francisco: Berrett-Koehler, 1996.

Lerner, Michael. *The Politics of Meaning*. Reading, Mass.: Addison-Wesley, 1996.

Levering, Frank, and Wanda Urbanska. *Simple Living*. New York: Viking, 1992.

Lewis, David, and Darren Bridger. *The Soul of the New Consumer*. London: Nicholas Brealey Publishing, 2000.

Lightman, Alan. *The Diagnosis*. New York: Pantheon, 2000.

Linden, Eugene. *The Future in Plain Sight*. New York: Simon & Schuster, 1998.

Linder, Staffan. *The Harried Leisure Class*. New York: Columbia, 1970.

Loh, Jonathan, ed., World Wildlife Fund, The UNEP World Conservation Monitoring Centre, Redefining Progress, and The Centre for Sustainability Studies. *Living Planet Report 2000*. Available through Redefining Progress and World Wildlife Fund International, October 2000.

Louv, Richard. *The Web of Life*. Berkeley: Conari Press, 1996.

———. *Childhood's Future*. New York: Houghton Mifflin, 1990.

Luhrs, Janet. *The Simple Living Guide*. New York: Broadway, 1997.

Luttwak, Edward. *Turbo-Capitalism*. New York: Harper/Collins, 1999.

Mack, Burton. *Who Wrote the New Testament?* San Francisco: Harper San Francisco, 1995.

———. *The Lost Gospel*. San Francisco: Harper San Francisco, 1993.

Macy, Joanna, and Molly Young Brown. *Coming Back to Life: Practices to Reconnect Our Lives, Our World*. Gabriola Island, B.C.: New Society Publishers, 1998.

Mander, Jerry. *Four Arguments for the Elimination of Television*. New York: William Morrow, 1978.

———. *In the Absence of the Sacred*. San Francisco: Sierra Club, 1991.

Marchard, Roland. *Advertising the American Dream*. Berkeley: University of California, 1985.

Marcuse, Herbert. *An Essay on Liberation*. Boston: Beacon, 1969.

———. *One Dimensional Man*. Boston: Beacon, 1964.

Martineau, Pierre. *Motivation in Advertising*. New York: McGraw Hill, 1971.

Marx, Karl, and Friedrich Engels. *Basic Writings on Philosophy*. Garden City, N.Y.: Anchor, 1959.

———. *Capital*. New York: Modern Library, 1906.

———. *Economic and Philosophical Manuscripts of 1844*. Moscow: Progress Publishers, 1974.

McCarthy, Eugene and William McGaughey. *Non-Financial Economics*. New York: Praeger, 1989.

McElvaine, Robert. *What's Left?* Holbrook, Mass.: Adams Media, 1996.

McKenzie, Richard. *The Paradox of Progress*. New York: Oxford, 1997.

McKenzie-Mohr, Doug, and William Smith. *Fostering Sustainable Behavior*. British Columbia: New Society Publishers, 1999.

McKibben, Bill. *The Comforting Whirlwind*. Grand Rapids, Mich.: Eerdmans, 1994.

———. *The Age of Missing Information*. New York: Random House, 1992.

———. *Hope, Human and Wild*. New York: Little Brown, 1995.

McNeal, James U. *Kids As Customers*. New York: Lexington, 1992.

Meadows, Donella, Dennis Meadows, and Jorgen Randers. *Beyond The Limits*. Post Mills, Vt.: Chelsea Green, 1992.

Miller, Perry, ed. *The American Transcendentalists*. Garden City, N.Y.: Anchor, 1957.

Molnar, Alex. *Giving Kids the Business*. New York Westview, 1996.

Moore-Ede, Martin. *The Twenty Four Hour Society*. Reading, Mass.: Addison-Wesley, 1993.

Morton, A.L., ed. *Political Writings of William Morris*. New York: International Publishers, 1973.

Myers, David. *The American Paradox*. New Haven, Conn.: Yale, 2000.

Myers, Norman, and Julian Simon. *Scarcity or Abundance?* New York: Norton, 1994.

Nabhan, Gary, and Stephen Trimble. *The Geography of Childhood*. Boston: Beacon, 1994.

National Conference of Catholic Bishops. *Economic Justice for All*. Washington, D.C.: National Conference of Catholic Bishops, 1986.

Naylor, Thomas, William Willimon, and Magdalena Naylor. *The Search for Meaning*. Nashville: Abiingdon Press, 1994.

Naylor, Thomas, and William Willimon. *Downsizing the USA*. Grand Rapids, Mich.: Eerdmans, 1997.

———. *The Abandoned Generation*. Grand Rapids, Mich.: Eerdmans, 1995.

Naylor, Thomas, William Willimon, and Rolf Ostenberg. *The Search for Meaning in the Workplace*. Nashville: Abingdon, 1996.

Needleman, Jacob. *Money and the Meaning of Life*. New York: Doubleday Currency, 1991.

Netherlands National Institute of Public Health and Environmental Protection. *Concern for Tomorrow*. Bilthoven, The Netherlands: Netherlands National Institute of Public Health and Environmental Protection, 1989.

New Road Map Foundation and Northwest Environment Watch. *All-Consuming Passion* (pamphlet). Seattle: New Road Map Foundation and Northwest Environment Watch, 1998.

New York Times. *The Downsizing of America*. New York: Times Books, 1996.

Northwest Earth Institute Discussion Courses. *Deep Ecology, Voluntary Simplicity*. Portland, Ore.: Northwest Earth Institute Discussion Courses, 1998.

O'Connell, Brian. *Civil Society*. Hanover, N.H.: Tufts, 1999.

O'Hara, Bruce. *Working Harder Isn't Working*. Vancouver, B.C.: New Star, 1993.

Oldenburg, Ray. *The Great Good Place*. New York: Paragon House, 1991.

O'Neill, Jessie. *The Golden Ghetto*. Center City, Minn.: Hazelden, 1997.

Packard, Vance. *The Hidden Persuaders*. New York: Pocket, 1973.

———. *The Status Seekers*. New York: Pelican, 1961.

———. *The Waste Makers*, New York: McKay, 1960.

Panati, Charles. *Extraordinary Origins of Everyday Things*. New York: Harper & Row, 1987.

Parker, Thornton. *What If Boomers Can't Retire?* San Francisco: Berrett-Koehler, 2000.

Perucci, Robert, and Earl Wysong. *The New Class Society*. Lanham, Md.: Rowman & Littlefield, 1999.

Phillips, Kevin. *The Politics of Rich and Poor*. New York: Random House, 1990.

Postel, Sandra. *Dividing the Waters: Food, Security, Ecosystem Health and the New Politics of Security*. Washington, D.C.: Worldwatch Institute, 1996, Vol. 132.

Postman, Neil. *Conscientious Objections*. New York: Vintage, 1988.

———. *Amusing Ourselves to Death*. New York: Viking, 1986.

Putnam, Robert D. *Bowling Alone*. New York: Simon & Schuster, 2000.

Rampton, Sheldon, and John Stauber. *Trust Us, We're Experts*. New York: Tarcher/Putnam, 2001.

Redefining Progress. *The Genuine Progress Indicator, 2000 Update*. San Francisco: Redefining Progress, 2000.

Rifkin, Jeremy. *The Age of Access*. New York: Tarcher/Putnam, 2000.

———. *The End of Work*. New York: Tarcher/Putnam, 1995.

———. *Time Wars*. New York: Simon & Schuster, 1987.

Robbins, John. *Diet for a New America*. Tiburon, Calif.,: H.J. Kramer, 1998.

Robbins, Ocean, and Sol Solomon. *Choices for our Future*. Summertown, Tenn.: Book Publishing Co., 1994.

Ropke, Wilhelm. *A Humane Economy*. Indianapolis: Liberty Fund, 1971.

Rosenblatt, Roger, ed. *Consuming Desires*. Washington, D.C.: Island Press, 1999.

Roszak, Theodore, Mary E. Gomes, and Allen D. Kanner, eds. *Ecopsychology*. San Francisco: Sierra Club Books, 1995.

Roth, Larry, ed. *The Simple Life*. New York: Berkley, 1998.

———. *The Best of the Living Cheap News*. Chicago: Contemporary, 1996.

Rubin, Lilian. *Families on the Fault Line*. New York: Harper Perennial, 1994.

Ryan, John. *Seven Wonders*. San Francisco: Sierra Club, 1999.

———. and Alan Durning. *Stuff: The Secret Lives of Everyday Things*. Seattle: Northwest Environment Watch, 1997.

Rybczynski, Withold. *Waiting for the Weekend*. New York: Viking, 1991.

Sakaiya, Taichi. *The Knowledge-Value Revolution, or, a History of the Future*. Trans. George Fields and William Marsh. Tokyo; New York: Kodansha International: Distributed in the U.S. by Kodansha America, 1991.

Saltzman, Amy. *Downshifting*. New York: Harper Collins, 1991.

Sanders, Barry. *A is for Ox*. New York: Pantheon, 1994.

Schleuning, Neala. *Idle Hands and Empty Hearts*. New York: Bergin & Garvey, 1990.

Schlosser, Eric. *Fast Food Nation*, Boston: Houghton Mifflin, 2001.

Schor, Juliet. *The Overworked American*. New York: Basic Books, 1992.

———. *The Overspent American*. New York: Basic Books, 1998.

Schut, Michael, ed. *Simpler Living, Compassionate Life*. Denver: Living the Good News, 1999.

Schwarz, Walter and Dorothy. *Living Lightly*. Charlbury, U.K.: Jon Carpenter, 1998.

Segal, Jerome. *Graceful Simplicity,* New York: Henry Holt, 1999.

Seiter,Ellen. *Sold Separately*. New Brunswick, N.J.: Rutgers, 1995.

Sessions, George, ed. *Deep Ecology for the 21st Century.* Boston: Shambala Press, 1995.

Shames, Lawrence. *The Hunger for More*. New York: Times Books, 1989.

Shi, David. *The Simple Life.* New York: Oxford University Press, 1985.

Shorris, Earl. *A Nation of Salesmen*. New York: Avon, 1994.

Shrady, Nicholas. *Sacred Roads*. San Francisco: Harper San Francisco, 1999.

Slater, Philip. *The Pursuit of Loneliness*. Boston: Beacon Press, 1970.

Smith, J.W. *The World's Wasted Wealth*, 2. Cambria, Calif.: Insitute for Economic Democracy, 1994.

Sobel, David. *Beyond Ecophobia: Reclaiming the Heart in Nature Education.* Great Barrington, Mass.: Orion Society, 1996.

St. James, Elaine. *Simplify Your Life with Kids*. Kansas City: Andrews McMeel, 1997.

Steamer, James. *Wealth on Minimal Wage*. Chicago: Dearborn Financial, 1997.

Stein, Herbert, and Murray Foss. *The New Illustrated Guide to the American Economy*. Washington, D.C.: The American Enterprise Institute, 1995.

Steingraber, Sandra. *Living Downstream: An Ecologist Looks at Cancer and the Environment.* Reading, Mass.: Addison-Wesley, 1997.

Strasburger, Victor C. *Adolescents and the Media*. Thousand Oaks, Calif.: Sage Publications, 1995.

Strasser, Susan. *Satisfaction Guaranteed.* New York: Pantheon, 1989.

Suzuki, David. *Earth Time.* Toronto: Stoddart Publishers, 1998.

Swenson, Richard. *The Overload Syndrome*. Colorado Springs: Navpress, 1998.

———. *Margin*. Colorado Springs: Navpress, 1992.

Theobald, Robert. *Reworking Success*. Gabriola Island, B.C.: New Society, 1997.

Thompson, William Irwin. *The American Replacement of Nature*. New York: Doubleday Currency, 1991.

Thurow, Lester. *The Future of Capitalism.* New York: Penguin, 1996.

Twitchell, James. *Adcult USA*. New York: Columbia, 1996.

Wachtel, Paul. *The Poverty of Affluence.* New York: The Free Press, 1983.

Wallis, Jim. *The Soul of Politics.* New York: New Press, 1994.

Walsh, David. *Selling Out America's Children*. Minneapolis: Fairview Press, 1995.

———. *Designer Kids*. Minneapolis: Deaconess, 1990.

Wann, David. *Biologic*. Boulder, Colo.: Johnson Books, 1994.

———. *Deep Design*. Washington, D.C.: Island Press, 1996.

Wattenberg, Ben. *Values Matter Most*. Washington, D.C.: Regnery, 1995.

Weil, Andrew. *Eating Well for Optimum Health*. New York: Alfred A Knopf, 2000.

Weil, Michelle, and Larry Rosen. *Technostress*. New York: John Wiley, 1997.

Williams, Terry Tempest. *Leap*. New York: Pantheon, 2000.

———. *Refuge*. New York: Vintage, 1991.

Worldwatch Institute. *Vital Signs 1995-2000*. New York: W.W. Norton Company, 2000.

———. *State of the World*. New York: W.W. Norton Company, 1995-2000.

Zablocki, Benjamin. *The Joyful Community*. Chicago: University of Chicago, 1980.

INDEX

ABOUT THE AUTHORS AND THE ILLUSTRATOR

John de Graaf has been a producer of public television documentaries for twenty-four years. More than a dozen of his programs, including *For Earth's Sake: The Life and Times of David Brower; Running Out of Time; Affluenza;* and *Escape from Affluenza*, have been broadcast nationally in prime time on PBS. He is a frequent speaker at colleges and universities and has been a visiting scholar at The Evergreen State College and a lecturer on documentary production at the University of Washington. This is his first adult book. He was the coauthor of a children's book, *David Brower: Friend Of The Earth*. He lives in Seattle.

David Wann has written four books and a hundred or more articles and has produced many videos and television programs about sustainable lifestyles. His book *Biologic* (1994) discusses individual actions based on biological realities, while *Deep Design* (1996) looks at the prospect of an entire economy grounded in sustainable enterprise. He has taught at the college level, worked for more than a decade as a policy analyst for the U.S. Environmental Protection Agency, and helped design and build the cohousing village in which he now lives, in Golden, Colorado.

Thomas Naylor is Professor Emeritus of Economics at Duke University, where he taught for thirty years. He has also taught at Middlebury College. He is a writer and social critic and has consulted with governments and major corporations in more than thirty countries. In 1993 he moved to Charlotte, Vermont, where he writes about the search for meaning and community and for simplifying all aspects of our lives. His articles have been published in the *New York Times*, the *International Herald Tribune*, the *Los Angeles Times*, the *Boston Globe*, the *Christian Science Monitor,* the *Nation,* and *Business Week.* He has appeared on ABC, CBS, CNN, NPR, and the CBC. He is the author or coauthor of thirty books.

David Horsey is the *Seattle Post-Intelligencer's* Pulitzer Prize–winning editorial cartoonist. His work is syndicated internationally by Tribune Media Services. The winner of numerous awards for his cartoons and written commentary, he has published five collections of his work. Currently, he is president of the Association of American Editorial Cartoonists. His career has taken him to Europe, Asia, Hollywood, and Washington, D.C., and through six presidential election campaigns. He lives in Seattle with his wife and two children.

Scott Simon (foreword) was the host of the TV program *Affluenza*. He is currently the host of *Weekend Edition Saturday* on National Public Radio and is a former host of the *Weekend Today Show* on NBC. The author of several books, he lives in Washington, D.C.

ABOUT REDEFINING PROGRESS

Redefining Progress (RP) is a nonprofit research and policy organization based in Oakland, CA, that believes that genuine progress entails providing a better life for all within the capacity of nature.

RP tools and policies emerge from three "Big Ideas":

Sustainability is rooted in the realization that ever more of us live on a planet with shrinking regenerative capacity. RP uses the Ecological Footprint to document overuse of resources and workshops to explore fair and effective ways to live once more within the means of nature.

Accurate Prices advances market mechanisms and incentives that provide accurate feedback about the full cost of our purchases and decisions to ourselves, others, and Nature.

Common Assets recognizes the value of our natural and community-based resources in strengthening our communities. RP fosters policies to improve the health of these resources so that they can efficiently and equitably meet the basic needs of our communities and households.

RP also applies these Big Ideas to the problem of global warming through two campaigns to promote fair and low-cost policies to address climate change.

Berrett-Koehler Publishers

BERRETT-KOEHLER is an independent publisher of books, periodicals, and other publications at the leading edge of new thinking and innovative practice on work, business, management, leadership, stewardship, career development, human resources, entrepreneurship, and global sustainability.

Since the company's founding in 1992, we have been committed to supporting the movement toward a more enlightened world of work by publishing books, periodicals, and other publications that help us to integrate our values with our work and work lives, and to create more humane and effective organizations.

We have chosen to focus on the areas of work, business, and organizations, because these are central elements in many people's lives today. Furthermore, the work world is going through tumultuous changes, from the decline of job security to the rise of new structures for organizing people and work. We believe that change is needed at all levels—individual, organizational, community, and global—and our publications address each of these levels.

We seek to create new lenses for understanding organizations, to legitimize topics that people care deeply about but that current business orthodoxy censors or considers secondary to bottom-line concerns, and to uncover new meaning, means, and ends for our work and work lives.

See next pages for other books from Berrett-Koehler Publishers

More books from Berrett-Koehler

Whistle While You Work
Heeding Your Life's Calling

Richard J. Leider and David A. Shapiro

We all have have a calling in life. It needs only to be uncovered, not discovered. *Whistle While You Work* makes the uncovering process inspiring and fun. Featuring a unique "Calling Card" exercise—a powerful way to put the whistle in your work—it is a liberating and practical guide that will help you find work that is truly satisfying, deeply fulfilling, and consistent with your deepest values.

Paperback original, 200 pages • ISBN 1-57675-103-1 CIP
Item #51031-364 $15.95

Repacking Your Bags
Lighten Your Load for the Rest of Your Life

Richard J. Leider and David A. Shapiro

Learn how to climb out from under the many burdens you're carrying and find the fulfillment that's missing in your life. A simple yet elegant process teaches you to balance the demands of work, love, and place in order to create and live your own vision of success.

Paperback, 234 pages • ISBN 1-881052-87-7 CIP
Item #52877-364 $14.95

Hardcover • ISBN 1-881052-67-2 CIP • Item #52672-364 $21.95

Audiotape, 2 cassettes • ISBN 1-57453-027-5 • Item #30275-364 $17.95

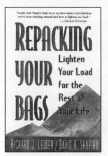

The Power of Purpose
Creating Meaning in Your Life and Work

Richard J. Leider

We all possess a unique ability to do the work we were made for. Concise and easy to read, and including numerous stories of people living on purpose, *The Power of Purpose* is a a remarkable tool to help you find your calling, an original guide to discovering the work you love to do.

Hardcover, 170 pages • ISBN 1-57675-021-3 CIP
Item #50213-364 $20.00

Audiotape, 2 cassettes • ISBN 1-57453-215-4 • Item #32154-364 $17.95

Berrett-Koehler Publishers PO Box 565, Williston, VT 05495-9900
Call toll-free! **800-929-2929** 7 am-12 midnight
Or fax your order to 802-864-7627
For fastest service order online: **www.bkconnection.com**

BK

Bringing Your Soul to Work

An Everyday Practice

Cheryl Peppers and Alan Briskin

This book addresses the gap between our inner lives and the work we do in the world. Case studies, personal stories, inspirational quotes, reflective questions, and concrete applications navigate readers through the real and troubling questions inherent in the workplace.

Paperback, 260 pages • ISBN: 1-57675-111-2 CIP
Item #51112-364 $16.95

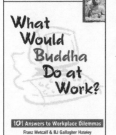

What Would Buddha Do at Work?

101 Answers to Workplace Dilemmas

Franz Metcalf and BJ Gallagher Hateley

What Would Buddha Do at Work? uses the gentle teachings of Buddha to help people discover deeper meaning in their work. It presents 101 typical situations or issues that people struggle with daily, ranging from coping with difficult bosses, serving customers, and working as a team to being creative, solving problems, and offering leadership. In response, the authors pass along Buddhist wisdom that will inspire and guide readers to "enlightened" answers to their problems—answers that are spiritual as well as practical and realistic.

Hardcover, 180 pages • ISBN 1-5697-5300-8 CIP
Item #53008-364 $16.95

Your Signature Path

Gaining New Perspectives on Life and Work

Geoffrey M. Bellman

Your Signature Path explores the uniqueness of the mark each of us makes in the world. Bestselling author Geoffrey M. Bellman offers thought-provoking insights and practical tools for evaluating who you are, what you are doing, and where you want your path to lead.

Hardcover, 200 pages • ISBN 1-57675-004-3 CIP
Item #50043-364 $24.95

Berrett-Koehler Publishers PO Box 565, Williston, VT 05495-9900
Call toll-free! **800-929-2929** 7 am-12 midnight

BK Or fax your order to 802-864-7627
For fastest service order online: **www.bkconnection.com**

Spread the word!

Berrett-Koehler books and audios are available at quantity discounts for orders of 10 or more copies.

Affluenza

The All-Consuming Epidemic

John de Graaf, David Wann, and Thomas H. Naylor
Illustrated by David Horsey

Hardcover, 275 pages
ISBN 1-57675-151-1 CIP
Item #51511-364 $24.95

To find out about discounts on orders of 10 or more copies for individuals, corporations, institutions, and organizations, please call us toll-free at (800) 929-2929.

To find out about our discount programs for resellers, please contact our Special Sales department at (415) 288-0260; Fax: (415) 362-2512. Or email us at bkpub@bkpub.com.

Berrett-Koehler Publishers
PO Box 565, Williston, VT 05495-9900
Call toll-free! **800-929-2929** 7 am-12 midnight
Or fax your order to 802-864-7627
For fastest service order online: **www.bkconnection.com**